The Political Language of Islam

The Political Language of Islam

◆

BERNARD LEWIS

The University of Chicago Press
CHICAGO AND LONDON

BERNARD LEWIS is the Cleveland E. Dodge Professor Emeritus of Near Eastern Studies at Princeton University and Director of the Annenberg Research Institute. Among his many books are *The Emergence of Modern Turkey* (2d edition, 1968); *The Arabs in History* (6th edition, 1980); *The Muslim Discovery of Europe* (1982); and *The Jews of Islam* (1984).

The University of Chicago Press, Chicago 60637
The University of Chicago Press, Ltd., London

Printed in the United States of America
97 96 95 94 93 92 91 90 89 88 5 4 3 2

The University of Chicago Press wishes to acknowledge assistance from the Exxon Foundation in the publication of this book.

LIBRARY OF CONGRESS CATALOGING-IN-PUBLICATION DATA

Lewis, Bernard.
The political language of Islam.

Includes index.
1. Islam and state. 2. Political science—Islamic Empire—History. 3. Political science—Terminology. 4. Symbolism in politics—Islamic countries. I. Title.
JC49.L48 1988 297'.1977 87-19222
ISBN 0-226-47692-8

Contents

Preface

♦

The main part of this book is based on lectures sponsored by the Exxon Foundation and the Committee on Social Thought of the University of Chicago, and delivered at the University 29 October–4 November 1986. In revising and expanding them for publication, I have maintained the structure of the lectures as delivered, and have tried to keep them in a form which will be accessible to readers interested in history and politics generally, and not only to specialists in Islam and the Middle East. For the latter, I have appended a detailed annotation, discussing some of the issues in greater detail and citing sources and bibliography.

This book is the work of one who is, by training and profession, a historian and an Islamicist. While aware of recent work by political scientists and psychologists and by semiologists on political language, and especially on the use of metaphors and symbols, I have made no attempt to intervene in their debate, but leave it to them to evaluate and interpret my findings in terms of their disciplines.

My thanks are due in the first instance to my hosts and audiences in Chicago, whose invitation gave me the opportunity to prepare and deliver these lectures, and whose questions and comments helped me to improve them for publication. It is also my pleasant duty to express my thanks, once again, to my friends and colleagues Professors Michael Curtis and Charles Issawi, for reading drafts of the text and offering suggestions for its improvement. Finally, I would like to express my gratitude to my research assistant Corinne Blake for her invaluable help, and to Leigh Faden, whose skill, devotion, and inexhaustible patience helped to carry this book through the long and difficult journey from first draft to final version.

Note on Transcription

♦

The terms discussed in this book are taken from the three major languages of Middle Eastern Islam, Arabic, Persian, and Turkish. Many of them, most but not all of Arabic origin, are shared by more than one language. Like the Greco-Roman words used in the languages of Europe, these terms have undergone changes of form, pronunciation, and sometimes even of meaning in their migration from one language to another. In transcribing Arabic and Persian, I have used the system of transliteration of the *Encyclopaedia of Islam,* with two changes; Arabic *jim* is represented by *j* as in James, not *dj;* Arabic *qaf* is represented by *q,* not *ḳ*. For Turkish, both Ottoman and modern, I have used the official Turkish orthography. In this c = j as in John; ç = ch as in church; ğ = approximately *y* as in *saying* or *w* as in *sowing;* ı = *u* in *radium;* ş = *sh* as in ship. Terms like "ulema" and "mufti," which have become accepted English words, are written without diacritical signs.

1

Metaphor and Allusion

◆

In 1979 a series of events began in Iran which brought profound changes not only in the government but also in the whole society of that country, with consequences reaching far beyond the Iranian frontiers. For these changes, those who accomplished them claimed the title "revolutionary"; most outsiders, with whatever reservations, have accepted that claim.

Revolutions express themselves differently, and each has its own way of formulating its critique of the past and its aspirations for the future. The French Revolution, with its ideological background in the eighteenth-century Enlightenment, formulated its ideals as liberty, equality, fraternity. The Russian Revolution, with a background in nineteenth-century socialism, set forth its plans for the future in terms of a classless state to be achieved through a dictatorship of the proletariat. The Iranian Revolution presents itself in terms of Islam, that is to say, as a religious movement with a religious leadership, a religiously formulated critique of the old order, and religiously expressed plans for the new. While the Jacobins thought of themselves as Roman Republicans, and the Bolsheviks were concerned to repeat or avoid the various events of the French Revolution, Muslim revolutionaries looked to the birth of Islam as their paradigm, and saw themselves as engaged in a struggle against paganism, oppression, and empire, to establish, or rather restore, a true Islamic order.

Major revolutions have a resonance far beyond the countries in which they occur. Both the French and Russian revolutions evoked an enormous response, and exercised immense influence in the whole European and Christian world of which both prerevolutionary France and prerevolutionary Russia were a part and with which they shared a common universe of discourse. The eager response of a young Englishman of the time to the earth-shaking events in revolutionary Paris was expressed by William Wordsworth in the famous lines,

> Bliss was it in that dawn to be alive,
> But to be young was very heaven!

Similar sentiments have been expressed, in somewhat different words, by Muslim observers of the Iranian Revolution, as far away as Southeast Asia and western Africa, and among the Muslim national minority in communist-ruled Yugoslavia.[1] The Iranian Revolution too has had an enormous impact all over the world with which it shares a common general and political culture. That culture is defined by Islam.

When we in the Western world, nurtured in the Western tradition, use the words "Islam" and "Islamic," we tend to make a natural error and assume that religion means the same for Muslims as it has meant in the Western world, even in medieval times; that is to say, a section or compartment of life reserved for certain matters, and separate, or at least separable, from other compartments of life designed to hold other matters. That is not so in the Islamic world. It was never so in the past, and the attempt in modern times to make it so may perhaps be seen, in the longer perspective of history, as an unnatural aberration which in Iran has ended and in some other Islamic countries may also be nearing its end.

In classical Islam there was no distinction between Church and state. In Christendom the existence of two authorities goes back to the founder, who enjoined his followers to render unto Caesar the things which are Caesar's and to God the things which are God's. Throughout the history of Christendom there have been two powers: God and Caesar, represented in this world by *sacerdotium* and *regnum*, or, in modern terms, church and state. They may be associated, they may separated; they may be in harmony, they may be in conflict; one may dominate, the other may dominate; one may interfere, the other may protest, as we are now learning again. But always there are two, the spiritual and the temporal powers, each with its own laws and jurisdictions, its own structure and hierarchy. In pre-westernized Islam, there were not two powers but one, and the question of separation, therefore, could not arise. The distinction between church and state, so deeply rooted in Christendom, did not exist in Islam, and in classical Arabic, as well as in other languages which derive their intellectual and political vocabulary from classical Arabic, there were no pairs of words corresponding to spiritual and temporal, lay and ecclesiastical, religious and secular. It was not until the nineteenth and twentieth centuries, and then under the influence of Western ideas and institutions, that new words were found, first in Turkish and then in Arabic, to express the idea of secular.[2] Even in modern usage, there is no Muslim equivalent to "the Church," meaning "ecclesiastical organization." All the different words for mosque denote only a building which is a place of worship, not an abstraction, an authority, or an institution. One might perhaps discern, in the postclassical evolution of the professional men of religion, some approximation to a clergy, and such terms as "ulema" and "mollahs" almost acquire this sense. But there is no equivalent to the term "laity," a meaningless expression in the context of Islam. At the present time, the very notion of a secular jurisdiction and authority—of a so-to-speak unsanctified part of life that lies outside the scope of religious law and those who uphold it—is seen as an impiety, indeed as the ultimate betrayal of Islam. The righting of this wrong is the principal aim of Islamic revolutionaries and, in general, of those described as Islamic fundamentalists.[3]

This definition of political identity and loyalty by religious belief, or to be more precise, by religious adherence, is not limited to the revolutionaries. For many years now there has been an active international grouping, at the United Nations and elsewhere, consisting of more than forty Muslim governments, which together constitute the so-called Islamic Bloc. This includes monarchies and republics, conservatives and radicals, exponents of capitalism and of socialism, supporters of the Western Bloc, of the Eastern Bloc, and of a whole spectrum of shades of neutrality. They have built up an elaborate apparatus of international consultation and, on many issues, cooperation; they hold regular high-level conferences, and despite differences of structure, ideology, and policy, they have achieved a significant measure of agreement and common action. In this the Islamic peoples are in sharp contrast with those who profess other religions.

The political relevance of Islam is internal as well as external. In all but one of the sovereign states with a clear Muslim majority, Islam is the state religion; many of them have clauses in their constitutions establishing the Holy Law of Islam as either the basis of law or the major source of legislation.[4] The one exception is the Turkish republic, which under the guidance of its first president, Kemal Atatürk, adopted a series of laws in the 1920s the effect of which was to disestablish Islam, to repeal the Holy Law, and to lay down the legal separation of religion and the state. These laws have remained in force, but their effect has been somewhat diminished by the reintroduction of compulsory religious education in the state schools, the full participation of Turkey in Islamic Bloc activities, and, as parliamentary democracy has taken root in the country, the increasing tendency of political parties to raise religious issues in order to bring out the peasant vote.

What then is the power, the attraction of Islam, both as a claim to allegiance and as a revolutionary appeal? This is a large and complex question, from which at this point I would like to bring a few major themes to your attention. The first which seems to me relevant is that in most Muslim countries Islam is still the ultimate criterion of group identity and loyalty. It is Islam which distinguishes between self and other, between insider and outsider, between brother and stranger. We in the Western world have become accustomed to other criteria of classification, by nation, by country, and by various subdivisions of these. Both nation and country are of course old facts in the Islamic world, but as definitions of political identity and loyalty they are modern and intrusive notions. In some countries, these notions have become more or less acclimatized. But there is a recurring tendency in times of crisis, in times of emergency, when the deeper loyalties take over, for Muslims to find their basic identity in the religious community; that is to say, in an entity defined by Islam rather than by ethnic origin, language, or country of habitation.

And just as the insider is defined by his acceptance of Islam, so in the same way the outsider is defined by his rejection of Islam. He is the *kāfir,* "the unbeliever," i.e., he who does not believe in the apostolate of Muḥammad and the authenticity of the revelation which he brought. The languages of Islam, like those of the civilizations of antiquity, of Christendom, and of Asia, have words to denote the stranger, the foreigner, the barbarian.[5] But from the time of the Prophet to the present day, the ultimate definition of the Other, the alien outsider and presumptive enemy, has been the *kāfir,* the unbeliever.

A second related point is that for many, probably most, Muslims, Islam is still the most acceptable, indeed in times of crisis the only acceptable, basis for authority. Political domination can be maintained for a while by mere force, but not indefinitely, not over large areas or for long periods. For this there has to be some legitimacy in government, and this purpose, for Muslims, is most effectively accomplished when the ruling authority derives its legitimacy from Islam rather than from merely nationalist, patriotic, or even dynastic claims—still less from such Western notions as national or popular sovereignty. In political life, Islam still offers the most widely intelligible formulation of ideas, on the one hand of social norms and laws, on the other, of new ideals and aspirations. And, as recent events have repeatedly demonstrated, Islam provides the most effective system of symbols for political mobilization, whether to arouse the people in defense of a regime that is perceived as possessing the necessary legitimacy or against a regime which is perceived as lacking that legitimacy; in other words, as not being Islamic or, perhaps, as having forfeited that legitimacy by no longer being Islamic.

In order to approach some understanding of the politics of Islam, of movements and changes which are perceived and expressed in Islamic terms, we must first try to understand the language of political discourse among Muslims, the way in which words are used and understood, the framework of metaphor and allusion which is a necessary part of all communication. And to achieve such an understanding, we must look beyond the contemporary language of politics in the Muslim world, which has been profoundly affected, some might say distorted, over the last century or more by external influences. To understand the changes brought by these external influences, and the responses and reactions of those whom they affected, we must go back to the time before the massive impact of Western power and thought, a time when the Islamic world was still developing according to other cultural traditions, some of them indeed pre-Islamic or non-Islamic, but all of them different from those of the modern West.

This culture was expressed in three languages, Arabic, Persian, and Turkish, which prevailed all over Southwest Asia and northern Africa. Linguistically, these three languages are of different and unrelated groups—as remote from each other as English, Hebrew, and Hungarian.[6] Culturally, however, they were very close, sharing a common script and an enormous vocabulary of loanwords, covering the whole range of both political thought and practice. Great numbers of Muslims live outside the Middle Eastern Islamic heartlands—indeed, by now the Muslims of South and Southeast Asia vastly outnumber the Arabic-, Persian-, and Turkish-speaking Muslims of the Middle East. But they have developed their own political and other cultures, much influenced by those of the regions in which they live. Their relevance to the Middle Eastern culture is minimal, and they are therefore not considered here.

The origins of Islamic political language, as of other aspects of Islam, must be sought in the Qurʾān, the Traditions of the Prophet, and the practice of the early Muslims. These in turn have their roots in ancient Arabia, and in the different religious beliefs, Christian, Jewish, and pagan, which existed there at the time of the advent of Islam. But the great extension of the Islamic polity and community under the early caliphs, until it embraced a vast region extending from Europe and the Atlantic at one end to the approaches to India and China at the other, subjected the new faith and civilization, when they were still young and malleable, to a great variety of influences. The Zoroastrians of the eastern provinces, the Christians of the central and western provinces, and—less important—the surviving Jewish minorities living among both, all made their contribution.

The practice of the Persian and Roman Empires, from which the new Islamic Empire acquired most of its provinces and most of its imperial administrative personnel, also helped to shape the processes and principles of government of Islam itself. The translation into Arabic, from the eighth century, of Persian manuals of statecraft and court etiquette[7] and of Greek treatises on political philosophy[8] gave a new sophistication to Islamic discourse on these matters. The rich and flexible Arabic language of politics was further enriched by loan-words and, to a vastly greater extent, loan translations of Persian and Greek and even Latin terms. Some of these go back to the earliest times. Even in the Qur'ān itself, Mecca is referred to as *Umm al-Qurā,* a literal translation of the Greek *metropolis*. The Straight Road, *al-Ṣirāṭ al-Mustaqīm,* which Muslims are enjoined to follow, is the straight Roman road, and *ṣirāṭ* is none other than the Latin *strata,* from which we also derive the English word "street."[9]

Closer acquaintance with Roman and Byzantine practice in the conquered provinces brought many more terms of this kind. Some are easily recognizable, such as *shurṭa,* the cohort charged with police duties. Others wear an Arabic-Islamic disguise, such as the *Muḥtasib,* a kind of inspector of morals and markets, who inherited the functions of the Byzantine *agoranomos*. There were similar borrowings from the eastern provinces. The administrative offices in which the servants of the government conducted their business, in Arabic called *dīwān,*[10] clearly derive their name from a Persian antecedent. The chief of the diwans, the *wazīr,*[11] bore a title which was etymologically Arabic but owed much of its development to Iranian imperial precedent.

By the eleventh century, Arabic had absorbed these cultural borrowings from the ancient empires, and merged them in a new and vigorous political culture that was distinctively Islamic. It was then compelled to undergo a second major transformation, resulting from the movement of the steppe peoples into the heartlands of Islam. From the north and from the east came first the Turks and then the Mongols, in a series of waves of migration extending from the eleventh to the fourteenth centuries.

Unlike the Persians, the Greeks, and the ancient peoples of the Middle East, the Turks and Mongols were never conquered by Islam. On the contrary, they entered the Islamic world as conquerors, some of them freely converted in their homelands, some of them, the Mongols, arriving as pagan aliens and imposing a pagan domination over the Muslims.

During these four centuries, and for long afterwards, the Islamic world of the Middle East was dominated by dynasties, and not only dynasties, but states and armies, of Turkish and Mongol origin.

These, as well as imposing a new domination, also established a new and different pattern of government and association, which reached its apotheosis in the great empires of the post-Mongol period, in Turkey, Iran, Central Asia, and India.[12] These empires had a stability, a permanence, and a regularity in their administrative structures without precedent in classical Islam. They also brought with them a new vocabulary from the steppe languages and gave new meanings to words already in use. In the civilization of the Ottoman Empire, Arabic, Persian, and Turkish were harmoniously combined as the three instruments of a general and, more specifically, a political culture which shaped the destinies of much of the Middle East for half a millennium and is by no means extinct even at the present day.

During the last two centuries or so—more in some areas, less in others—the thought world of Islam has once again been transformed by an external impact, this time from Europe. This was, in many ways, the most difficult of all to absorb. The Europeans who came in the nineteenth and twentieth centuries were not conquered subjects like the Persians and the Greeks, ready and indeed eager to serve their new masters. Nor were they teachable recruits to the Islamic faith and culture, like the Turks and the Mongols, who came as conquerors but soon became the valiant defenders of Islam against its enemies.[13] These came and remained as aliens, accepting neither the faith nor the culture of the Muslim peoples over whom they ruled. This time it was the Muslims who were either conquered or in imminent danger of conquest, and who were forced to learn the ways of the new masters of the world, in order to survive. Some Muslims, incorporated in the four great empires of Russia, Holland, Britain, and France, had, perforce, to submit to European political rule or influence. Others tried to master the secrets of European political success, so to resist domination or, failing that, to end it.

The result of all this was a transformation of government, both as practiced and as perceived, and a recasting of ideas and words more comprehensive than anything that either the Greco-Persian renaissance of the early Middle Ages, or the Turko-Mongol domination of the later, had accomplished.[14]

If we compare Western and Islamic political language, we shall find that they have much in common. Some of this resemblance is due to our common human predicament—to our living in the same physical world, experiencing the same basic needs, and, often, encountering the same problems. Similar problems may naturally produce similar solutions. Part of the resemblance is historical, and it is attested by a shared vocabulary, of Greek and Latin loanwords and loan translations in Arabic and, to a lesser extent, words of Arabic origin in the languages of Europe.[15] Islamic and Christian civilizations were never as remote and alien to one another as were for example the ancient civilizations and religions of India and China. Islamic civilization first flourished in or near the Mediterranean lands, and in many important areas shares a common heritage with Christendom. Greek philosophy and science, Judeo-Christian revelation and law, have an important place in the Islamic culture and heritage, and made possible a level of communication between Christians and Muslims, even in the most fanatical medieval societies, that was intellectually impossible for either to achieve with, say, Hindus or Buddhists.

But despite these resemblances, there are still enormous differences, and these are particularly clear in the language of political assertion, denunciation, and appeal. Muslims revere different scriptures—not the Bible but the Qur'ān. They are nurtured on different classics, and draw inspiration and guidance from a different history. Few if any civilizations in the past have attached as much importance to history as did Islam, in its education, in its awareness of itself, in the common language of everyday talk. Even today, in the bitter war that is being waged between Iraq and Iran, the war propaganda of both sides makes frequent allusions to events of the seventh and eighth centuries.[16] There can be little doubt that these references are recognized by the vast majority of people in both countries and indeed elsewhere in the Muslim world, and that the force of the allusions is well understood.

Until very recently, history—that is to say significant, usable history—for Muslim historians meant the history of Islam. And of the events in the history of Islam, the most significant, thus the most usable, were those of the early centuries, the life of the Prophet and his immediate successors, which constitute the sacred history, one might even say the salvation history, of Islam and form the core of the historic self-awareness of Muslims everywhere. In Christendom, the sacred history is imprinted on the minds of the faithful in a number of ways—through teaching and texts, but also through statuary, through pictures, through stained-glass windows, through music. Apart from certain deviant groups, Islam has none of these. The ban on images has effectively precluded any development of religious representational art, while the Islamic mistrust of music inhibited the development of liturgy. Islam has no hymns, no fugues, no icons. The interior decoration of the mosque consists of texts, mostly from the Qurʾān. In Islamic lands the art of calligraphy, in particular the writing of sacred texts, attained the level of a major votive art, of great depth and subtlety. In a profound sense, the Qurʾanic and other texts that adorn the walls and pillars of Muslim mosques are the hymns and fugues and icons of Islam.

And the texts, of course, consist of words, and part at least of their impact is through the words which they record. Much that in other faiths is expressed through art and music is, in Islam, expressed through the word, giving to verbal communication a unique importance.

This importance was recognized by some of the earliest Arabic classical writers, who speak of poetry and oratory as the two arts which the Arabs most admired and in which they most excelled.[17] Both of them are of course arts of verbal persuasion; both were extensively used for political purposes. Much classical Arabic poetry was written to be recited in public; much of it consists of eulogy and satire. Many of the poets were employed or retained by rulers and other political personages. Their task was to burnish the image of their patron and tarnish that of his opponents, the one by eulogy, the other by satire. In earlier times, and perhaps to some extent even today, there was also a magical quality in the blessings lavished on a ruler, and in the imprecations hurled against an enemy. It is surely significant that the Arabic term for satire, *hijāʾ*, is the etymological cognate of the Hebrew *hagah,* with the meaning, among others, of "weaving spells against someone."[18] In the days before the advent of the media, the poet had an important role in the field of propaganda and of what we nowadays call public relations, and poetry could often be an important weapon of political warfare. For the modern historian, it is often an invaluable source of information on the language of political discourse, and on the allusions to which the poet knew his listeners would respond. In addition to poetry, we have at our disposal a vast mass of literary and documentary evidence, the former including a wide range of historical and political writings, the latter reflecting many different aspects of both the conduct of government and the waging of political warfare among Muslims from medieval to modern times.

Islamic political language, like virtually all forms of language, is full of metaphor, some of it dead, buried, and forgotten, some of it to varying extents alive and conscious. When we use the English word "government," few of us think of its origins in an ancient Greek noun meaning "rudder" and an ancient Greek verb meaning "to steer"; but when we—that is, the verbally less gifted or fastidious among us—speak of the man at the helm steering the ship of state, there is still some faint awareness of a maritime metaphor contained in these words. Similarly, when Muslims use the word *siyāsa,*[19] the Arabic word which, with minor variations, denotes politics in virtually all the languages of the Islamic world, few of them connect it with an ancient Middle Eastern word meaning "horse," or a classical Arabic verb meaning "to groom" or "train a horse." But when the Ottomans used the horsetail as an emblem of authority, and designated certain high officers of the sultan as "the *Ağa*s of the Imperial stirrup," they were clearly evoking the image of the man on the horse as the symbol of effective power.

Probably the commonest metaphors, in Islamic as in Western language, are those which are called spatial, denoting position and direction in space. These are the metaphors with which political relationships, and changes in these relationships, are indicated in terms of up-down, front-back, in-out, near-far. In Islamic as in Western language, "up" and "front" generally indicate greater power, status, or wealth; movement upward or forward indicates improvement, while movement downward or backward indicates deterioration or loss of power, status, etc. But while Western language, from the earliest times, makes extensive use of up-down and front-back imagery to indicate domination and subordination, early Arabic political language makes very little use of these images. Where they do occur, they are often specific allusions rather than metaphors. Thus, the common use of verbs from the roots *qdm* and *ʾmm,* both with a root meaning of "in front of" or "before," to indicate precedence or authority, derive from leadership in battle or in prayer. In ancient, in contrast to modern, times, both kinds of leadership were necessarily exercised from the front, not from the rear, and the use of these terms thus represented facts on the ground, not metaphors in the mind. Similarly, the use of the term "high" as an adjective qualifying the doors or gates or buildings at the centers of power, as in the famous Ottoman Sublime Porte, refers at least in part to the actual height of buildings which, in earlier times, must have dwarfed all other structures with the exception only of places of worship. The terms "high," and more especially "low," are commonly used to express human status and relationships, but in a social and even moral rather than in a political sense. Thus the usual connotation of the Arabic word *safil,* "low," would be something like "vile," "base," "lowborn."

Power relationships are more commonly indicated in Islamic usage by the imagery of near and far, in and out, or, to borrow a social science expression, center and periphery, and, of course, movement in either direction. Thus, according to an early text, the caliph ʿUmar explained his refusal to employ Christians in positions of power in these words: "I will not honor them when God has degraded them; I will not glorify them when God has humiliated them; I will not bring them near when God has set them far."[20] A Western speaker or writer would almost certainly have expressed this idea by saying that he would not raise them up when God had cast them down.

In Persian and Ottoman usage the word "high" (but not "low") appears more frequently, particularly in titles and in honorific language. Most of this is formulaic, while the discussion of real relationships and changes continues to make much more extensive use of the imagery of near and far, in and out, center and periphery. Clearly, the centrality of the ruler, and the importance of nearness and access to him, is reflected in this language.[21]

One of the roots most frequently used to connote power and authority, the triliteral *wly,* whence such familiar terms as *vali* and *vilâyet* from Turkey, *mollah* from Iran, and *maulvi* and *maulana* from India, has the primary meaning of "to be near."[22]

Between the near and the far, there is the middle. And the Arabic word *wasaṭ,* "middle," has given rise to a wide range of terms connoting mediation, intermediaries, intercessors, and interventions of various kinds. At the court of Fatimid caliphs of Egypt, the *Wasīṭ*,[23] or "middleman," was a high court official, corresponding more or less to the wazir of the ʿAbbasid caliphate in Baghdad. Supreme sovereign power is at the center. The nearer to the center, the greater the power; the further from the center, the less the power. In the Ottoman Imperial Palace, the entire complex of buildings was divided into three zones known as the Inside, the Inbetween, and the Outside. The officers of the Inbetween, in Turkish *mabeynci*,[24] in large measure controlled access to the seats of power and thereby themselves wielded great power and influence.

Another spatial or orientational metaphor familiar to us from both ancient and modern Western usage is that of revolution or, as it often becomes in practice, movement in circles. This is rare in classical political language. When it occurs, it is usually in the context of cyclical or even astrological explanations of the accession and overthrow of dynasties.

Changes in power relationships are indicated by the same metaphors. In Western language contenders for power may rise or fall. If they rise, it may be as climbers or as rebels, engaged in an uprising. In Islam, verbs meaning "to rise" are commonly used to convey religious, especially mystical, experience, but rarely political ascent. Ambitious Muslims move inward rather than upward; rebellious Muslims secede from, rather than rise against, the existing order. The earliest—indeed the paradigmatic—movement of rebellion against the existing order was that of the *Khawārij*, "those who go out." Significantly, their movement was expressed as horizontal, not vertical; even more remarkably, it was outward, not inward. The same concept is expressed in the extensive social and political use of the two verbs *jamaʿa*, "to gather or join," and *faraqa*, "to separate or divide." Gathering is good—hence the *jamāʿa*, "the community," ruled by *ijmāʿ*, "consensus." Separation is bad, and gives rise to *firqa*, "sect," and other forms of disunity. The two notions are combined and contrasted in the prophetic injunction to the Muslim not to separate himself from the community, the *jamāʿa*.[25]

The language of right and left, now universally adopted, is not primarily a spatial or orientational metaphor, but an historical allusion, and derives from the seating arrangements of the French National Assembly after the Revolution, themselves influenced by the seating of government and opposition in the British Parliament. Underlying this there is of course a much older metaphor derived from the body in which, by almost universal belief, the right is good and the left is somehow ill-omened and suspect.[26] If we look at the Latin, French, and Anglo-Saxon components of our own English vocabulary, we shall find that while the associations of the right are dexterity, adroitness, rightness, rightfulness, and even righteousness, those of the left are somewhat gauche, and can be positively sinister. These terms have their equivalents in many other languages. The classical Arabic *mash'ūm,* "ill-omened," and the modern Arabic *mutashā'im,* "pessimistic," are both participial forms of a verb derived from a root meaning "left," while *yumn,* "good fortune," and *yamīn,* "oath," both come from the common Arabic word for "right." A particularly interesting example is the Russian use of "on the left" for an illicit or black-market transaction. Our own familiar expression "right-hand man" is given formal status in such titles as "Wazir of the Right Hand" for the sovereign's senior and most powerful minister.

This older imagery of right and left is physiological rather than spatial, and is part of a large group of metaphors derived from the human body. In Islamic as in Western languages, the head in its usual place, on top and in charge, and our references to this organ, both visible and hidden, as in "head," "chief," "capital," have their Islamic equivalents in the use of the Arabic *ra's* and *ra'īs,* the Persian *sar,* and the Turkish *baş.*[27] The use of the term "member," or "limb" (Arabic *ʿaḍuw,* Turkish *aza*), to denote an individual forming part of some larger group or assembly is purely modern, and dates from the period of Western influence. The names of the individual limbs or parts of the body, however, figure prominently in Islamic political metaphor. A much-used physiological metaphor is that of the chest or breast, in Arabic *ṣadr,* which in early usage sometimes denotes centrality (e.g., in a building), prominence, leadership, or command, and in later Ottoman usage becomes the formal title of the Grand Vizier.

The terms for forearm (*sāʿid*) and upper arm (*ʿaḍud*)[28] appear occasionally to designate helpers or ministers of the ruler, while the words for hand, in Arabic *yad* and in Persian *dast,* are very widely used with a connotation of power, authority, or protection. In legal language, *yad* means "actual possession or control." In other usages, it has a connotation of competence, capability, or active help. The Persian word *dast* appears to have had the sense of "power and authority" from pre-Islamic times. The term *dastūr* or *dastvar* meant "a person exercising authority," whether religious or political, and was later specialized to denote members of the Zoroastrian priesthood. Arabic derivatives include the senses of "rule," "regulation," and, in modern times, "constitution."

The tongue, the foot, and the blood figure in various idioms, while the eye serves two important purposes, the one for spies, the other for notables or prominent persons.

The imagery of birth and rebirth, renaissance and resurrection, so important in Western usage, have no place in classical Islamic times, probably because of its specifically Christian associations. The great movement of Arab cultural and then political revival in the nineteenth and twentieth centuries, which Westerners have often called the Arab Renaissance, is denoted in Arabic by the word *nahḍa,* from a classical root meaning "to rise to one's feet," in other words from a seated or recumbent position. The political use of the Arabic term *baʿth* and the Persian *rastākhīz,* both with the original theological meaning of "resurrection," dates from the middle years of the present century.

But if Muslim political language spurns the themes of birth, death, and resurrection, it does, however, make use of the metaphors of sickness and more particularly of weakness. The Arabic word *ḍaʿīf,*[29] with the primary meaning of "physically weak," has been used since ancient times to denote those who are socially weak, i.e., in a socially inferior position. A derived participial form, *mustaḍʿaf,*[30] "made weak" or "deemed weak," has acquired the meaning of "deprived" or "oppressed" and has been used from medieval times to the present day in revolutionary appeals.

Another common feature in political language is the imagery of youth and age. Muslims in the past seemed to have shared the common belief that age and experience bring wisdom and confer authority. This belief was once universally held; it is now generally abandoned outside the communist world, and is under attack even there. Examples of this former attitude are not difficult to find. In English, the Latin word for an old man gives us "senator," "senior" and, in a somewhat different vein, "senile." From the equivalent Anglo-Saxon term, we have such words as "elder" and "alderman." The Arabic word *shaykh,* literally "an old man," has become the archetypal term connoting dignity and authority in all the lands of Islam and is widely known in the rest of the world.[31]

Youth is quite another matter. In classical times, the social and political connotation of youth was expressed mainly in two forms, one with a connotation of subordination and service, the other of youthful energy and valor. The best-known example of the first is the term *ghulām,* meaning "a young man," then "a servant," and finally a general term for "young male slaves," particularly those in the service of rulers and governors. The term was also applied to the slave pretorians and other slave troops of these rulers, and thus also acquired a military connotation. Two other terms for a young man, *ḥadath* and *fatā,* have a quite different military connotation, and are applied to the bands of young men, apprentices and others, who formed a kind of militia in the Muslim cities of the Middle Ages.[32] *Futuwwa,* an abstract noun connoting the qualities and characteristics of the *fatā,* is often contrasted with *muruwwa,* the qualities of the grown and mature man. Both terms have a connotation of valor and chivalry. Neither, however, connotes any authority, nor any claim to it.

It was not until the nineteenth and early twentieth centuries that such European movements as Young Germany and Young England evoked their Middle Eastern analogues. The idea that youth constituted a claim to authority was still so alien and indeed shocking, that even the leaders of these movements seem to have had some difficulty in accepting the term. The first such movement was a group of Turkish radicals and reformers who flourished in the 1860s. They were known in Europe as "the Young Ottomans," but in Turkish they called themselves *Yeni Osmanlılar,* or "New Ottomans." Similar caution affected even the vastly more important Young Turks who accomplished the Revolution of 1908. They were known all over Europe as "Young Turks," and even in Turkey, and in the Turkish language, they called themselves and were called by others *Jön Türk,* with a French, not a Turkish adjective. Even that was used by them only when they were in opposition, and abandoned once they were in power. Several decades later, political leaders in the Arab and other Islamic countries began to describe themselves as young, with the expectation that they would thereby gain rather than forfeit the respect of the people.[33]

Metaphors drawn from the family, the household, and the dwelling figure prominently in Islamic political language. The notion of the ruler as the father of his country or people, common in the West and expressed in such terms as the Latin "paternal" or the Greek "patriarchal," is absent in Islam, again probably because of its Christian connotation. The Christian notion of the fatherhood of God, shared in a limited sense by Judaism, is perceived by Muslims as a blasphemous absurdity, and this rejection seems to have extended to the use of the image of the ruler as father. Only in Turkish does a term meaning "father," *ata,*[34] acquire a political connotation, and there it is used of an uncle and tutor rather than a father in the strict sense. Among the Turks, though not among the Muslim Arabs, the term *baba,*[35] "father," is often used as a term of respect for older men, and among the Dervishes is used as a kind of title for Dervish santons and leaders. It has no political connotation. The image of the ruler as mother seems to have been equally abhorrent, and it is probable that the Qurʾanic word *umma,*[36] "the people" or "community," which some have connected with the Arabic *umm,* "mother," is in fact a loanword from either Hebrew or Aramaic.

If, however, the state has no parents, it certainly has children, and terms denoting sons and brothers are in common political use. These may be literal, as for example in indicating membership of a tribe or dynasty, or figurative, indicating a relationship to the state. The term "brother," with its various equivalents, is in common use for members of the same group, by allegiance as well as by kinship, and in Turkish usage "elder brother," *ağa,*[37] is a common term of respect for holders of authority. The best-known example is the *abnāʾ,*[38] "sons," of the ʿAbbasid dynasty, an elite group of slaves and freedmen, both soldiers and civilians, who served the state and thus freed it from dependence on Arab tribal support. This extension of the meaning of "son" was a natural development.

The medieval Muslim family, like that of most of the ancient societies, included slaves as well as kinfolk, and these are regarded in many ways as members of the family. There are many different words for slave in Arabic and other Islamic languages, depending on their functions and their racial origins. "Slave" is commonly used as a metaphor of man's relation to God. It is rarely if ever used as a metaphor for the subject's relation to the sovereign. Various words for slave are often used for the agents and employees of the ruler, but these indicate a legal, not a metaphorical, relationship. The Arabic legal and social terms for "master," the head of the household and owner of the slaves, never underwent the political semantic development of the Greek *despotes* or the Latin *dominus*. Significantly, the best-known Arabic term for "master," *ṣāḥib,*[39] has a primary meaning not of "mastery" but of "companionship." It is the term applied to the companions of the Prophet, the nearest Muslim equivalent to the apostles of Christ; it was sometimes applied, in later times, to the associates and intimates of rulers. Its development into a term of authority, usually delegated or subordinate authority, is a striking example of the potency of nearness.

The pastoral image of government, familiar from the Old Testament and much loved by medieval Christian writers on politics, also appears in both classical and early modern Islamic writings. The first major statement on politics, the introduction to *The Book of the Land Tax,*[40] written for the caliph Hārūn al-Rashīd by his chief qadi Abū Yūsuf, develops the theme of the ruler as shepherd at considerable length.

One of the duties of a shepherd is to feed his flock, and the imagery of food—both cooking and eating—was sometimes used to denote the holding of public offices. Servants of the ruler were said to eat or break his bread. A common Ottoman term for the recipient of a government stipend is *vazifehor,* literally job-eater. In the corps of Janissaries, higher and lower officers were called soupmakers and cooks, and the *kazan*—cookpot or kettle—came to be the emblem of the corps' identity and loyalty. When the Janissaries overturned their cookpots and symbolically refused the sultan's food, this was the recognized signal for mutiny.

Another major group of metaphors derives from travel. The almost universal religious metaphor of God's path or way, which mankind must follow, is familiar to Muslims from the start. It appears in various forms in the Qur'ān, and is reiterated in the daily prayer. The Holy Law of Islam is poetically designated by the term *sharī'a,* the primary meaning of which is "the way to a watering place." If to follow the way is good, to deviate from it is bad, and a variety of terms denoting misbelievers, propounders of error, and rebels have the primary meaning of "to stray from the right path."[41]

While in most Western languages the imagery of travel is maritime, in the Islamic lands it derives from travel by land, and more particularly on horseback. The rider, the horse, the accoutrements, the stirrups, the reins, and even the tail are brought into service as metaphors and sometimes as symbols of authority. Western usage contains two dead metaphors, both derived from the man and his horse—chivalry and management, the one from French *cheval,* "a horse," the other, via French, from Italian *maneggio,* "the handling or training of a horse," whence "horsemanship" and "riding school." Both lines of development are present in Islamic political language, in such words as *furūsiyya,*[42] "equitation," "knightliness," "valor," and *siyāsa,* "horse-handling," "statecraft," "politics."

Travel is not undertaken at random, and rarely alone. Starting point, route, and destination provide a number of metaphors. So too—indeed more particularly—do the guides and leaders and those who follow them. Sometimes the guidance is military, as that of the *qā'id,* "the guide and leader into battle." Sometimes it is perceived as religious, as the guidance of the *murshid,* who leads men into the path of righteousness.[43] A special kind of guidance is that given to the *Mahdī,* "the guided one," a messianic figure who, according to Muslim belief, will be sent and guided by God to end the time of sin and evildoing and fill the world with justice and equity.

The metaphoric journey may be undertaken for a variety of purposes—economic, for pasturage or trade; religious, to a place of pilgrimage; or military, to raid or make war. All these different images appear in the language of power.

From the earliest time, the dwelling and its various parts figure prominently in political metaphors. In ancient Arabian literature, the tent and its components—the peg, the pole, the canopy, etc.—serve as metaphors for the ruler, his government, and his supports. Under the caliphate, the tent was replaced by more sophisticated structures, often denoted by the same words, with the tent pole becoming a column, the canopy a cupola, and the tent peg the foundations of the buildings.

By far the commonest of these metaphors, from ancient to modern times, is the use of words denoting the entrance to the building, or some part of it, to represent the government as such. In modern European history, the Sublime Porte is the familiar Ottoman equivalent of Downing Street, the Elysée Palace, the Ballplatz, the Wilhelmstrasse, and more recently, the Kremlin and the White House. The Sublime Porte was in fact the entrance to the premises of the Grand Vizier, who conducted the business of government on behalf of the sultan. It is the last example of an elaborate system of metaphors going back to remote Middle Eastern antiquity, in which not only the door or gate but also the lintel, the threshold, the portals, the anteroom, the curtains, and all the other approaches to the seat of power were used to represent the power itself.

In Ottoman chancery usage, this metaphor in various forms becomes a standard formula. Thus, Sultan Murad III, writing to Queen Elizabeth of England in 1583 to acknowledge the receipt of her letter, remarks that "your friendship-encompassed letter has . . . reached our Splendid Threshold, the Orbit of Felicity, and our lofty Lintel of Justice, which is the refuge of puissant Sultans and the sanctuary of mighty and revered Khaqans."[44]

Looked at from below, even the threshold might seem exalted. A petition from an imprisoned dragoman addressed to the Ağa of the Janissaries in about 1769, begins, "Having bowed my head in submission and rubbed my slavish brow in utter humility and humbleness and complete abjection and supplication to the beneficent dust beneath the feet of my mighty, gracious, condescending, compassionate, merciful, benefactor" and then addresses a petition to "the might of the dust of the condescending residence." The inscription on the outside of the petition reads, "In the name of almighty God. Petition to the mighty dust beneath the feet of my mighty, gracious, merciful, bounteous, compassionate benefactor, most generous master, now Aga of the Janissaries of the Lofty Court of the Sublime Porte."[45]

In a sense, this imagery is an elaboration of the more basic themes of in and out, near and far. In most Muslim courts, there were chamberlains who guarded the points of access to the ruler from the Outside—beyond the door. They are known by such names as the Arabic *ḥājib,* an active participle of a verb meaning "to screen or veil or cover," or the Persian *pardadār,* "the curtain holder."[46]

Sometimes the metaphors of power are not merely verbal but material, and appear as symbols—as the insignia of authority. In the Islamic lands as elsewhere in the world, the commonest and most widely used of these were weapons. The Prophet himself, we are told, when he first celebrated the two major Muslim festivals, was preceded by one of his followers carrying a spear. During the ceremonies the spear was planted in the ground and indicated the direction towards which the congregant turned in prayer. The caliph ʿUmar is said to have carried a riding switch, and most of the early caliphs, as well as their provincial governors, made it a practice to carry a spear or a staff on ceremonial occasions. It became usual even for the preacher, when ascending the pulpit during the Friday service, to hold or lean on a sword, or a staff, or a bow. Both the staff and the pulpit itself had been tokens of authority among the ancient Arabs, and were used by orators and by arbitrators settling disputes. According to ancient custom, in cities which submitted peacefully to the rule of Islam, the preacher carried a staff. In those that were conquered by force, he carried a sword.

This double tradition continued in a modified form in later times. On the one hand, the staff or sword was attenuated to a purely symbolic scepter, held by the sovereign in person; on the other it was replaced by a symbolic weapon, usually a lance or a mace, carried by a functionary who preceded the ruler in ceremonial public appearances.[47]

In France, the king was proud to be called *le roi-soleil.* In the Middle East, the sun was not a beneficent friend but a terrible enemy, and the metaphoric role of the ruler was not as sun but as shadow—providing shade to protect the people under his authority from the merciless sun. According to an early dictum, "The sultan is the shadow of God upon Earth, with whom all creatures seek shelter."[48] This was materially symbolized by a parasol, carried by a parasol bearer,[49] who accompanied the sovereign at his public appearances. In later Persian and Turkish usage, the imperial shade (*sāye-i humāyūn*) is a common metonymy for the imperial person and the imperial authority.

Not all the metaphors and symbols of power are as beneficent as pasturage and shade. Sometimes the names of various ferocious beasts and birds of prey are used in royal titulature, and some are even portrayed pictorially. Such, for example are the pictures in early Umayyad palaces, depicting panthers and eagles pouncing on their prey. The implied message was no doubt well understood by those who attended the palace.

The crown and the throne, surely the most familiar emblems and metaphors of royal power in the Christian world, are of limited significance in Islamic political symbolism and discourse, and even that little can be attributed to extraneous, usually Persian influence. Though Muslim historians were acquainted with these insignia as used by the ancient kings, and Muslim artists even portrayed them in miniatures, Muslim sovereigns, in no doubt conscious rejection of pagan trappings of monarchy, began their reigns with neither coronation nor enthronement. The nearest equivalent to any such ritual of accession was the ceremony of the girding of the sword of Osman on a new Ottoman sultan. The symbolism of the sword was familiar from the earliest days of Islam.

In most Muslim dynasties, the crown, in Arabic *tāj,*[50] a loanword from Persian, was a turban studded with jewels; in classical times, the functional, though never the symbolic, equivalent of the throne was the *sarīr,* not a high chair but a low couch, on which the sovereign might sit or, more commonly, recline, while holding court. Both were used by provincial governors and other dignitaries, as well as by the sovereign; naturally enough, neither served as a metaphor of supreme power. Another Arabic term, *ʿarsh,* which might be more accurately translated as "throne," is used only of God, in a frequently recurring image in the Qurʾān. The *sarīr* is hardly more than a dignified place to sit or recline.[51]

This contrast between Islamic and Western usage illustrates very clearly the Muslim perception of power relationships in horizontal rather than, as in Christendom, in vertical terms. This is a society which always in principle, and often, at least to some extent, in practice, rejects hierarchy and privilege, a society in which power and status depend primarily on nearness to the ruler and the enjoyment of his favor, rather than on birth or rank.

Movement inward may be beset with difficulties and obstructed by chamberlains and other barriers; but it is incomparably easier than movement upward through the well-defended layers of a stratified society. In this as in much else, Muslim political language reflects the Muslim ideal of social mobility. The Arab historians tell us that when the caliph al-Manṣūr, the architect of the ʿAbbasid Empire, built his new capital in Baghdad in A.D. 758, "he traced the city plan, making the city round."[52] His reason for this, according to the chroniclers, was that "a circular city has advantages over a square city, in that if the monarch were to be in the center of the square city, some parts would be closer to him than others, while, regardless of the divisions, the sections of the Round City are equidistant from him when he is in the center."[53] Nearness is what counts, and justice requires equidistance, at least as a starting point.

The Arab geographers give further reasons for the choice of site. Iraq is the center of the world, Baghdad is the center of Iraq, and the caliph's residence is the center of Baghdad. To emphasize this centrality, the classical authors use a striking metaphor—"the navel of the world."[54] A navel presupposes a body and the body politic is one of the most universal and most enduring of metaphors.

2

The Body Politic

In the year 1653, according to the chroniclers, the Ottoman sultan Mehmed IV convened a meeting of the high officers of the state to discuss a problem that was troubling him. Under his father and his predecessors, he said, the revenues of the state had been sufficient to cover expenditure and even leave some surplus. "My expenditure is not as great as that of my father, and the revenues are the same. Why then does the income of the state no longer suffice to cover the expenditure and why is it that money cannot be raised for the fleet and other important matters?" Those present, beginning with the Grand Vizier, gave various answers to these questions, and in due course, officials conducted some inconclusive investigations and applied some ineffective palliatives.

Among those present at some of these discussions was a famous Ottoman writer and scholar of the time, who was employed in the department of finance. Known as Kâtib Çelebi, he wrote a booklet containing his own explanation of the persistent financial problems of the Empire and the best way to deal with them. The framework of Kâtib Çelebi's analysis is provided by a sustained metaphor. Human states (by which he clearly means dynasties), like human individuals, are organic; they are born, go through the three phases of growth, maturity, and decay, and finally and inevitably, they die. In states as in persons, the relative lengths of these phases may vary according to the health and strength of the individual. The Ottoman state, thanks to its strong constitution and its sound limbs, had enjoyed a long and healthy life. Its current troubles were the symptoms of the approach of the stage of decline. It was the task of physicians for individuals, and of statesmen for states, to recognize these symptoms, and to devise and apply appropriate treatment. In this way old age could be eased and death delayed, by good physic in the human body, by sound statesmanship in the body politic.[1]

In the course of the centuries, Muslims have devoted a great deal of thought and attention to the features, functions, and also ailments of the body politic—the nature of sovereignty, how it is acquired, how it should be exercised; the characteristics of good and bad government; and, in general, the relations between the ruler and the ruled. From early times there has been a rich and ramified literature devoted to these topics, mainly in Arabic but also in Persian, Turkish, and other languages which became vehicles of Islamic civilization.

There is an important historical difference between medieval Islamic and medieval Catholic writings on history and politics. Western Christian civilization was born amid the chaos of the barbarian invasions, in a political context dominated by two contrasting yet related facts—the fall of the Roman State and the rise of the Christian Church. For St. Augustine, the first Christian political theorist, the body politic was man-made and evil, and government a punishment or at best a remedy for original sin. Cain, after all, had founded the first city. In this perception, drawn from the teachings of the ancient Hebrew prophets and shaped by the events of the time, defeat and destruction were divine instruments, designed to bring mankind to the Church, in which alone they could attain salvation. It was not until the thirteenth century that Thomas Aquinas, recognizing the emergence of a Christian polity, accorded some legitimacy to the state and some positive value to political institutions.

Muslim historical observation and political analysis moved in the opposite direction, and began not with defeat but with triumph, not with the fall but with the rise of empire. For the Muslim observer of these early days, political authority was not a human evil, not even a lesser or a necessary evil: it was a divine good. The body politic and the sovereign power within it are ordained by God himself, to promote his faith and to maintain and extend his law. The Muslim, like the Christian, sees God as involved in human affairs and as subjecting his people to a variety of tests. But for the Muslim, God's main concern is to help rather than to test his people, in particular to help them achieve victory and paramountcy in this world. For the Muslim historian, therefore, the holders of power and their activities are not secondary or marginal to the true purpose of history; they are its very essence. Even later, in times of decadence, when pious Muslim authors saw the body politic as diseased and the service of the state as a contamination,[2] they held firm to the principle that the authority of the Muslim ruler, however obtained and however exercised, was a divinely ordained necessity, and that the Sunni community, organized in the body politic, was the unchanging medium of God's guidance. These beliefs are reflected in a number of ways in classical Muslim historical and political writings, and notably in the sharp perception and calm acceptance of the realities of power.

Classical Islamic writings on politics fall into several well-defined categories. Probably the best known in the Western world is the philosophical literature, much of which has been translated into Western languages. Some of these translations date back to the Middle Ages, and exercised a significant influence on the development of political thought in Europe. This Muslim school of political philosophy had its origins in the first Arabic translations and adaptations of ancient Greek texts, notably the political writings of Plato and Aristotle. Muslim philosophers were concerned to relate the philosophic doctrines which they had inherited from antiquity with the religious teachings of Islam. In confronting these dilemmas, they produced a new and original philosophical literature, often containing fresh insights into some of the major problems of politics. In doing so, they forged a new political vocabulary, devising Arabic equivalents for Greek political terms and blending it with the other and more original language which had grown up to express the religio-political traditions of Islam.[3]

This literature, however, despite its undoubted interest and despite the considerable attention which, perhaps because of its familiarity, it has received in the West, is nevertheless of marginal importance in the political and intellectual history of Islam. The Muslim philosophers of the Hellenistic school were a comparatively small, relatively minor group. Their kind of philosophy flourished for a time in the Islamic academies during the Middle Ages, but it died out and had only a limited impact on later generations.

It did, however, contribute substantially to the vocabulary of other types of political writing, of far greater significance for the study both of Muslim ideas and of Muslim attitudes and practices as reflected in history. Medieval Islam, unlike medieval Christendom, had not one but two literate elites, each of which produced its own distinctive literature and even language. In Western Christian lands, for centuries, the clergy were virtually the only literate class. In the Islamic lands in the same period, there was a second literate elite, consisting in the main of what one might call the scribal class—those who in various ways served the central and regional bureaucracies. The scribes produced an immense literature, including history, literary history and—what concerns us here—lengthy discussions of politics. Their concern was practical rather than theoretical, with statecraft rather than political philosophy. Their writings include whole books, or chapters in larger books, devoted to the arts of government, and variously addressed to rulers, ministers, or secretaries of state. These writings reflect very clearly the professional skills, aims, and outlook of medieval Islamic bureaucracies.

The term commonly applied in classical Arabic to these writings is *adab,*[4] a word which, as used in medieval texts, comes close to expressing the meaning of the modern term "political culture." In the most ancient Arabic examples, from pre-Islamic Arabia, it has the meaning of "custom or precedent," more particularly the examples set by revered ancestors and predecessors. In this sense it approximates in meaning to the term *sunna,* which came to denote the sanctified example set by the Prophet and his companions. In later usage it acquires both an ethical and a practical content. In the first sense, it has a connotation of good breeding, courtesy, and urbanity; in the latter sense, of civility, etiquette, and correct behavior in both social and political contexts. In order to meet these requirements, the *adīb,* the possessor of *adab,* needs to achieve a certain elegance in behavior and a certain level of intellectual sophistication. In time, the latter is understood to require knowledge of Arabic poetry, history, and antiquities, as well as of the increasingly ramified nonreligious literature available to medieval readers of Arabic. By the ninth century, *adab* is frequently used in the sense of "literature"—a usage which survives to the present day. At the same time, we find it appearing in the sense of the specialized knowledge or skill required to discharge some office, and more particularly, public offices such as those of the wazir, the qadi, or the civil servant.[5]

Adab was thus the creation and the pabulum of the educated scribal class, on which they were educated and in which their corporate ethos is accurately reflected. It is often contrasted with *ʿilm,* meaning "knowledge," and more particularly, the knowledge of the professional men of religion, the ulema (*ʿulamāʾ*), the possessors of *ʿilm*. These, like the scribes, produced their own specialized literature, primarily concerned with religious matters, which in Islam include law and jurisprudence. The latter is called *fiqh,* and one who engages in it is called *faqīh,* conventionally translated as "doctor of the Holy Law." The most innovative aspect of the political system devised by the Ayatollah Khomeini is his doctrine of the "Authority of the *Faqīh*"[6] which provides for the establishment of a single *faqīh* as the supreme legal authority in the state—a kind of constitutional supreme court, with powers to declare invalid any action or enactment of the government seen as contrary to Islam. There is no precedent for such an office in past Islamic doctrine and practice.

The standard treatises on *fiqh,*[7] almost without exception, include sections on government, and some authors devote whole works to this topic. From the point of view of the *faqīh,* these writings are not concerned with philosophic speculation, nor with political theory, nor even with practical statecraft, but with constitutional law. The *sharīʿa,* the Holy Law of Islam, embraces the whole range of human activities, and is therefore naturally concerned with the conduct of government in all its aspects. Since the law, in the Muslim conception, is divine and immutable, that part of it concerned with government shares these attributes. The function of the jurist, in this as in other areas of the law, is not to speculate, still less to innovate; his task is to formulate and where necessary to interpret the explicit rules and to elaborate the general principles contained in the Qurʾān, the Traditions of the Prophet, and the other recognized sources of Islamic jurisprudence. The *faqīh* is concerned with the state neither as a philosophical abstraction nor as a historical phenomenon, though clearly he is aware of both these aspects. He sees the state primarily as a divine instrument—as a necessary and inherent part of God's providential dispensation for mankind.

The principal function of government is to enable the individual Muslim to lead a good Muslim life. This is, in the last analysis, the purpose of the state, for which alone it is established by God, and for which alone statesmen are given authority over others. The worth of the state, and the good and evil deeds of statesmen, are measured by the extent to which this purpose is accomplished. The basic rule for Muslim social and political life, commonly formulated as "to enjoin good and forbid evil,"[8] is thus a shared responsibility of the ruler and the subject, or in modern terms, of the state and the individual.

In principle, the Holy Law, in politics as in other matters, is based on revelation and is therefore not subject to change. In fact, with the passage of time, differences of interpretation appeared among the jurists, reflecting the impact of new ideas, sometimes from inside, sometimes from outside the Muslim community, and also—indeed more especially—the practical changes which were taking place. During the fourteen centuries that have passed since the *hijra* of the Prophet, there have been many states established by Muslims and called "Islamic." As is natural in the course of human affairs, these reflect a wide variety of different circumstances, different challenges, and different responses. While the jurists, in principle at least, remained faithful to the basic precepts of the Holy Law, there was room for disagreement and development concerning the interpretation and application of those precepts. Muslim jurists, at least in Sunni Islam, have usually accepted the principle that men of learning and piety might disagree in good faith, within certain limits, while remaining orthodox. It is in this way that they sometimes justify the coexistence and mutual tolerance of different schools of legal interpretation. The accommodation of such changes and developments was facilitated by the doctrine of *ijmāʿ*,[9] usually translated "consensus," though perhaps "climate of opinion" might be a closer rendering.

There are two very common misapprehensions concerning Islamic political thought and government, the one perceiving them as theocratic, the other as despotic or even dictatorial. These judgments are based on misunderstandings. The question whether the Islamic polity is or is not theocratic is more semantic than substantial, and the answer depends largely on the definition of theocracy that is adopted. If by theocracy we mean a state governed by the church, that is, by priests, Islam clearly is not and until recently could not be a theocracy. There is no church or priesthood in Islam, neither theologically, since there is no priestly office or mediation between God and the individual believer, nor institutionally, since there are no prelates and no hierarchy.

At least, there were none in classical Islamic times. In postmedieval, and more especially in recent, times, there have been some changes. The Ottomans adopted the institution of territorial muftis (Arabic *muftī*, Turkish *müftü*),[10] each with his own diocese, forming part of a hierarchy presided over by the chief mufti of Istanbul. There was no such system in medieval times, when the mufti operated as a jurisconsult, without public appointment and without defined jurisdiction. In Iran, because of the official adoption of Shiʿite Islam in the sixteenth century, the professionalization of religion followed a somewhat different path, but there too, the *mujtahids,*[11] as the Shiʿite divines are called, began to function, at least in the sociological sense, as a clergy. This tendency was accentuated in the late nineteenth century, with the emergence for the first time of the office of *āyatollāh*[12]—the first Muslim equivalent to an episcopate.

Despite these developments, there is still no priesthood in the strictly theological sense and, therefore, no true theocracy as thus defined. But there is another interpretation of the word "theocracy," based on its original and literal meaning, that is, "the rule of God."[13] In the juristic conception of the Muslim state, God alone is the supreme sovereign, the ultimate, indeed the sole legitimate source of authority. In this conception, only God makes law; only God confers, or at least legitimizes, authority. God thus becomes the formal expression of supreme sovereignty, and is often named in much the same way, and in much the same contexts, as the city, the crown, or the people in various Western polities. This did not, of course, mean the rule of the clergy, which, in the sacerdotal sense, did not exist. In most Muslim countries it was not the practice for professional men of religion to hold political office. There is no papacy in Islam, and there are no equivalents in Muslim history to cardinals Wolsey or Richelieu, Mazarin or Alberoni. In this respect too, the regime of the mollahs in present day Iran is a radical departure from all Islamic precedent.

There is even less foundation for the portrayal of Islamic government as a system in which the ruler is an all-powerful despot and the subject his helpless slave, entirely at his mercy. This picture is false in both theory and practice. Muslim law has never conceded absolute power to the sovereign, nor, with few exceptions, have Muslim sovereigns ever been able to exercise such power for any length of time. It is true that the predominant view of the jurists is authoritarian, that is to say, that the sovereign, once installed, has a very considerable authority, and that the subject's duty of obedience is a religious obligation as well as a political necessity. Nevertheless, the authority of the ruler, though paramount, is subject to a very important limitation.

The principle which underlies this limitation derives from the Muslim conception of law. In the traditional Muslim view, the state does not create the law, but is itself created and maintained by the law, which comes from God and is interpreted and administered by those who are skilled in these tasks. The ruler's duty is to defend and uphold, to maintain and enforce, the law, by which he himself is bound no less than the humblest of his subjects. For these purposes he may make rules and regulations, to clarify and apply the law. He may in no way abrogate or amend the law, nor may he add to it.

Since the ruler cannot change the Holy Law, he cannot legally exceed the degree of authority assigned to him by that law. If he attempts to do this, if he acts, or commands others to act, in a manner that is contrary to the law, he is guilty of an offense against the law, for which he is liable to punishment.

While classical Muslim political writers did not normally make the modern distinction between the state and the government, they nevertheless developed a wide range of technical terms to denote and discuss the polity, the sovereign authority ruling over that polity, the nature of the power which that authority exercises, and the manner in which it is or should be exercised.

Each of the different schools or groups of political writers developed its own terminology. In the writings of the jurists and theologians, the constitutional lawyers of classical Islam, the term invariably used to denote the supreme sovereign authority is *imāma,* "the office or function of the *imām.*" From a root meaning "in front of," the *imām* comes to be the leader in prayer, and hence, by extension, the religio-political head of the whole Islamic community, whose God-given task it is to lead them in the fulfillment of God's commandments. It is noteworthy that the jurists chose this word, rather than the more obvious *khilāfa,* "caliphate," in their formulations of the qualifications, functions, and duties of the supreme sovereign.[14]

The polity or community over which this sovereign rules is the *umma,* the single universal Islamic community embracing all the lands in which Muslim rule is established and the Islamic law prevails. The term *umma* is pre-Islamic, occurring in early Arabic as well as in other Semitic languages, and can be used of groups defined in various ways. It occurs several times in the Qur'ān, with interesting variations. It can be ethnic, since the Qur'ān speaks of the *umma* of the Arabs. It can be religious, since the Qur'ān also speaks of the *umma* of the Christians. It can be moral, since the Qur'ān speaks of the *umma* of good people, as opposed to the *umma* of bad people. It can be ideological, since the Qur'ān speaks of the *umma* of those who do well and behave well among the Christians. In ancient southern Arabia, the obviously related term *lumiya* meant a "tribal confederacy," and it is probably in something like this sense that the term *umma* was used during the lifetime of the Prophet, for the first constituted Islamic community in Medina.

In classical Islamic literature, the word *umma* is frequently used in both religious and ethnic senses, sometimes with no clear differentiation between the two. Thus, mentions by medieval Arabic writers of the Persian and Turkish *umma*s may, in different contexts, refer to their pre-Islamic past, or may serve to contrast them, as Muslims, with the Arabs. Increasingly, however, Muslim writers came to speak of a single *umma* of the Muslims, without ethnic or regional subdivisions, and when they speak of other *ummas* (the Arabic plural is *umam*), these are usually religious groups such as, for example, the Christians or the Zoroastrians. They may also be ethnic nations, such as the Franks or the Slavs, though from late medieval times *umma* is rarely used of ethnic groups within Islam.[15]

The Arabic philosophical literature, beginning with translations and adaptations from Greek texts and developing into an important branch of Islamic literature, uses a somewhat different vocabulary to denote the body politic. The word commonly used for the polity or political society is *madīna,* and it clearly represents an attempt to render the meaning of the Greek words *polis* and *politeia.* The various types of cities named in the Greek classifications—the oligarchic city, the aristocratic city, the democratic city, etc.—are all rendered as *madīna,* each with a suitably devised adjective.[16]

The word itself has an interesting history in Arabic usage. In origin, it is clearly a loanword from either Aramaic or Hebrew, and comes from the same root as *dīn,* which has the related meanings of "religion" in Arabic and "law" in Hebrew and Aramaic. The *madīna* is the area of jurisdiction of a judge, *dayyān.* The word *madīna* occurs frequently in the Qur'ān. Most of the occurrences are in stories told about the ancient prophets, but in four places it is applied to the oasis town of Yathrib, to which the Prophet and his followers had moved from Mecca, and in which they established the first Muslim polity. Already during the lifetime of the Prophet, *al-Madīna,* "the city," was used as a kind of honorific name for Yathrib, and before long, the old name passed out of use. In the first few centuries of the caliphate, the word *madīna,* most frequently in the plural, *mudun,* was used to designate the administrative centers of the provinces. Aramaic was still widely spoken, and it is not unlikely that the term retained its original meaning of "a jurisdiction." In another plural, *al-madā'in,* it provided the Arabic name of the ancient Persian city of Ctesiphon, the only imperial capital to fall into the hands of the Arab conquerors. In the singular form *madīnat al-salām,* "the city of peace," it was adopted by the ʿAbbasid caliphs as the official designation of Baghdad. In a similar honorific sense, *madīna* is also used of other Islamic cities, such as Cairo, Isfahan, Samarqand, and Bokhara. In North Africa *madīna* remained in use until modern times, to designate the inner or walled city or citadel, in contrast to the outer suburbs.

It was not only the jurists and the philosophers who discussed the nature of government. The basic questions of politics are discussed in a wide range of other writings—literary, bureaucratic, historical, etc.—and these devote much space to the theory as well as the practice of government, to statecraft as well as administration. While these writers of what we might call the literary and practical schools make some use of the language of the jurists and the philosophers, they tend to use a somewhat different vocabulary of their own, more literary, and also more practical, in discussing the conduct of government and the agencies through which it is conducted.

Two Arabic roots in particular are laid under heavy contribution. The word *amr,* which is used in the Qurʾān and in other early texts in the sense of "authority" and "command," is of frequent occurrence. A person who holds a command or an office or position of authority is referred to as a *ṣāḥib amr.* The holder of a high *amr* is, of course, an *amīr.* In later medieval times, the adjective *amīrī* is often used in the sense of "governmental or administrative," while in the Ottoman Empire the slightly shortened form *miri,* with its Turkish translation *beylik,* comes to be the common word for "governmental," "public," "official." In Ottoman usage, *miri* is also used of the state treasury, of government storehouses, and of government property in general.[17]

Another root much used in the early texts is *wly,* which, from the primary meaning of "to be near or close to someone or something," comes to have the general meaning of "to be in charge," "to run or administer," "to govern or rule," "to exercise power or authority." This verb, and the nominal forms *walī* and *wilāya,* appear frequently in the Qurʾān, the Traditions, and the early literature, to denote, respectively, the ruler and the exercise of rule. Ibn al-Muqaffaʿ, writing in the mid–eighth century, uses these two words currently in his discussions of politics. A vivid example is his dictum *wilāyat al-nās balāʾ ʿaẓīm*[18]—"governing people is a great tribulation." Shakespeare expressed the same notion in the phrase "uneasy lies the head that wears a crown." Al-Ghazālī, writing in the twelfth century, still uses the term *wilāya* when he wishes to discuss the office and function of government, or the exercise of state authority. *Wilāya,* he says, is validly executed by sultans who profess allegiance to the caliph. His point is to provide a legal and theoretical justification for the kind of de facto authority being exercised by the sultans. *Wilāya,* he says, in these days, is a consequence solely of military power. To whatever person the holder of military power professes allegiance, that person is caliph.[19]

By Ottoman times, *wilāya* had even acquired a territorial significance. In early Ottoman usage, *wilāya*—in Turkish *vilâyet*— meant "a governorship," and hence the area over which the governor exercises his authority. The governor, of course, is the *vali*.

Another word used with the general abstract sense of authority is *sulṭān*. This appears a number of times in the Qur'ān, with the meaning of "power," sometimes of "proof" and more particularly of "effective power," often with the adjective *mubīn—sulṭān mubīn,* "manifest authority." It also occurs in the Qur'ān in the sense of authority exercised by someone over someone else, and it seems to retain this meaning in early Islamic usage. In a famous speech said to have been delivered by Ziyād when he was sent by the caliph Muʿāwiya to govern Iraq, he told the Iraqis, "We govern you by the authority [*sulṭān*] of God which He has given us."[20]

This use, in the early Islamic period, is attested in a number of other sources. The scribe ʿAbd al-Ḥamīd, writing in the early eighth century, commonly uses *sulṭān* for "rule" or "government."[21] What is perhaps more striking is the use of the term in administrative papyri coming from Egypt in this period, where it has the sense of "the public authorities." Thus, the land tax accruing to the government is called "the tax of the *sulṭān*"; the public or state treasury is called "the treasury of the *sulṭān*." These are clearly the practical administrative equivalents of what in the juridical literature would be called the taxes of God or the treasury of God or sometimes of the Muslims. Even later, when the word *sulṭān* came to be used more and more of a person, it still retained the general sense of authority in certain specific contexts, as for example in the formula often found in construction inscriptions by rulers and dignitaries, *adām Allāh sulṭānahu,* "may God prolong his authority" (i.e., his reign).[22]

By far the commonest term for the state and the polity, from the eighth century onwards, is *dawla,* which, with its phonetic variations in other Islamic languages, is now the almost universal word for the state. It comes from the Arabic root *dwl,* with the basic meaning of "to rotate, turn, change, alternate, or succeed one another." It is used, for example, when speaking of the alternation of seasons in the year. It occurs in the Qur'ān (III, 140), speaking of the alternation of good days and bad days. At a very early stage in Arabic, it acquires a meaning close to the idiomatic English use of the word "turn," and there are many passages in ancient Arabian poetry in which *dawla* refers to somebody's "turn" at success and power or merely of favor and attention, as for example, a wife's "turn" with her husband in a polygamous household. In the form *dūlatan,* it occurs in the Qur'ān (LIX, 7) in the sense of something held in common, the ownership of which is taken in turn by a number of persons. These and other similar expressions are based on the familiar image of the wheel of fortune, the slowly turning wheel of fate which brings one man or group up and another man or group down.

Common political use of *dawla* dates from the accession to power of the ʿAbbasid caliphs in the mid-eighth century. The Umayyads had had their turn, and now it was the turn of the House of ʿAbbās. There are many texts of the period, expressing this notion and using this terminology. When Ibn al-Muqaffaʿ remarks, *"Al-dunyā duwal,"* it is clear that he does not mean that the world consists of dynasties or states, as the phrase would mean in modern Arabic; his meaning is rather that the world is full of ups and downs, of vicissitudes.[23] The word "vicissitude," incidentally, comes from the Latin *vicissim,* "in turn."

The turn of the ʿAbbasids lasted a long time, and the word *dawla,* by a process of gradual transformation, came to mean the reigning ʿAbbasid house, and then, more generally, the dynasty and ultimately the state. This evolution of the word from the primary meaning, "to turn around," to a connotation that is governmental, imperial, in a sense even aulic, is not unparalleled, as a glance at some recent and current uses of the terms "revolution" and "revolutionary" may demonstrate.

At the present time, the common word in Arabic, Turkish, and some other languages for "government" is *ḥukūma*. Though by now almost universal in Islamic lands, its use in this sense is very recent, and dates back no further than the nineteenth century. The word *ḥukūma* itself is very ancient. The root *ḥkm* in Arabic and in some other Semitic languages expresses the related basic notions of judgment and wisdom. In some Semitic languages, notably Hebrew, it is the sense of "wisdom" that prevailed. In Arabic, the sense of "wisdom" or even "knowledge" is present, as for example in *ḥakīm,* "a sage" and hence "a physician," but it is the sense of "judgment" or "adjudication" that is most usual. *Ḥukūma* meant "adjudication," the administration and dispensing of justice, usually by a qadi or some other judicial functionary.

During the Middle Ages, by a natural development, the range of meaning of the root and of its various derivatives was extended to include political as well as judicial authority, and *ḥukūma* often denoted the office or function of governorship, or even the seizure, tenure, or term of office of a governor. By the end of the eighteenth century, the word had acquired a more general sense of authority. Thus, in a letter of January 1801 sent by the French general Jacques (later ʿAbdallāh) Menou to the diwan in Cairo, he describes himself as a commander of the armies of the French Republic and the representative of its authority (*muẓāhir ḥukūmatihā*) in Egypt.

In early nineteenth-century Turkish writings, the Turkish form of the word, *hukûmet,* is commonly used in the senses of rule, political authority, dominion, and occasionally even regime. It had much the same range of meaning in contemporary Arabic works, as for example in the Arabic translation of the first part of William Robertson's *History of the Reign of Charles V,* published in 1844. This usage seems to have been new in Arabic and still did not have the precise meaning of the European term "government." An Arabic translation of Machiavelli's *Prince,* completed in 1825, and a translation of the French constitutional charter, published in 1834, use other terms and expressions to render the Italian *governo* and the French *gouvernement.*

The first unambiguous occurrence of the new meaning that has so far come to light is in a Turkish memorandum of about 1837, in which the writer, Sadık Rıfat, speaks of "the governments of the states of Europe" (*düvel-i Avrupa hukûmetleri*). In this the writer is clearly distinguishing between the state (*devlet, dawla*) as an abstraction, and the government (*hukûmet, ḥukūma*) in the sense of the group of men exercising the authority of the state. Thereafter this distinction becomes commonplace, and the use of this term conforms almost exactly to the common practice of Western languages.[24]

Among numerous other terms used with a connotation of power or authority, two are of particular interest, coming from opposite ends of the spectrum of political perceptions. *Shawka,* from *shawk,* "thorn," "spike," or "prickle," means "power," and is used more particularly of physical military might, irrespective of any question of legitimacy, legality, or religious sanction. It is often used, as for example, by al-Ghazālī, in discussing the difference between brute force and religious legitimacy. By Ottoman times, it had undergone a subtle change, and had acquired a much more positive connotation. Linked with such other words as *ijlāl* and *iqbāl,* it connotes the imperial pomp and majesty of the sultan, and a number of compound words, combining *shawka* (Turkish *şevket*) with some other element, figure prominently in the sultan's titles and mean something like "imperial," "august," or "majestic."[25]

If *shawka* represents brute force, another term, *ḥaḍra,* represents the sacral, in a sense the mystical, aspect of royalty. With the literal meaning of "presence," from the verb "to be present," it was in common use by the high Middle Ages. Initially, it seems to refer to the physical presence or nearness of the sovereign, who by this time is secluded from the mass of the people by an army of chamberlains, courtiers, and guards. In time the word itself was, so to speak, sacralized. It no doubt derived additional force from its contemporary use in the language of the mystics, who spoke in similar terms of the presence or nearness of God. *Ḥaḍra* is also used of holy places, notably of the tomb of the Prophet in Medina, which is also secluded and protected from general access by the guardians of the sanctuary.[26]

While later usage added many new words to the early Islamic terminology for the ruler and the government, it added very little to the terminology used to denote the society or community as a whole. *Umma* remains by far the commonest word to denote both the Islamic community and those other communities, at home and abroad, with which it had dealings. A few other words, however, came into general use and acquired a new and specialized significance.

The word *milla,* more familiar to us in its Turkish form *millet,* is a Qur'anic Arabic word of Aramaic origin, originally meaning "a word," and hence a group of people who accept a particular word or revealed book. In Christian Aramaic it is used to translate *logos.* In Qur'anic and subsequent usage, it is more strictly religious in its connotation than *umma.* It is used of the religious community of Islam; it is also used of other, including non-Muslim, religious groups, and of some deviant groups within the Islamic world. In the Ottoman

Empire it became a technical term, and was used for the organized, recognized, religio-political communities enjoying certain rights of autonomy under their own chiefs.[27]

Again, the primary basis was religious rather than ethnic. Either interpretation is possible for the Armenians and the Jews, since these could be defined in both religious and ethnic terms. But the composition of the largest and most important of the non-Muslim *millets,* the Greek *millet,* makes it clear that the basic classification was religious. The Greek *millet* in the Ottoman empire meant the Greek Orthodox Church and all its followers, including Serbs, Rumanians, Bulgarians, Albanians, and Arabs, as well as Greeks. It was not until a very late date, and under the influence of European nationalist ideas, that separate ethnic *millets* began to appear.

Similarly, there was only one Muslim *millet* in the Ottoman Empire, and the term was not used of Turks, Albanians, Arabs, Kurds, or other ethnic groups within the larger Muslim community. The Ottomans saw even the outside world in similar terms. When the sultans first began to send letters to Queen Elizabeth I of England, they addressed her as "Glory of the virtuous ladies of the Christian Community, Elder of the revered matrons of the Sect of Jesus, Moderator of the peoples of the Nazarene Faith, who draws the trains of majesty and reverence, Mistress of the tokens of grandeur and glory, Queen of the *vilâyet* of England, may her end be happy." For the Ottoman chancery scribes, the important thing about Elizabeth was that she was a Christian princess, and this comes first, second, and third in the list of titles. It is only in the fourth place that her realm of England is named, and then with the somewhat dismissive designation of *vilâyet.*[28]

Though Muslim protocol usually despised territorial limitations, regarding them as something to be applied to others rather than to their own rulers, they were nevertheless aware of the existence of territorially defined kingdoms. The commonest term in Arabic and other languages is *mamlaka,* Turkish *memleket,* with the plural *mamālik.* From an Arabic verb meaning "to own or rule," and associated with *malik,* "king," and *mālik,* "proprietor," this word might be generally translated as "realm," "dominion," or even "kingdom." The commonest usage, when speaking of one's own territories, was some such formula as the "Islamic realms" or the "divinely guarded realms." Specific territorial or dynastic limitations were normally applied only to others, though in the later Ottoman period, the term "Ottoman realm," possibly under European influence, came to be accepted.[29]

In modern times a new word has entered the political vocabulary and is now in almost universal use. It is the Arabic term *waṭan,* with its phonetic variations and equivalents in the other languages of Islam. In classical usage, *waṭan* means "one's place of birth or residence." It is often used in the sense of "homeland" or "birthplace," and appears frequently with a connotation of sentiment and nostalgia. Longing for one's *waṭan* is often associated with lamenting for one's departed youth. It had no political connotation, and there is no suggestion that the *waṭan* could in any sense be the focus of allegiance or identity or the basis of some political structure.

The new meaning dates from the last years of the eighteenth century, and can be traced to foreign influence. The earliest examples of its use in a clearly political sense that have so far come to light occur in the report of the Turkish ambassador to Paris after the French Revolution. There he uses the word *vatan* in a number of contexts where it obviously represents the French *patrie,* with the normal political connotations which the word held at that time and in that place.

In the course of the nineteenth century, the word *waṭan,* with derivatives for "patriot" and "patriotism," passed into common use as part of the new nationalist terminology, and a number of older terms, part of the political languages of Islam, began to acquire new meanings. The ideological influences coming from Europe after the French Revolution suggested new concepts of political identity and authority, based, not on communal loyalty and dynastic allegiances, as in the past, but on country or nation.[30]

Countries and nations had of course existed from time immemorial, and had evoked sentimental attachment and ethnic pride, both well attested in the literature of the Islamic peoples. But countries and nations had not hitherto been seen as constituting either the basis of corporate identity or the legitimizing source of political power. This was a new idea, and its general acceptance in the twentieth century transformed the political scene and even the political map of the Islamic world. The universal Islamic monarchy of the Turkish sultans was destroyed and that of the Persian shahs transformed, and in their place the ancient lands of the Middle East were covered with a patchwork quilt of soi-disant nation-states. With a few exceptions, their frontiers and sometimes their very identities were new and invented, typified by straight lines on the map, such as often appear in America but never in Europe; even some of their very names were exhumed from the forgotten past or borrowed from the alien West.

For these new and imported political structures, a new vocabulary was needed. "Country"—a land, a place, tangible and visible—was easy enough, and the word *waṭan* quickly acquired and has ever since retained the emotional and ideological overtones and undertones of *patrie, vaterland, rodina,* and the rest. "Nation" was much more difficult. What, after all, is a nation, by what criteria is it defined, by what common attributes and values is it held together? These questions are difficult enough to answer in Europe; they become much more difficult when posed amid the kaleidoscopic ethnic diversity and deep communal loyalties of the Islamic world.

Arabic, Persian, and Turkish all possess numerous words denoting ethnic groups. It is surely significant that these words did not furnish the terminology of emergent nationalism. Instead, Arabs, Persians, and Turks alike preferred to take old terms, with a religious meaning, and refurbish them to meet the new need. In both Persian and Turkish, the words for "national" and "nation" are *milli* and *millet,* from the old *milla* or *millet,* "a religio-political community." Even today, in the secular Turkish republic, "nation" is *millet,* "nationalism" is *milliyet,* and "nationalist" is *milliyetci.* In modern Arabic *milla* and *millī* are virtually obsolete, but the Arabs have adopted a word of equally religious content, *umma,* to designate the Arab nation.

Clearly, such words, when acquiring a new value, do not entirely lose the old, and the proportions of old and new meanings, of religious and national content with which they are used, may vary considerably according to time, place, circumstance, and the user. Sometimes different, indeed contrasting, meanings may be found in the same document, as for example in the great Ottoman reform edict of 1839, which proclaims an Ottoman *millet* that includes all Ottomans irrespective of religion, and goes on to discuss the need for good relations between "the people of Islam and other *millets*" within the Empire.[31]

These and similar ambiguities have persisted, in the language of political discourse in Islamic lands, to the present day. In recent years, indeed, they have increased rather than decreased, as political involvement and participation have spread beyond the small, mostly westernized elites who for long dominated political life in their countries, and are reaching ever wider circles of the population, where Western political notions are less acceptable or even familiar and where traditional beliefs and aspirations still predominate. Amid the fearful strains and stresses of our time, it is clear—and not surprising—that older and deeper loyalties are stirring beneath the cracking surface of the modern nation-states.

3

The Rulers and the Ruled

♦

There is in the books of Muslim tradition a *ḥadīth,* a saying attributed to the prophet Muḥammad, in which we find, conveniently listed in the descending order of merit and preference, some of the main titles of sovereignty used by Muslims. According to this tradition, the Prophet said, "After me, there will be caliphs; and after the caliphs, amīrs; and after the amīrs, kings; and after the kings, tyrants. . . ."[1]

The tradition is certainly spurious, and is of a familiar type, in which some judgment or argument concerning the events of the early centuries of Islam is projected backwards into the mouth of the Prophet. It is one of many messianic traditions, probably dating from the second century of the Muslim era, and it refers to the patriarchal, early and late Umayyad caliphs.

This, however, in no way affects its value for the purposes of our study. Indeed, this listing, with the value judgments implied, forms a convenient starting point for the study of Muslim sovereign titles, of their origins, development, and transformations, and the associations which they had for Muslims in their time.

The first in sequence, and obviously the most highly esteemed, is caliph, which is also the Muslim sovereign title of the Middle Ages best known in the outside world. Indeed, it has become customary in modern historiography to refer to the medieval Muslim polity as a whole as the caliphate. The English word comes from the Arabic *khalīfa,*[2] a root to be found in a number of Semitic languages, sometimes with the meaning of "pass on" or "pass over," in Arabic usually with the meaning of "come after" or "come instead of." The word thus combines the meanings of deputy, replacement, and successor—an ambiguity significant for the later development of the title.

The term is first attested in pre-Islamic Arabia, in an Arabic inscription of the sixth century A.D., in which the *khalīfa* appears to be some kind of viceroy or lieutenant acting for a sovereign[3] elsewhere. *Khalīfa* occurs twice in the Qurʾān, once referring to Adam (II, 28) and once to David (XXXVIII, 257)—the latter in a context which carries a strong suggestion of sovereignty. "We have made you *khalīfa* on Earth," says God to David, "judge justly among men." David, it will be recalled, was for Muslims both prophet and king, combining religious and political authority. The word also occurs several times in the Qurʾān in two plural forms, *khulafāʾ* and *khalāʾif*. These occur in contexts where they may be translated as "successors," sometimes as "heirs," as "possessors," or possibly as "viceroys."[4]

The historic caliphate, the first and by far the greatest and most important sovereign institution in Islamic history, begins with the death of the Prophet and the appointment of Abū Bakr as his successor in the headship of the community. He was the first of a long series. There is an interesting conversation, recorded in several versions by later Arabic writers, which runs something like this: "When Abū Bakr succeeded the Prophet, he was called *Khalīfatu Rasūl Allāh,* the deputy of the prophet of God. Then ʿUmar succeeded [or perhaps replaced] him [the Arabic word is *istakhlafahu*]. A man came to hear ʿUmar and addressed him as *Khalīfat Allāh,* deputy of God. ʿUmar cursed him, and said: 'That is David.' The man then called him *Khalīfatu Rasūl Allāh,* deputy of the prophet of God, and ʿUmar said: 'But that was Abū Bakr, who is now dead.' So the man addressed him as *Khalīfatu Khalīfati Rasūl Allāh,* deputy of the deputy of the prophet of God, and ʿUmar said: 'That is correct, but it will grow longer,' and the man said: 'Then what shall we call you?' And ʿUmar said: 'You are the believers and I am your commander, therefore call me 'commander of the believers.'"[5] We shall return to this title a little later.

This narrative is no more likely to be authentic than the tradition of the Prophet already cited. Like it, the conversation reflects the preoccupations of a later date, and seeks early authority for a particular point of view. The issue at stake was profoundly important. Granted that the supreme sovereign of the Muslim polity and community is a viceregent, of whom is he in fact the viceregent: of the Prophet, or of

God? The view of the jurists, frequently expressed in narratives like this and more directly in the form of argument, is that the sovereign is the *khalīfa* of the Prophet, and in no sense of God. From quite an early date we find many dicta specifically rejecting the notion of any viceregency or vicariate of God. Clearly, the jurists and others felt an urgent need to make and to repeat this point. They make it, however, to denounce usage and abusage, not to refute any contrary argument. There is no formal theoretical statement of the vicariate of God in Sunni juridical, philosophical, or political literature, and the caliphs themselves seem, on the whole, to have been rather careful not to take up a formal position on this question. The coins and inscriptions in which the title is used for the most part simply describe the ruler as *khalīfa,* without stating of what or of whom, nor indeed over whom he exercised his caliphate.

With three exceptions, the title *khalīfat Allāh,* "deputy of God," with the vastly more extensive claim that it implies, was used in a tentative, one might even say an unofficial, way. It appears, for example, in odes of praise addressed to the Umayyad caliphs and later to the ʿAbbasid caliphs, by their court poets, or as we might nowadays call them, their public relations officers. It appears occasionally in speeches and letters cited in books, or in historical narratives and other writings. Its use, however, in what one might call official contexts is exceedingly rare and, when it does occur, highly significant. The first who appears to have used the title in inscriptions was the Umayyad caliph ʿAbd al-Malik (r. 685–705). He was also the first caliph with a conscious and explicit imperial purpose, a Muslim rival to the Christian Roman Emperor in Constantinople. His imperial ambitions were expressed in the creation of a new, centralized administration working in the Arabic language and, most dramatically, in the issue of a new gold currency with Arabic, Islamic inscriptions. Until then, only the Roman emperors, in Rome and Constantinople, had struck gold coins, and ʿAbd al-Malik's infringement of this hitherto unchallenged world prerogative provoked the emperor to make war.

There are also coins of the ʿAbbasid caliph al-Maʾmūn (r. 813–33) in which he describes himself as *khalīfat Allāh.* Al-Maʾmūn, it will be recalled, was one of the very few caliphs who ever attempted to assert the authority of the state over religious teachings, and was the author of what has been well described as the one and only—and unsuccessful—attempt by a Sunni ruler at an Erastian Islam.

The third to use this title in an inscription was the late ʿAbbasid caliph al-Nāṣir (r. 1180–1225). In this he not only calls himself *khalīfat Allāh,* "deputy of God," but further maintains that he exercises this function over *Kāffat al-Muslimīn,* "all the Muslims." Al-Nāṣir too, it will be recalled, was engaged in an attempt unique in Islamic religious politics, to create a sort of caliphal Vatican state. By this time, the real political power of the caliphate had long since been lost, but the emergence of separate and rival military powers in the eastern and western lands of the caliphate allowed to the caliph who still reigned in Baghdad a brief interval of semi-independence, which al-Nāṣir tried to transform into a local political principality with universal religious suzerainty.[6]

The title *khalīfat Allāh* clearly marks a claim to something like a divine right of monarchy, an authority deriving directly from God. By far the more usual interpretation, that of the totality of Sunni ulema, was that the caliph was the deputy or successor of the Prophet—that is to say, the custodian of the moral and material heritage of the Prophet, in his double capacity as founder of the faith and creator of the Islamic polity and community, but not in his spiritual office as Prophet and as the bringer and interpreter of God's word.

In principle, there could be only one *khalīfa,* one supreme sovereign. This was perceived as a universal, in a different perspective one might say an imperial, title, an Islamic equivalent of the Hellenistic and Hellenistic-Christian idea of the pan-basileus, the "all-king," presiding over a single, universal empire. Indeed, right through the Middle Ages, the title *khalīfa* was only used by those who held, or at least claimed, the office of supreme Muslim ruler, and never by lesser sovereigns with more limited claims. There was one God in heaven, who gave one law to mankind and established one ruler to maintain and enforce that law in his one community.

In principle, therefore, there could be only one caliph, and, with a single exception, this principle was maintained right through the Islamic Middle Ages. That exception was the challenge of the Fatimid caliphs,[7] who appeared in North Africa at the beginning of the tenth century, ruled Egypt and Syria and western Arabia, and tried unsuccessfully to conquer the East. Just as the popes of Rome, for a while, faced the challenge of an antipapacy, so too did the caliphate for a while confront an anticaliphate. The Fatimid caliphs were no local dynasty, of a kind that had by then become common in the Islamic world, trying to carve out an autonomous or independent principality from caliphal territories. They were the leaders of a major religious and political movement, inspired by Ismāʿīlī Shiʿism, which denied the legitimacy of the ʿAbbasid caliphs, and sought to supplant them as heads of all Islam. The challenge lasted for centuries, and at times came very near to success. It ultimately failed, and the nominal supremacy of the Sunni ʿAbbasid caliphate in Baghdad was restored. The first, and for a long time the only, example of a purely local caliphate was that established by the Umayyad amīr of Cordova, the capital of Muslim Spain, in 929. Until then, the rulers of Muslim Spain, though effectively independent of the Muslim powers of the East, had been content with the title of amir, and had given token recognition to the ʿAbbasid caliph in Baghdad. The proclamation of the Fatimid caliphate in North Africa was, however, too near and too dangerous a challenge, and the Spanish amirs could hardly rely on Baghdad for their protection. The Spanish caliphate never exercised or claimed authority outside its own immediate domain, and it disappeared after a little more than a century, in 1031.

With the decline in the effective power of the line of caliphs, the title *khalīfa* also suffered a process of devaluation. In time it ceased to connote sovereignty or indeed to connote any kind of effective authority. This is already clear in the last centuries of the ʿAbbasid caliphate in Baghdad, and the process was completed after the destruction of the caliphate in Baghdad by the Mongols in 1258 and the establishment of a sort of puppet caliphate in Mamluk Cairo. But even before these events, the transfer of effective power from the caliphs to other rulers was recognized and in a sense formalized, and when the ʿAbbasid caliph al-Nāṣir attempted to reassert some political authority for the caliphs against the military rulers, this was regarded as a usurpation. In 1194, according to the Persian historian Rāvandī, the military leaders, complaining of the caliph's action, addressed the populace as follows: "If the caliph is the Imam, then his constant occupation must be prayer, since prayer is the foundation of the faith and the best of deeds. His preeminence is this respect and the fact that he serves as an example for the people is sufficient for him. This is the true sovereignty; the interference of the caliph in the affairs of government is senseless; they should be entrusted to the sultans."[8]

This passage, and many others that could be added, reflect a decline in the power and prestige of the caliph that was accompanied and to some extent caused by a corresponding rise in the power and prestige of another authority, most commonly designated as the sultan. This title carries with it a connotation of military and political authority.

With the loss of real power by the caliphate, many titles which had once been exclusive caliphal prerogatives, and eventually even the title "caliph" itself, passed into common usage, and a situation was ultimately reached in which almost every Muslim ruler could be a caliph in his own realm.

In 1258, when the heathen Mongol invaders captured the city of Baghdad and executed the last of the ʿAbbasid caliphs to reign in that city, the historic institution of the caliphate was finally laid to rest, and effective power, in theory as well as in practice, passed to the sultans. The caliphate did, however, survive in a kind of shadowy afterlife. In 1261 Baybars, the Mamluk sultan of Egypt, welcomed an ʿAbbasid prince fleeing from Baghdad, and installed him at his court in Cairo with the title and style of caliph, but with no effective power whatsoever.[9] Even after the decline and fall of the caliphate, Sunni Muslim rulers still felt the need for some legitimizing authority, providing a formal expression of the supremacy of Islam and the unity of the Islamic world. For two and a half centuries a line of ʿAbbasids held office as nominal caliphs under the rule of the Mamluk sultans in Cairo. The Mamluks were even able to gain some limited recognition for their caliph in other Sunni countries, especially in the Ottoman empire and among the Muslim states in India. With the conquest of the Mamluk sultanate by the Ottomans in 1517, and the deposition of the last of the ʿAbbasid shadow caliphs in Cairo, this shadow caliphate came to an end.

According to what became an official legend, the last of the ʿAbbasid shadow caliphs in Cairo transferred the caliphate to Selim I, the Ottoman conqueror of the Mamluk sultanate, who thus became the first of a series of legitimate Ottoman caliphs.[10] There can be not the slightest shadow of doubt that this story is apocryphal. Neither the Egyptian nor the Ottoman historians of the sixteenth century make any allusion to it, and it is inconceivable that so important an event would have passed unnoticed. The Ottomans, from time to time, used caliphal titles, but so did many other relatively minor Muslim monarchs. What gave added weight to the Ottoman use of these titles was, of course, the great military and naval power of the Ottoman empire and its position as the champion of Islam against Christian Europe on the one hand and Shiʿite Iran on the other. This seems at times to have won a certain recognition for the Ottomans, in other Muslim states, as leaders, though not rulers, of the Sunni Islamic world. This did not, however, represent any claim on the part of the Ottoman sultans to jurisdiction, as distinct from a vague primacy, over non-Ottoman Muslims. The age of the universal caliphate had come to an end, and no Muslim sovereign advanced a claim to the universal caliphate until the revival of the idea by the Ottomans in the late eighteenth century.

Such a claim appeared for the first time in the treaty of Küçük Kaynarca of 1774. By this treaty, it will be recalled, the Ottomans were compelled by Russia to recognize the independence of the Crimean Tatars, as a first step towards the annexation of the Crimea by Russia a few years later. As a face-saving device, the Ottoman sultan, while renouncing political sovereignty over the Crimeans, was permitted to put forward the claim that "as the supreme religious head of Islam,"[11] he was the religious chief of the Tatars, to whom they therefore owed a religious, though not political, loyalty. This also served as a face-saving counterpart to the claim asserted by the czars of Russia, by abusive extension of a clause in the same treaty, to what became a kind of protectorate over the Orthodox Christian subjects of the Ottoman empire. But while the czar's protectorate of the Ottoman Christians gave rise to frequent and extensive interventions,[12] the parallel claim of the sultans to religious authority over the Muslim inhabitants in the territories conquered by the czars was never effectively recognized or enforced.[13] It did, however, give rise, at a later date, to another kind of caliphal policy, known in the West as "pan-Islamism."

The story of the transfer of the caliphate from the last of the Cairo ʿAbbasids to the Ottoman sultan Selim appeared for the first time in 1788, in a famous book by a famous author—written in French by a Turkish Armenian in the Swedish diplomatic service. His name was Ignatius Mouradgea, Baron d'Ohsson in the peerage of Sweden.[14] The appearance of the story at this time was undoubtedly connected with the new idea of an Ottoman religious pontificate. That the idea was already being discussed—and questioned—in the late eighteenth and early nineteenth centuries is clear from an interesting passage in a contemporary English novel located in the Middle East, in which a character, commenting on the general dishonesty of officials, remarks that even the sultan "cheated Allah himself, when he assumed the title of caliph of the Faithful."[15] But if lie it was, it won increasing acceptance, and developed rapidly in the late nineteenth century. Associated with the new pan-Islamism, it appealed strongly to Muslim loyalties at a time when the western and eastern European imperial powers were asserting themselves as the effective rulers of most of the lands of Islam. The Ottoman Empire, as the last independent Muslim state of any size and power, served as a rallying point, and the claim that the Ottoman sultan was the head of all Islam had a ready appeal. This claim was formally asserted in the first Ottoman constitution of 1876.[16] It remained official Ottoman doctrine until the caliphate was abolished by the Turkish Republic in 1924.

After the caliphs, according to the tradition cited above, came the amirs, and this—the text is obviously intended to convey—was the first step downward, the first step on the way to tyranny. *Amīr,* like *khalīfa,* comes from a common Semitic root, this time with the meanings of "speech" or "command." In Arabic it usually has the meaning of "command," and an *amīr* is one who commands, a military commander, a provincial governor, or—when the position of authority is in some measure hereditary—a prince.

The title *amīr al-muʾminīn* is said to have been introduced by the caliph ʿUmar. It soon became the standard and most common title of the caliphs, and the one which for the longest period remained an exclusive caliphal prerogative, long after most other titles had been adopted by all kinds of lesser rulers. The reference in the tradition, however, is not to the *amīr al-muʾminīn,* but simply to the *amīr,* usually translated as "commander" or "prince." This was a title used by a variety of lesser rulers, who appeared as governors of provinces, and even mayors of the palace in the capital, and who arrogated to themselves effective sovereignty, while giving a purely symbolic recognition to the sovereignty of the caliph as the supreme legitimizing authority in Islam.

The age of the amirs was a time of fragmentation, both of power and of territory. First the caliphs lost their authority over the provinces, which came to be ruled by independent and eventually hereditary dynasts. Before long, the caliphs lost power even in their own capital and metropolitan province, and in 935 the amir in Baghdad, in order to assert his primacy over the amirs in the provinces, used the title *amīr al-umarāʾ,* the "amir of amirs" or "chief amir."[17] This title was adopted shortly afterwards by the Persian Buyid dynasty, who made it an effective title of sovereignty, distinct from the caliphate and indeed in many ways superior to the caliphate, since the caliph had now become little more than a puppet in the hands of his mayors of the palace. This was the first stage in the evolution towards what eventually became the characteristic term of sovereignty in Islam—namely, "sultan."

Sulṭān in Arabic is an abstract noun meaning "authority" or "government." Originally it was used only as an abstraction and never of a person. Even later, when it was commonly used for persons, we still find it occasionally in the abstract sense. It seems at first to have been applied rather informally to ministers, governors, or other important figures. This is, incidentally, an example of a general tendency in political language, by which words denoting abstractions become personal titles of sovereignty. The title *sulṭān* is said to have been given for the first time by the caliph Hārūn al-Rashīd to his wazir. This is doubtful but not impossible. We find it occasionally used of the caliphs, both ʿAbbasid and Fatimid. By the tenth century it had become a common designation, though still only informally, of independent rulers and potentates, used to distinguish them from those who were still subject to the effective authority of the central power.

There are many literary references, in poems, letters, and historical narratives, to such use, but there are no coins or inscriptions in which *sulṭān* is used as a personal title. From this it is clear that it had not yet been officially recognized. It became official in the eleventh century, when it was used by the Turkish dynasty known as the Great Seljuqs, who adopted it as their principal title.[18]

In Seljuq usage, *sulṭān* had a new sense and embodied a new claim, no less than a title to universal empire. For the Seljuqs, there was one sultan just as there was one caliph, and the sultan was supreme political and military head of Islam. I prefer to say political and military rather than secular and temporal, since this is not really a division between spiritual and temporal, secular and religious, as these terms are used in the West. For Muslims the sultanate too was religious, at least in theory. The Seljuq sultan claimed a religious base for his authority as chief of Islam, but he limited his claim to military and political functions and left the religious headship—as one writer put it, "preaching and prayer"—to the caliphs. It is from this time that we see developing the theory, as well as the practice, of a division between caliphate and sultanate as two supreme authorities.[19]

For a while, the so-called Great Sultanate of the Seljuqs was respected as a single, universal sovereignty. But the sultanic copyright was of far shorter duration than that of the caliph. Before long, the title *sulṭān* was used informally by a number of regional rulers, such as the famous Zangi of Mosul and the much more famous Saladin. It even appears in some of their inscriptions, though not on their coins. Muslim rulers often show more caution in their coins, which may be widely circulated and where excessive claims might be seen as a *casus belli,* than in their inscriptions, which have a more limited readership, all safely under their own jurisdiction.

With the decay of the Great Seljuq sultanate, that title went through the familiar processes of devaluation and decline. After the Seljuqs it was adopted for a while by the Khwarizmshahs as claimants to the succession to the universal sultanate of the Seljuqs. Thereafter it was used by many other dynasties. Before long it was no longer even a title exclusively applied to rulers, but was widely used by princes and even by princesses. In Ottoman usage the title *sulṭān,* placed after instead of before the personal name, was given to the daughters of a reigning sovereign or of a prince of the blood; the grand-daughter through her mother of a male Ottoman had the lesser title of *hanım sultan,* "lady sultan." The mother of the reigning sovereign had the title of *valide sultan* (mother sultan), and exercised both power and authority as supreme head of the imperial harem.[20]

In the post-Seljuq period, *sulṭān* became the usual Islamic title of sovereignty. That is to say, it was the standard title used by a monarch claiming to be the head of a state and not recognizing any suzerain or superior. Thus, it was used in the late Middle Ages by the Mamluk sultans in Egypt, by the Ottoman sultans in Turkey, and by many others. In this sense it survived into modern times, when it began to give way to a new title, very old in one sense, but clearly the result of Western influence in another sense—the title "king." The evolving significance of this term is vividly illustrated in the changes of title by the dynasty which ruled Egypt from Muḥammad ʿAlī (1805–49) to Fārūq (1936–52). The rulers of Egypt, as of other Ottoman provinces, were entitled *pasha.* When they achieved autonomous and hereditary status in the nineteenth century, they adopted the eastern Iranian title *khedive,*[21] to indicate their increased stature. The khedives were still subject to Ottoman sovereignty, but as hereditary and autonomous rulers, they were more than mere pashas. The twentieth century brought two further changes. To assert his independence against the Ottoman sultan, the khedive of Egypt became a sultan; to assert his independence against the king of England, the sultan of Egypt became a king. Similar changes elsewhere—as for example, in Morocco, where independence from France was accompanied and in some measure indicated by a change in title from "sultan" to "king"—also attest to the high prestige of the term "king," accruing from its use by the mighty sovereigns of the European imperial powers. Along with the title "king," Muslim rulers adopted the European honorific "Majesty," a term previously used only of God. A first sign of a return to more traditional Islamic perceptions of kingship and majesty may perhaps be seen in the Saudi royal decision, in October 1986, to renounce "Majesty" and assume the traditional title of "Custodian of the Two Holy Places."[22]

The Arabic word for king, *malik,*[23] has not always had so positive a connotation, and in the tradition cited above, it marks the third step in the decline of legitimacy and the last before naked tyranny. That the term "king" should have conveyed so negative a meaning among the early Muslims is in no way surprising. The ancient Arabs, like the ancient Israelites in their tribal phase, mistrusted kings and the institution of kingship. When the Israelites, dissatisfied with the administration of the prophet Samuel's sons, came to him and asked, "Now make us a king to judge us like all the nations," Samuel was displeased, and God, it seems, shared his displeasure. "And Samuel told all the words of the Lord unto the people that asked of him a king." He warned them what they might expect of a king—a descending spiral of taxation and conscription, confiscation, forced labor, and servitude—"and ye shall cry out in that day because of your king which ye shall have chosen; and the Lord will not hear you in that day." Nevertheless, the Israelites persisted in their desire for a king, and had to endure the consequences, which the later prophets frequently pointed out to them (1 Samuel, chapters 8 and 9).

The ancient Arabs were, of course, familiar with the institution of sovereignty in the surrounding countries, and some were led to adopt it. There were kings in the states of southern Arabia and in the border principalities of the north. But all of these were, in different degrees, marginal to Arabia. The sedentary kingdoms of the south used a different language and were part of a different culture. The border principalities of the north, though authentically Arab, were deeply influenced by Persian and Byzantine imperial practice, and represented a somewhat alien, or at least alienated, element in the Arab world. But even among the tribes, the royal title was not unknown. The earliest surviving inscription in the Arabic language, a funeral inscription of A.D. 328, commemorates a "king [*malik*] of all the Arabs."[24]

The pre-Islamic history of Bedouin Arabia is little known and is encrusted with all kinds of myths and legends. The corporate memory preserves the recollection of an attempt to establish a monarchy, the short-lived kingdom of Kinda,[25] which flourished in the late fifth and early sixth centuries. The realm of Kinda disintegrated, and the general attitude of the Arabians, sedentary as well as nomadic, was hostile to monarchy. Even in an oasis town like Mecca, the Arabs preferred to be led by consensual chiefs, rather than commanded by monarchs.

This negative attitude towards monarchy is in general reflected in the Qurʾān and in the Traditions. The word *malik* occurs frequently as one of the divine epithets, and as such is endowed with sanctity. When applied to human beings, however, it usually has an unfavorable connotation. Thus, in the Qurʾān (XII), in the story of Joseph, the word "king" is used of Pharaoh, hardly the model of a good and just ruler.[26] In the early Islamic centuries, it became customary to contrast kingship with caliphate. While the latter represented Islamic government under God's law, kingship was taken to mean arbitrary personal rule, without this religious and legal basis and sanction. The historian al-Ṭabarī tells of a conversation between the caliph ʿUmar and the first Persian Muslim, Salmān: "Salmān said that ʿUmar said to him: 'Am I a king or a caliph?' and Salmān answered: 'If you have taxed the lands of the Muslims one dirham, or more or less, and applied it to unlawful purposes, then you are a king, not a caliph.' And ʿUmar wept."[27]

A similar distinction is made by the Arabic historians writing in the ʿAbbasid period, to separate the regime of the dethroned Umayyads from those of both their predecessors and successors. In their narratives, and even in their tables of contents, the historians speak of the "caliphate" of the first four rulers of Islam, followed by the "kingdom" of the Umayyads, until the return of the caliphate with the accession of the ʿAbbasid dynasty. Only one of the Umayyads, ʿUmar II (r. 717–20), in recognition of his piety, is accorded the title of "caliph" in subsequent historiography. All the rest are designated—perhaps more accurately denigrated—as kings, and their periods of rule as kingdom or kingship (*mulk*).

The point is made quite explicitly in the early ninth century by al-Jāḥiẓ in a propaganda tract putting the ʿAbbasid case against the Umayyads. Under the rule of the latter, he says, the imamate became a Persian kingdom and the caliphate a Byzantine usurpation, literally "a Chosrean kingdom and a Caesarian usurpation."[28] Given this connotation of the title "king," it is not surprising that it was used by Muslims for the rulers of the infidels—for the Byzantine emperor, the king of Nubia, and the various monarchs of Christian Europe collectively known as *mulūk al-kuffār,* "the kings of the unbelievers," or even *mulūk al-kufr,* "the kings of unbelief."

In early Islamic times, the term "king" was most commonly used to diminish others rather than to aggrandize oneself. There are, however, some signs of another attitude persisting, or perhaps recurring, in Islamic usage. Court poets and other professional eulogists, seeking for fresh titles with which to glorify their patrons or employers, sometimes had recourse to the word "king." But this remained rare and entirely unofficial. It is not until the middle of the tenth century that we find the word *malik* in official usage, occurring in inscriptions and coins, and used by rulers to describe themselves.

The significance of this return to royal style is clear. By this time the central caliphal authority of the Islamic empire has lost all effective control of the provinces, which were ruled by what began as hereditary governors and in time became local dynasties. The use of the title *malik* does not indicate a claim to equality with the caliphs or, later, with the sultans. It serves, rather, to assert a local sovereignty under the loose suzerainty of a supreme imperial ruler elsewhere. In this it is roughly equivalent to the contemporary use of the title "king" by the various monarchs in Europe under the nominal supremacy of the Holy Roman Emperor.

The reason for the choice of this title, among the many possibilities offered by the rich lexical resources of the Arabic language, is not difficult to guess. Those who used it, the Samanids and their successors, ruled in lands of Iranian culture, where the monarchical traditions of ancient Iran were still very much alive. Iranian court style, etiquette, and even titulature had already affected the court of the ʿAbbasid caliphs. These influences were all the stronger in the capitals of the new states that were still arising in the actual territory of Iran. The old Persian title *shāh* was still too alien and too heathen to be adopted by Muslim rulers, but its Arabic equivalent, *malik,* served in its place. From the use of *malik* to the revival of Persian and later of Turkish royal titles was only a step, and the reappearance of such old Persian titles as *shāh* and *shāhanshāh* was certainly part of a conscious Iranian cultural revival. There is some rather dubious evidence on the use of the Persian title by the Samanids, and quite definite evidence of its use by the Buyids. Indeed, their use of these titles was so characteristic that they are even designated by some historians as the *shāhanshāhiyān*. Thereafter, we find these Persian titles used informally in eulogies and poetry, and more formally in titles adopted by a variety of rulers in the Iranian and Turkish territories of the Islamic world.[29]

The most famous, of course, were the Safavids, who, in the early sixteenth century founded a new line of shahs ruling over a united Iranian state. This line continued through several different dynasties, until the establishment of the Islamic republic in 1979. Along with *shāh,* "king," came *shāhanshāh,* "king of kings," and *pādishāh,* meaning something like "super shah" or "head shah." This title was much used by the Ottomans, by the Mogul rulers of Muslim India, and by some other dynasties in the lands of Iranian and Turkish culture.[30]

Khan and *khaqan* are Turkish and Mongol titles, occasionally encountered in the earlier Islamic period on the central Asian margins of the Islamic world, but acquiring a new importance after the Mongol conquests. Now, *khan* became the exclusive prerogative of the line of Jenghiz Khan, and only those who were blood descendants of the great conqueror were entitled to put *khan* after their names. Even Tamerlane, one of the greatest conquerors, never dared to call himself *khan*. The most that he used was *kürgän,* a Mongol word meaning "son-in-law." His highest title of honor—appearing even on his tombstone in Samarqand—was that he had allied himself by marriage to the Imperial House of Jenghiz. But in time, *khan* too suffered a devaluation. It was used by the Ottoman sultans and then by other, lesser rulers, and in modern times, in Iran and in the Indian subcontinent, it has come to be little more than "mister" or, perhaps, "esquire."[31]

Muslim sovereigns, as we have seen, were neither crowned nor enthroned. There were, however, certain ceremonies by which the accession of a new caliph or, later, sultan was solemnized and celebrated. From the simple and direct actions of the early caliphs, these rites of accession developed in time into a complex and highly charged language, full of symbolism and often of polemic. The language of ritual and ceremony was, of course, a major means of communication, one might even say of communion, between the ruler, his ministers, and his subjects. Its purpose was to express, symbolically and ritually, certain basic Muslim beliefs and principles concerning the nature of sovereignty and authority and the purpose of government.

In times of conflict, it could serve the additional purpose of proclaiming the superior rights of a ruler, a dynasty, or a sect and refuting the pretensions of a rival.[32]

While the ceremonies and rituals of investiture vary from time to time and from place to place, one part was universal, and was seen by jurists and theologians on the one hand, and political and military leaders on the other, as the essential act of validation, by which the sovereign accepted the duties of a Muslim head of state and received the power to discharge them, and the subjects undertook the duty of obedience to him. This act, in Arabic called the *bayʿa*,[33] is often translated as "oath of allegiance." In time, an oath of allegiance came to be a normal part of the proceedings. But that is not what the word means, and in principle an oath of allegiance is not a necessary component of the *bayʿa*, which is perceived rather, in principle, as an agreement between two parties. The term used to denote this validation of authority clearly reveals the concept that underlies it. It derives from a root meaning "to barter," hence to buy and to sell, with the related, and perhaps original, meaning of the clasping or slapping of hands with which it was customary, in ancient Arabia, for the parties to symbolize agreement on a transaction. In commercial law and usage, a slightly variant form of the same word, *bayʿ*, is the normal term for "a sale" and hence for a contract or agreement between two parties, the one to sell and the other to buy. In the language of government, in the form *bayʿa*, the term denotes a contractual agreement between the ruler and the ruled, by which both sides undertake certain obligations towards one another—or, as we might say, a covenant. The *bayʿa* itself is neither an election nor an oath of allegiance, but is preceded by the one and followed by the other. The party of the one hand is, of course, the ruler himself, and this does not change. The party of the other hand, in the law books usually described simply as "the Muslims," in practice normally consists of the small group of men, officers of the court, the army, the bureaucracy, and, exceptionally, the religious leadership, at the center of power.

Under the caliphs, though the ceremonies became more complex and more elaborate, the *bayʿa* remained the central symbol of the investiture of sovereignty. Under the sultans, the *bayʿa* remained a necessary part of the proceedings, but it was usually overshadowed by other symbols of more directly military content. The best known among these is the famous ceremony of "the Girding of the Sword" by a new Ottoman sultan on his accession.

The tyrants and usurpers, the infidels and apostates who come at the end of the sequence will be discussed elsewhere. But the survey of titles of sovereignty must include some which have been added in modern times, though with roots in a remoter past. Two in particular are of importance—indeed, of universal importance in the Islamic world of the present day. One is the term *ra'īs,* the usual translation of "president"; the other is *za'īm,* "leader," as that term developed in continental Europe in the second quarter of the twentieth century.

Ra'īs,[34] literally "head" or "chief," goes back to pre-Islamic times, and was one of the terms used for a tribal chief, though it was less common than such other terms as *sayyid* and *shaykh.* In the earliest Islamic period it seems to have been little used, but in the caliphate it appears as the title given to the chiefs of various services and departments in the administration, of non-Muslim religious communities,[35] and, on occasion, as a personal title accorded by the sovereign to one or another dignitary. In the tenth century, the philosopher al-Fārābī, discussing the organization of the city—the *madīna* or *polis*—uses the term *ra'īs* for its head or ruler.

In Seljuq times and after, *ra'īs* acquired a quite different connotation. In this very military regime, the *ra'īs* became a kind of civil affairs officer in a city under military rule or occupation. He might be a local notable, or he might himself be an officer appointed by and in the service of the military ruler. In the Ottoman Empire,[36] *ra'īs* (Turkish *reis*), following the name, was the title of an admiral, and in modern usage, dating from the nineteenth century, it has come to mean the president of the republic. At first, it was used only of the presidents of European and American republics, since there were no others, and then of the presidents of Muslim republics, when these came into being. It is by now the most widely used title of sovereignty in the Muslim world, having replaced almost all the others that have been enumerated and discussed. This single title may express a very wide variation of content and meaning.

Za'īm[37] is the common modern Arabic term for the charismatic political leader, the equivalent of *duce, führer, vozhd, caudillo,* and the rest, with all the range of different contents implied in that list. It is curious that the earliest use of the term *zaʿīm* in classical Arabic indicates that it was not a compliment. It is a word suggesting pretention, with the stress on the pretense, and is most commonly used of leaders of whom the user disapproves. Thus, for example, the chief of the Assassins, the famous Old Man of the Mountain, was often referred to by Sunni historians of the time as the *zaʿīm* of the Ismāʿīlīs.[38] The Zaydī Imam of the Yemen, who dared to call himself "commander of the faithful," was addressed in the protocol of the Mamluk chancery of Egypt as the "*zaʿīm* of the faithful"[39]—in other words, "he thinks he is, but we know better." The Almohade ruler of the Maghrib was called *Zaʿīm al-Muwaḥḥidīn,* obviously with the same sense.[40] A similar reserve is expressed in the form of words used by the Caliph's wazir in confirming the appointment of the exilarch, the head of the Jewish community in Baghdad, in the year 1247: "I appoint you *zaʿīm* over the people [*ahl*] of your community [*milla*], over the people of your superseded religion, which was superseded by the Muhammadan holy law."[41] Even in modern Arabic, the negative meaning survives in the passive participle *mazʿūm,* meaning "so-called" or "soi-disant." In an Arabic-Spanish vocabulary published in Granada in 1505 by Pedro de Alcalà, *zaʿīm* is translated as *hablador de soberbias, vanaglorioso,* "braggart," "vainglorious."[42]

Its use, however, was not exclusively negative. In the Mamluk sultanate, for example, there was a military title *zaʿīm,* usually followed by *al-juyūsh* or *al-junūd,* "the leader of armies." There was even a *zaʿīm al-dawla,* and this title was clearly intended to be a compliment rather than an insult to a high military officer.[43] It seems to have acquired the modern meaning of "leader" sometime in the nineteenth century. The earliest example known to me of its domestic use is for the Egyptian Nationalist leader Muṣṭafā Kāmil, who is called *al-zaʿīm al-amīn,* "the faithful leader." This title was later revived by President Qāsim of Iraq, who also called himself *al-zaʿīm al-awḥad,* "the unique leader." These adjectives were no doubt intended as a corrective to the negative implications which the term *zaʿīm* might still have carried at that time. In modern Syria, *zaʿīm* is also used of a military rank, in Lebanon of a local chieftain.

Such were the rulers, the monarchs, the leaders. But whom did they rule, whom did they lead, over whom did they reign?

In discussions of the generality of the population over whom Muslim sovereigns and rulers held sway, three terms have predominated: *raʿiyya, tabaʿa,* and *muwāṭin.*[44] From the earliest times until the penetration of European political and juridical notions, *raʿiyya*[45] was the universal term for "the subjects of the ruler," without specific differentiation. In common administrative and colloquial use, the term penetrated into the English dictionary in two forms, "rayah," via Western travelers in the Ottoman Empire, and "ryot," via the British administration of India. The entries in the *Oxford English Dictionary* show an interesting variation. According to this source, "ryot" was first used in English in 1625. Of Urdu and ultimately of Arabic origin, it meant "an Indian peasant, husbandman or cultivating tenant." "Rayah," according to the same source, came much later, and is first attested in 1813. It is defined as "a non-Muhammadan subject of the sultan of Turkey, subject to the payment of the poll tax."

Neither definition is entirely wrong; neither accurately reflects the Islamic usage of the term. In classical Arabic usage, *raʿiyya* means "the population as a whole," in contrast to "the ruler." It expressed the pastoral metaphor of government common to Islam, Judaism, and Christianity, perceiving the ruler as the shepherd and the people as the flock which he tends and protects. By the mid-eighth century, the term, sometimes with a further development of the image which it expresses, was in common use. A notable example is the introduction to the *Book of the Land Tax* written by the chief qāḍī Abū Yūsuf and addressed to the caliph Hārūn al-Rashīd (r. 786–809).[46] This is a sustained homily on the caliph's duties as shepherd to his flock. The term *raʿiyya* occurs in literary and scribal writings as well as religious and legal writings, with the same meaning. The contrast is usually between the *raʿiyya* and the ruler, depicted as a relationship between the flock and their shepherd, who is responsible to God for their care.

In Ottoman usage, the first for which we have detailed archival documentation, there is a certain shift in the significance of the term *raʿiyya* (Turkish *raiyyet,* plural *reaya*). As well as in tracts and homilies of various kinds, it also appears in innumerable fiscal and administrative documents, and in these is clearly a technical term with a well-defined meaning. It is commonly contrasted, not with the person of the ruler, as in earlier times, but with the apparatus of government—with the ruling institution, or with its personnel. The former is normally designated as the *miri,* the common Ottoman term for "the state," "the government," "the administration"; the latter, "the personnel," is often called *ʿaskarī* (Turkish *askeri*),[47] a term which goes beyond its original meaning of "soldier" to denote a member of the ruling military class.

Another group not included, in Ottoman usage, among the *reaya* was the bureaucratic and religious classes—the *kalemiye,* "men of the pen" and the *ilmiye,*[48] "men of (religious) learning" in traditional Ottoman terminology. Together with the *askeri*s, these formed the military, religious, and bureaucratic establishments maintaining the Ottoman state. While *reaya* is still sometimes used in Ottoman literature in the general sense of all the subjects of the sultan, its most common and precise usage was to denote all those elements of the population which did not belong to any of the privileged groups. In this sense, it included both townspeople and peasants, both Muslims and non-Muslims. It did not include slaves, who were totally owned chattels and did not belong even to this component of society.

The earliest European visitors to the Ottoman Empire traveled mainly in the European provinces, and had contact mainly with the Christian townspeople and peasants who formed the majority of the population in these provinces. This gave rise to the widely held but erroneous belief that *reaya* was an Ottoman term for non-Muslim subjects of the state. This became standard in virtually all European writings about the Ottoman Empire, and by the nineteenth century was beginning to affect even the usage of the European-influenced Ottomans themselves.

But by this time, another term was becoming current in the Ottoman and other Muslim states, to denote the subjects of the ruler. This was the Ottoman term *tebaa* (Arabic *tabaʿa*), with its equivalents in other languages. The word derives from *tābiʿ,*[49] the Arabic active participle of the verb "to follow." In classical Ottoman administrative language, it was the normal term indicating "subordination" or "dependence," and could be used equally of persons, places, and offices. Thus, a village was *tābiʿ* to the chief town of the district, the chief town of the district was *tābiʿ* to the capital of the province. The same word was used to indicate the relationship of the rulers or governors or administrators of these various units to their superiors. In the course of the nineteenth century, as the Ottoman Empire joined the "concert of Europe" and became more and more involved in the diplomatic and other conventions which governed the relations between European powers, *tābiʿ* acquired a new usage, becoming the Ottoman equivalent of the English word "subject." In other words, it denoted what we nowadays call nationality or citizenship. Ottoman *tebaa* were those who owed allegiance to the Ottoman sultan as their sovereign, and to the Ottoman Empire as their country—another alien term now used for the first time with a political connotation. When, as began to happen more frequently in the course of the nineteenth century, they traveled abroad, they could carry passports indicating their status as Ottoman subjects. The Ottoman empire was a monarchy, and the Ottoman, like the Briton or the Dutchman, was a subject; unlike the Frenchman or the American, he was not a citizen.

Indeed, the term "citizen," with its connotation of the right to participate in the formation and conduct of government, and with its origins going back from the French and American revolutions to the city-states of ancient Greece, was totally outside the Muslim political experience, and therefore, unknown to Islamic political language. When ancient Greek political writings were translated into Arabic in the high Middle Ages, and served as the basis of a new and original political literature in Arabic, there was an equivalent for the city; there was none for the citizen. The Greek word *polis,* "city," was rendered as *madīna;* the Greek word *polites,* "citizen," found no true equivalent, and the word *madanī,* by which it is usually translated, means something more like "statesman."[50] It was not until the general adoption of Western ideas of nationality and citizenship in the Islamic world that a term was needed and was found. It is now in common administrative usage in virtually all Muslim states.

The choice that was made among the rich lexical resources of the Arabic language is significant. The Arabic term is *muwāṭin;* its Persian and Turkish equivalents are *hamvaṭan* and *vatandaş*. All three come from the Arabic root *waṭan,*[51] which in classical usage means "the place of one's birth or residence," and in the course of the nineteenth century became the equivalent of the French *patrie,* with all its patriotic connotations. The literal meaning of *muwāṭin* and its equivalents is thus "compatriot" or "fellow countryman," and its content is patriotic and nationalistic but not libertarian.

Islam has often been described as an egalitarian religion and, in a profound sense, this is true. The world into which Islam came at the time of its advent in the seventh century was very far from egalitarian. To the east, there was the elaborately structured and rather rigid class system of pre-Islamic Iran, and beyond that the even more rigidly discriminatory caste system of Hindu India. To the west, there were the systems of hereditary and privileged aristocracy, which Christendom had inherited from the Greco-Roman world and the Germanic tribes, and which, though somewhat softened by Christian values and teachings, had never been abrogated and in many ways were even confirmed and extended.

Islam in principle never recognized either caste or aristocracy. As far as caste is concerned, the Islamic rejection was in fact as well as in theory. The denial of aristocracy was a much more difficult matter. In the Islamic world, as in every other human society, successful men found ways to transmit their power, wealth, and privilege to their children, and there was an inevitable tendency to the formation of hereditary privileged groups. Under Islam this happened in spite of and not as part of the prevailing ideology, and it received only limited recognition from the law. The prevailing conditions of insecurity further weakened the position of privileged groups. Islamic aristocracies were precarious and often of brief duration. Many were overthrown and replaced by successive waves of conquest, each creating a new and short-lived conqueror ruling class. There is nothing in Islamic law and little in Islamic usage to parallel the patricians and plebeians of ancient Rome, the nobles and villeins of feudal Europe, or the peerage and baronage that flourished in almost every Christian country. From the beginning to the present day, there are no hereditary titles, other than royal, in the Islamic lands, except on a very limited and local scale, and even there by courtesy rather than by law.

But if Islamic usage rejects privilege, it admits—in certain situations it even imposes—inequality. Three inequalities in particular were established and regulated by law and developed through centuries of usage—the unequal status of master and slave, of man and woman, of Muslim and non-Muslim. These are, of course, three different kinds of classification, which may overlap or intersect, and the practical effects of belonging to one or other of these categories varied greatly from time to time and from place to place. In principle, equality of status, and with it the right to participate at whatever level in the exercise of power, belonged only to those who were free, male, and Muslim, while those who lacked any of these qualifications, the slave, the woman, and the unbeliever, were excluded.

The extent to which this exclusion was in fact enforced varied enormously. The least effectively enforced was the ban on slaves exercising power. From the ninth century onwards, slaves appeared in growing numbers in the apparatus of government, as rulers came to rely on slave soldiers rather than on free levies to carry out their commands. In time, the military and governmental apparatus was dominated by slave commanders and generals leading slave armies, and gave rise, in at least two cases, in Egypt and India, to slave dynasties, with succession by purchase and enfranchisement instead of by filiation. The Islamic languages developed a rich vocabulary of terms for "slave," denoting the whole range of the vast slave population, from the humble toilers in fields, mines, and kitchens to the sultan's slaves who commanded armies, governed provinces, and controlled the central administrations. Used of these last, such words as the Arabic *mamlūk* and Turkish *kul,*[52] though technically meaning "slave," carried a connotation not of enslavement or servility but of power and dominance.

The Islamic terms for "free,"[53] until the eighteenth century, had a primarily legal, and occasionally social, significance, and meant one who, according to the law, was a free man and not a slave. Neither term, "free" or "slave," was used in a political context, and the familiar Western use of the terms "freedom" and "slavery" as metaphors for citizen's rights and oppressive rule is unknown to the language of classical Islamic political discourse. There too, there is much discussion of good and bad government, but the issue at stake is not freedom but justice.

Women and non-Muslims were in a somewhat different position from slaves. Legally, socially, and in most cases economically, the free woman or the non-Muslim was better off than even a Muslim slave, but not politically. In principle, the non-Muslim was excluded from the polity. He could have a place in Muslim society either as a *dhimmī*, a permanent resident with a certain status, or as a *musta'min*, a temporary resident from the non-Muslim world.[54] Both had well-established and in general recognized legal rights. Neither had any political rights. Islamic literature from early to modern times is full of injunctions not to employ infidels in political office or, more generally, in "conducting the affairs of the Muslims." The frequent repetition of such injunctions shows that they were not always heeded, and indeed, from the earliest times, non-Muslims were employed in great numbers in the various departments of government. Almost invariably, however, this was in administrative and usually subordinate capacities. The appointment of non-Muslims to positions of real power was extremely rare, and, when it happened, almost invariably gave rise to bitter, and sometimes active, hostility.[55]

The bottom of the social pile was, of course, the non-Muslim female slave. But even the free Muslim woman was at a considerable disadvantage and was virtually excluded from the political process, except by what was seen and condemned as palace intrigue. There are no queens in Islamic history, and the word "queen," where it occurs, is used only of foreign rulers in Byzantium or in Europe. There are a few instances where Muslim dynastic thrones were briefly occupied by women, but this was perceived as an aberration and condemned as an offense.[56]

In each of these three basic divisions, there were some intermediate categories. Between the freeman and the slave, there was the freedman or *mawlā* (plural *mawālī*). The *mawlā* was a liberated slave who stood in a certain legal relationship to his former master, one that imposed obligations on both parties. In early Islamic times this was a significant relationship, and men in this position constituted a distinct social group with an important political role. In later times, this relationship, and the freedmen as a group, ceased to signify.

Between the Muslim and the unbeliever, seen as an enemy and an outsider, there were, as we have noted, such intermediate categories as the *dhimmī* and the *musta'min*. Even between men and women, there was a kind of intermediate category, the eunuch, who alone could move freely between the male and female worlds and who, at certain periods, had some political significance.[57]

While the strict application of the law made no distinction between free male Muslims, the social and economic, and therefore ultimately also the political, facts of life were somewhat different, and in the literature, a number of terms appear which denote the different social divisions among the Muslim general population. The commonest of many pairs of terms distinguishing between the upper and lower layers of society is *khāṣṣa and ʿāmma,*[58] which may be literally translated as "the special" and "the general." The first of these terms corresponds to what has at various times been known in the West and elsewhere as the elite, the establishment, the *nomenklatura;* the second covers the rest of the population. It is in this sense that Shakespeare, speaking of a somewhat elitist taste in theater, remarked: "The play, I remembered, pleased not the million; t'was caviar to the general" (Hamlet, act II, scene 2).

We have no precise definition of the *khāṣṣa*. The term has generally been understood to denote the literate, urban classes associated with government; the political, bureaucratic, and military elements; and the holders of religious offices. It includes in particular the two learned classes, the religious and the scribal, the former represented by the ulema, the latter by the bureaucracy. It may include the educated merchants and landowners, though this is not always clear. It is, briefly, the cultivated, more or less affluent society of cities, families who are related to each other by descent and intermarriage, who move in the same social circles, and have, broadly, the same relationship to authority. In all this, they are clearly marked off from the illiterate or semiliterate mass of the population. In Ottoman times, the first for which we have archival documentation, we find evidence of a more precise division, between the ruling elite on the one hand, consisting of political, military, bureaucratic, and religious personnel, and the rest of the population, on the other.

Another division occurring frequently in early Islamic times is between *sharīf* and *ḍaʿīf,*[59] the first meaning "noble," the second "weak." Originally, the term *sharīf* corresponded fairly closely to the English word "noble" in its two senses, the one denoting high birth, the other moral elevation of character. It is commonly contrasted with *ḍaʿīf*, "weak." In some cases this seems to mean "weak of pedigree," i.e., not wellborn; in others, it clearly means "unarmed." In medieval Islam as in most other societies, one of the most important social distinctions was between those who bore arms as of right and those who were precluded from doing so, by law, custom, or usage. In an arms-bearing society, the disarmed were, in a very real sense, weak.

By classical Islamic times, *sharīf* was specialized to one particular line of high birth—the descendants of the Prophet. This came to be the only form of noble birth formally recognized by Islam. In the Ottoman Turkish registers, for example, the descendants of the Prophet are listed by name in every province, city, and village, and noted as exempt from most forms of taxation. Similar exemptions are granted by some, though by no means all, other Muslim states. This exemption was, of course, by its very nature, hereditary, but it carried with it no other immunities or privileges comparable with those of European aristocracies. It was based, not on conquests or positions or power, but simply on descent, in the male line, from the founder of the faith. In later Ottoman times, the *sharīfs* were often organized in a kind of guild, with a syndic or leader of their own, and were sometimes able to play a significant role in city, through rarely in imperial, politics.

Muslim political literature devotes a great deal of attention to the problems of the duties and obligations of both the rulers and the ruled. This discussion centers on three major issues: (1) the choice, appointment, and accession of the ruler; (2) the obligations owed by the ruler to the subject and the subject to the ruler; and, arising from these, (3) the extent and limits of authority and obedience.

On all three topics, there is a substantial area of agreement among writers, and particularly among the jurists. On the first point, it is generally accepted that the ruler, in order to accede legally to power, must be qualified; that is to say, he must possess certain necessary qualifications specified by the law. There are differences between schools and sects on the nature of these qualifications, but there is general agreement that such a set of requirements exists under God's law, and that the ruler must meet them. It is further agreed that the ruler must accede to his office by means of certain procedures, laid down and approved in the law. Here again there are differences between the schools and sects as to the rules to be followed, but all agree that succession must be in accordance with accepted procedures, and that the accession of a new ruler is legally validated by a kind of contract agreed between himself and a number of qualified persons who, acting individually or collectively and on behalf of the Muslim community, recognize him as their sovereign. By this contract, the ruler undertakes certain obligations toward the Islamic community and towards the individual Muslims of whom it is composed. The subjects on their side undertake the duty of obedience to the sovereign.

Each side thus owes a duty to the other; each has an expectation of the other, and it is this expectation that comes nearest to the modern Western notion of rights. All the jurists, and indeed other writers on politics, agree that the subject owes a duty of obedience to the sovereign. This duty is, however, justified, and at the same time transcended, by the subject's basic duty as an individual Muslim, to do and enjoin good and to avoid and forbid evil. Since the purpose of the existence of the state, the basis of legitimacy in authority, and the justification for the obedience owed to the ruler by the subject, all derive from the need to fulfill the basic precepts of Islam and, on the part of the ruler, to create situations in which their fulfillment is possible, it would follow that when the individual's religious duty as a Muslim and his political duty as a subject come into conflict, it is the individual's duty as a Muslim that must prevail.

There is general agreement on certain basic principles. The ruler's obligations are both religious and practical. His prime duty is, of course, to respect and enforce the Holy Law. In order to accomplish this, he must safeguard the worldly interests of the Islamic state and community—the defense or expansion of the frontiers, the waging of war against the unbelievers, the administration of public property and the collection and expenditure of state revenues, the dispensing of justice, and the maintenance of internal security.

The expectations of the ruler and of the subject have been defined by many jurists, sometimes at considerable length. There is general agreement on certain basic principles. The ruler owes a collective duty to the Islamic community as a whole, to defend its interests, protect it against enemies, and advance its cause; he also owes a duty to the individual believer, to enable him to live the good Muslim life in this world, and thus prepare himself for the next. In return for these services, he is entitled to command the obedience of his subjects in everything except sin. The duty of the subject is to render this obedience, as thus defined and as thus delimited. His expectation is that the ruler will fulfill his obligations and conduct himself in accordance with what is usually called justice.[60] The notion of justice becomes central to Muslim discussions of the duties owed by the ruler on the one hand to God, on the other to his subjects. While definitions of justice vary from period to period, from country to country, from school to school, even from jurist to jurist, the basic principle remains that justice is the touchstone of the good ruler. It is the counterpart of obedience, the converse of tyranny (*ẓulm*).[61]

This again raises the question of limits and sanctions. A common view has been that since the limits are set by God, only God can determine an offense and impose a punishment. The sovereign must be obeyed. This, it is said, is the first rule of politics, and it is further buttressed by the argument that even a bad and oppressive government is better than anarchy. According to an often repeated dictum, found mainly in literary rather than religious works, if the sovereign is oppressive, the subject must be patient and endure. In due course, the sovereign will be punished for his crimes and the subject rewarded for his patience, both of them in the hereafter. Religious writers take a less lenient, or perhaps one should say less pragmatic, view of oppressive government. They are more insistent in reminding the ruler of the worldly limits of his power, more explicit in asserting that obedience also has its limits. Two *ḥadīths* are frequently cited in this connection. According to one, the Prophet said, "Do not obey a creature in transgression against the Creator." According to the other, he said, "There must be no obedience in transgression [against God]," i.e., in sin. The meaning of both is clear. If the ruler commands something which is contrary to God's law, the subject's duty of obedience lapses. Some go even further and assert what amounts to a right, or even a duty, of disobedience. The definition of this right or duty, and the determining of the point at which it comes into operation, constitute one of the most fundamental problems of Islamic political thought and life.

4

War and Peace

◆

One of the ideas most commonly associated, in Western minds, with Islamic political thought and practice, is the notion of holy war. Islam is perceived, from its inception, as a militant, indeed as a military religion, and its followers as fanatical warriors, engaged in spreading their faith and their law by armed might. It may, therefore, come as something of a surprise that classical Arabic usage has no term corresponding to holy war. There is, of course, a word for war, *ḥarb,* and many words for different acts and types of warfare. There is also a word for holy, *muqaddas*. It is, however, of comparatively rare occurrence in classical usage, and appears more often than not in contexts with a Jewish or Christian rather than a strictly Islamic connotation. In the Qurʾān, it is used of the holy soil on which Moses stands before the burning bush (XX, 12; LXXIX, 16); of the Holy Land which God promised to the children of Israel (V, 23); and, most frequently, in another form from the same root, of the Holy Spirit (*rūḥ al-quds*) in the Muslim version of the annunciation (II, 87; II, 253; V, 113; XVI, 102). The notion of the sacralization of place or space is familiar and indeed central to Islam, and there are many "holy places."[1] The holiest of all are the Kaʿba in Mecca and the tomb of the Prophet in Medina, but the terms usually applied to these derive not from the root *qds,* "holy," but from another root, *ḥrm,* with the base meaning of "forbid" and with a connotation, dating back to ancient Arabia, of awe and inviolability.[2]

Some of these holy places are the tombs of revered local personages, whom Westerners, but not Muslims, call "holy men" or "santons." The Islamic term is *walī,*[3] from a root meaning "to be near." The same root gives rise to a whole scatter of terms denoting power and authority, i.e., nearness to the center of sovereignty. For the santon, of course, it means nearness to God.

In general, while the sacralization of places is common and widespread in the Islamic world, the sacralization of living persons and human actions is not practiced by Muslims. In particular, the collocation of the adjective "holy" and the substantive "war" does not occur in classical Islamic texts. Its use in modern Arabic is of recent and extraneous origin.

While, however, the translation "holy war," like "holy law," is in some measure a distortion, it is by no means, as are some other such attributions, a mere invention. Both renderings, "holy war" and "holy law," rest on a certain basis of fact. In Western parlance, the adjective "holy," preceding the word "law," is necessary, since there are other laws of other origins. In Muslim parlance, the adjective is tautologous. The *sharīʿa* is simply the law, and there is no other. It is holy in that it derives from God, and is the external and unchangeable expression of God's commandments to mankind.

It is on one of these commandments that the notion of holy war, in the sense of a war ordained by God, is based. The term so translated is *jihād*, an Arabic word with the literal meaning of "effort," "striving," or "struggle." In the Qurʾān and still more in the Traditions, commonly though not invariably followed by the words "in the path of God," it has usually been understood as meaning "to wage war." The great collections of *ḥadīth* all contain a section devoted to *jihād*, in which the military meaning predominates.[4] The same is true of the classical manuals of *sharīʿa* law. There were some who argued that *jihād* should be understood in a moral and spiritual, rather than a military, sense. Such arguments were sometimes put forward by Shiʿite theologians in classical times, and more frequently by modernizers and reformists in the nineteenth and twentieth centuries. The overwhelming majority of classical theologians, jurists, and traditionists, however, understood the obligation of *jihād* in a military sense, and have examined and expounded it accordingly.

In the law books, elaborate rules are laid down governing the initiation, the conduct, and the termination of hostilities, and dealing with such specific questions as the treatment of prisoners and of conquered populations, the punishment of spies, the disposal of enemy assets, and the acquisition and distribution of booty. While the regulations show a clear concern for moral values and standards, it is difficult to accommodate them in a moral and spiritual interpretation of *jihād* as such.

According to Muslim teaching, *jihād* is one of the basic commandments of the faith, an obligation imposed on all Muslims by God, through revelation. In an offensive war, it is an obligation of the Muslim community as a whole (*farḍ kifāya*); in a defensive war, it becomes a personal obligation of every adult male Muslim (*farḍ ʿayn*). In such a situation, the Muslim ruler might issue a general call to arms (*nafīr ʿāmm*). The basis of the obligation of *jihād* is the universality of the Muslim revelation. God's word and God's message are for all mankind; it is the duty of those who have accepted them to strive (*jāhada*) unceasingly to convert or at least to subjugate those who have not. This obligation is without limit of time or space. It must continue until the whole world has either accepted the Islamic faith or submitted to the power of the Islamic state.

Until that happens, the world is divided into two: the House of Islam (*dār al-Islām*), where Muslims rule and the law of Islam prevails; and the House of War (*dār al-Ḥarb*),[5] comprising the rest of the world. Between the two there is a morally necessary, legally and religiously obligatory state of war, until the final and inevitable triumph of Islam over unbelief. According to the law books, this state of war could be interrupted, when expedient, by an armistice or truce of limited duration. It could not be terminated by a peace, but only by a final victory.

The leader of the Muslims in the *jihād* is the sovereign or ruler of the Muslim state. In classical times, this meant the caliph; later it meant whatever sultan or amir was in charge. At a time when Islamic standards of legitimacy and of justice were being whittled down to accommodate the harsh realities of military power, the jurists were careful to insist that the obligation of *jihād* survived every change of government or regime, and was owed to any ruler actually possessing the necessary power. According to a saying improbably ascribed to the Prophet: "*Jihād* is incumbent upon you under every amīr, whether he be godly or wicked, and even if he commits major sins."[6] In *jihād*, the subject's normal duty of obedience becomes one of active armed support.

A number of terms, mostly Arabic, are used in Islamic languages to designate the various forms of warfare and those engaged in them. *Mujāhid* or *jihādī* means a fighter in the *jihād*. The latter term, used adjectivally, often appears where modern usage would employ the word "military." *Jihād* was of course normally fought on the frontier, and there are several specialized terms for the frontiersmen, the march warriors who defended the far-flung frontiers of Islam and carried the war, by invasion or by raiding parties, into the territory of the enemy.[7]

The word *razzia*, which came to English via France from Algeria after the French conquest in 1830, means, according to the Oxford English Dictionary, "a hostile incursion, foray or raid, for purpose of conquest, plunder, capture of slaves, etc., as practiced by the Mohammedan peoples in Africa." In the forms *ghazw* and *ghāziya*, the word dates back to pre-Islamic Arabic, when it was used with much the same meaning. The active participle, *ghāzī*, in Turkish *gazi*, "one who takes part in a razzia," became a technical term for Muslim frontier fighters and then, by extension, a title of honor assumed by or given to Muslim rulers who won distinction in the fight against the infidels. It was particularly favored in Turkey, the bastion and the advance post of Islam in Europe, and was used both by the first Ottoman sultans and the first president of the Turkish republic.[8] In 1974 it reappeared in the Turkish press, to describe the Turkish forces that landed in Cyprus in that year.

Another kind of fighter, against another kind of enemy, is denoted by the term *fidāʾī*, first used in the high Middle Ages, and now enjoying a new popularity. Literally meaning "one willing to lay down his life for another," the term was originally adopted, in Iran and in Syria, by the emissaries of the Ismāʿīlī leader known as the Old Man of the Mountain. Their mission was to serve their master and terrify his enemies by the dramatic murder of some prominent figure; from these missions it was not their practice to return alive. They enriched the languages of the West with the word "assassin," which the Crusaders brought back from the Levant, and the languages of Islam with a term connoting a totally committed devotee, ready to sacrifice his own life and that of others for his cause.[9]

After the suppression of the Assassins by the Mongols in Iran and by the Mamluks in Syria in the thirteenth century, the term went out of use. It was revived in mid-nineteenth-century Turkey by a group of conspirators against the sultan and has since been used by several groups in Iran, the Arab lands, and elsewhere.

In the early days, there seemed no reason to doubt that the extension of Islam to all the world belonged to a near rather than a distant future. With breathtaking speed, the Arab Muslim armies advanced out of Arabia, westwards to the Atlantic and the Pyrenees, eastwards to India and China. They had overcome the two greatest empires of the time, in Persia and Byzantium. The one was utterly destroyed and conquered, the other badly defeated and deprived of some of its richest provinces. Some utterances at the time clearly reflect the belief that the God-given task of bringing Islam to all the world would soon be completed. Thus, in one tradition, the Prophet is quoted as saying, "You will certainly conquer Constantinople. Excellent will be the amir and the army who will take possession of it." In another tradition, of early date but certainly spurious, the Prophet goes even further, and predicts that the imminent fall of Constantinople would be followed by that of Rome.[10]

By the early ninth century, Muslims began to realize that this fulfillment was not imminent, and in popular religion and legend it was postponed to a remote, indeed a messianic, future. With this realization came important changes in the Muslim perception of the frontier, and of the nature and conduct of relations with the powers that existed on the other side.

Since war was, in certain circumstances, a legal obligation, it was also legally regulated. From very early times, Muslims were at some pains to formulate, and where possible to enforce, their version of the rules of war. A very early text quotes the caliph Abū Bakr as instructing his armies in these matters, in the year A.D. 632:

> O people! I charge you with ten rules; learn them well!
>
> Do not betray, or misappropriate any part of the booty; do not practice treachery or mutilation. Do not kill a young child, an old man, or a woman. Do not uproot or burn palms, or cut down fruitful trees. Do not slaughter a sheep or a cow or a camel, except for food. You will meet people who have set themselves apart in hermitages; leave them to accomplish the purpose to which they have done

> this. You will come upon people who will bring you dishes and various kinds of food. If you partake of them, pronounce God's name over what you eat. You will meet people who have shaved the crown of their heads, leaving a band of hair around it. Strike them with the sword.
>
> Go, in God's name, and may God protect you from sword and pestilence.[11]

Abū Bakr, it seemed, had nothing against monks, but disapproved of tonsures.

The jurists discuss these and related matters, concerning the conduct of *jihād,* at considerable length. The rights and immunities of envoys, including those from hostile rulers, were recognized from the start, and enshrined in the *sharīʿa.*[12] The biography of the Prophet furnishes numerous examples of embassies sent and received, in the course of the Prophet's complex diplomatic dealings with the Arab tribes surrounding Medina. Several words are used to denote envoys, but there seems to have been no accepted technical term until centuries later, when *safīr*[13] was used, first in Arabic and then in Persian and in Turkish, for "ambassador." It remains in use to the present day.

Traditional Muslim rulers did not maintain resident embassies abroad, and had no professional diplomats. They sent an envoy when one was needed. A suitable high official was appointed, who returned home when he had delivered his message. Resident foreign embassies were accepted in the Ottoman capital from the sixteenth century, but the sultans did not establish permanent embassies abroad, or appoint diplomats, until the last years of the eighteenth century.

European consuls, first from the Italian merchant city-states, then from the larger European countries, had long been familiar in the seaports of the Levant and of the North African littoral, and were known by the loanword *qunsul,* already attested in Mamluk times. They were seen as chiefs of their communities and as hostages, or rather pledges, for their good behavior. As a fifteenth-century Arabic writer puts it, "The consuls are the chiefs of the Franks and are hostages for each community. If anything happens from any community dishonoring to Islam, the consul is answerable."[14] In fact, official action against foreign consuls, based on this principle, was rare. For the most part, the foreign merchant communities, like the native *dhimmīs*, took care to avoid anything that might be construed as dishonoring to Islam, and the consuls were allowed to pursue their avocations. In the Ottoman Empire, with the steady spread and acceptation of European international practice, ambassadors and consuls were, with one exception, normally accorded the same status and treatment as in other countries. The one exception was the long-maintained Ottoman practice, on the outbreak of war with a European state, of interning its official representatives, usually in the Castle of the Seven Towers, until the resumption of peaceful relations.

Of immediate relevance to the political language of Islam is the legal classification of enemies, against whom it is legitimate to wage war. They are of four kinds: the unbeliever, the bandit, the rebel, and the apostate.[15]

Of these four, the unbeliever is, in principle though not always in practice, by far the most important. It is against him that the *jihād* par excellence is waged; it is with him that jurists and historians alike are primarily concerned, in their discussion of relations with the foreigner, the outsider, the enemy. The unsubjugated unbeliever is by definition an enemy. He is part of the *Dār al-Ḥarb,* "the House of War," and is designated as a *ḥarbī,* an attributive form of the word for war. He is sharply differentiated from the *dhimmī,* the unbeliever who submits to Muslim rule, accepts Muslim protection, and pays the poll tax to the Muslim state. This term derives from the *dhimma,* a kind of contract between the Muslim state and the leader of a non-Muslim community, by which members of that community are granted a certain status, with certain duties and privileges, under Muslim authority.

Between the *ḥarbī* and the *dhimmī,* there is the *musta'min,*[16] a *ḥarbī* who lives for a while in a Muslim country as a temporary visitor. He is granted safe conduct, allowed to practice his religion, and is exempted from the payment of the poll tax and other disabilities imposed on the *dhimmīs*. He may enjoy a modified form of the autonomy allowed to the *dhimmīs*, and band together with others of his own nation to form an autonomous community, subject to their own laws, under the governance of a consul appointed by their own ruler. The *musta'min* is so called because he is the holder of an *amān,* a "safe conduct," for entry and temporary residence, issued to a *ḥarbī* by the Muslim authorities. The *amān* may be personal, granted to a single individual. It may be collective, granted to a foreign state, which may then extend this privilege to its own citizens traveling abroad. The growth in the later Middle Ages of resident communities of European merchants from Venice, Genoa, and other Christian states was made possible by this procedure.

According to the jurists, the natural and permanent relationship between the world of Islam and the world of the unbelievers was one of open or latent war, and there could, therefore, be no peace and no treaty. Truces and temporary agreements were, however, possible, and for these the jurists found precedent even in the Qurʾān. The legal term for truce is *hudna,* from a root meaning "calm" or "tranquillity." Another term for truce or armistice is *ṣulḥ.*[17] This occurs in the Qurʾān in the sense of a composition or settlement in a dispute over property, and it retains this meaning in later Islamic law. In Islamic law and usage, the status of the conquered lands and peoples depended, in certain significant respects, on whether they had been brought into the House of Islam *ʿanwatan,* i.e., "by force," "by assault," or *ṣulḥan,* i.e., "by agreement," which in practice meant "by surrender on terms."[18] In the form *ṣulḥa,* the latter term figures prominently in Bedouin customary law, to denote the settlement of a tribal feud. In Ottoman texts, *sulh* was the term commonly used to denote the kind of peace that is concluded between governments.

The commonest Arabic word for peace, also widely known in many other languages, is *salām.*[19] This word occurs many times in the Qurʾān, and figures prominently in everyday conversation in virtually all Muslim languages. Its associations are, however, overwhelmingly nonpolitical. In Muslim usage, *salām* denotes peace both in this world, i.e., tranquillity, and in the next, i.e., salvation. It figures in the commonest of all Muslim greetings, *salām ʿalaykum,* "peace be upon you," and its connotation is most clearly indicated by its frequent association, in such greetings, with God's mercy and blessing. There are texts, purporting to be letters written by the Prophet to the Jews of Maqna and to the Christians of Ayla, which conclude with this greeting.[20] At an early date, however, the principle came to be universally accepted that the salutation *salām* should only be used between Muslims, and that other forms of greeting should be adopted if it became necessary, in speech or in writing, to address non-Muslims. In Muslim diplomatics, *salām* is always used when addressing a fellow Muslim, even in a state of war;[21] it is never used in addressing a non-Muslim ruler, even in a condition of alliance. For friendly non-Muslim rulers, the common practice was to use a formula derived from the Qur'anic account of Moses' appearance before Pharaoh, whom he greeted with the words: "Peace be on whosoever follows the guidance [of God]" (Qur'ān XX, 49). This formula is found in other early letters ascribed to the Prophet and addressed to non-Muslims; it appears in Arabic papyri of the early eighth century, in communications addressed to Christian tax officials in Egypt. It later became standard usage in the chanceries of Muslim states.[22] For the senders, it maintained the principle that *salām* was only for Muslims and those who embraced Islam. For the recipients, it presented the appearance of a polite salutation—an appearance which could be enhanced by the creative translations on which such recipients normally had to rely.[23]

While the connotation of *salām* is thus primarily religious—indeed, the word "Islam" itself is derived from the same root—it does sometimes have the sense of more mundane "safety" or "security," i.e., the lack of trouble or danger. It was not, however, normally used, in classical political or legal contexts, to denote the ending of war. For this, Arabic usage preferred, and in some contexts continues to prefer, the term *ṣulḥ,* in spite of its earlier connotation of a truce of limited duration. Thus, in modern Arabic history textbooks, even purely European peace treaties, where no Islamic interest or party was involved, are usually denoted by the term *ṣulḥ*—for example, *ṣulḥ Utrecht, ṣulḥ Versailles.* In the last century or so, the use of *ṣulḥ* and *salām* in Arabic has undergone a considerable change. In classical usage *ṣulḥ* alone was used for "peace" as opposed to war. In early modern Arabic *ṣulḥ* was confined increasingly to the sense of "a transition from war to peace"—i.e., the process or ratification of peacemaking—while the previously nonpolitical *salām* acquired the broader and more general sense of "a *state* of peace," as opposed to a *state* of war.[24] More recently, Arabic usage has begun to approximate more closely to common international practice, with *salām* as the accepted term for a state of peace between nations.

Both terms remained in use, though with some changes in meaning. A cessation of hostilities might involve some kind of agreement, in the early texts commonly called *ʿahd,* which might be approximately translated as "covenant." *ʿAhd* is widely used in Islamic political parlance, its most frequent occurrence being to denote the agreement between a ruler and the successor whom he designates in his lifetime, the *walī ʿahd.* It is also used of the *dhimma,* and of agreements of one kind or another, with non-Muslim states. It is sometimes almost a synonym of *amān.*

Some—by no means all—jurists even recognize an intermediate zone between the *Dār al-Ḥarb* and the *Dār al-Islām,* called the *Dār al-ʿAhd* or *Dār al-Ṣulḥ,*[25] in which the non-Muslim rulers continue to govern their people through their own agents, with a measure of autonomy under a form of Muslim suzerainty. The extent of the autonomy and the weight of the suzerainty vary considerably in the examples known to history.

The chroniclers preserve the text of an agreement said to have been concluded by the Arab governor of Egypt in the year A.D. 657 with the Christian kingdom of Nubia. This agreement, regarded as a *locus classicus* by the jurists, placed the Nubians under a kind of protectorate, whereby the Muslims guaranteed their security and they in return accepted certain obligations. No Muslim governors ruled over them, and no poll tax was collected from them. Their main obligation was to pay an annual tribute in slaves. Since Muslim law categorically prohibits the enslavement of free subjects of the Muslim state, whether Muslim or *dhimmī,* such an arrangement had obvious advantages. The Nubian treaty is known in Muslim annals as the *Baqt,* a word obviously derived from the latin *pactum,* or "pact." As far as is known, this term did not become part of the Muslim vocabulary, but was used exclusively of this agreement.[26]

Further north, the Armenian princes were able to conclude an agreement with the Umayyad caliph Muʿāwiya, by which they retained their lands and their autonomous rule. Centuries later, during the Ottoman expansion in southeastern Europe, the status of *Dār al-ʿAhd* was often a stage in the incorporation of these lands in the Ottoman Empire. Similarly, during the Ottoman retreat, it was sometimes a way station on the road to independence.

According to the law books there are two categories of Muslim enemies against whom it is lawful for the Muslim state to wage war—bandits and rebels. Bandits, including brigands, highwaymen, pirates, and the like, are to be combated in the same way as rebels, but with certain significant differences. These are listed by the jurist al-Māwardī (d. 1058)[27] under five headings. (1) It is lawful to fight and kill them coming or going, whereas it is not lawful to pursue rebels in flight. (2) It is lawful to wage a war of extermination against those of them who have committed murder, whereas it is not lawful to wage a war of extermination against rebels. (3) They are held accountable for whatever blood and property they have taken in war or otherwise, contrary to the case of rebels. (4) When captured, they may be jailed pending investigation, while captured rebels may not be put in jail. (5) Taxes collected by them are not deemed to have been lawfully collected, but are considered as theft; the taxpayers are still liable for these taxes to the treasury, and must claim reimbursement from the rivals.

The general purport of these differences will be clear. Their purpose is to distinguish between mere criminals and the armed forces of a rival power, possessing certain belligerent rights. The use of the term "rebel" to define this category is an interesting example of how the doctors of the law confronted those situations where the manifest facts of life around them were in sharp contrast with the provisions of the law; and how they contrived to provide legal regulation and judicial sanctions for situations which, according to a strict interpretation of the law, did not and could not exist. According to the political and constitutional provisions of the *sharīʿa,* there is only one Muslim community, administered by one Muslim state, and ruled by one Muslim sovereign. The juristic discussion of war, truce, and peace, and in general of external relations, is almost entirely in terms of dealings between the Muslim state and a non-Muslim state. There may be many of the latter; of the former there can, in principle, only be one.

In fact, the unity of the Islamic society and polity, however firmly maintained in theory, had been lost in practice from the mid–eighth century onward. Many different Muslim states came into existence, often in conflict with one another, sometimes at war. The paramount need to accommodate this fact in the legal framework was met through the law relating to rebels. The rebel, *bāghī,* as discussed in the law books, is obviously rather more than a mere insurgent or mutineer. From the legal texts it is clear that he may in fact represent a sovereign Muslim state other than the caliphate. Muslim rebels have virtually full belligerent rights. According to some law books, they may be killed only on the battlefield and not otherwise. Unlike apostates, they may be given quarter; unlike unbelievers, they may not, if captured, be enslaved or held to ransom. When defeated, rebel regimes are not, like non-Muslim states, required to pay tribute, and captured rebel property may be taken and used only if it belongs to the state. Private property must be respected and, when practicable, returned. A qadi appointed by a Muslim rebel chief is validly appointed, and decisions given by him are lawful and valid. Taxes collected by rebel authorities are lawfully collected, and cannot be collected again from the same taxpayers.

The purpose of all this is clear. If an established group maintain themselves in power, then even though they may reject the suzerainty of the caliph, they nevertheless constitute a legal and valid Muslim government, with the power to act and to empower others to act, in all matters where a Muslim authority is required. As long as the Sunni caliphate survived, its nominal suzerainty was recognized by virtually all Muslim rulers. After the demise of the caliphate, there was no single recognized authority in the Muslim world. For each Muslim ruler, or at least for each major Muslim ruler, he himself was the Lord of Islam, and his neighbors and rivals were established rebels. This can be seen in the titulature of Muslim monarchs, who used sovereign titles the clear meaning of which was the headship of all Islam. Territorial and ethnic titles might follow as corroborative detail in their own titulature; put in first place or alone, their purpose was to belittle a rival. The Sultan of Turkey and the Shah of Persia were titles which each used of the other and neither of himself.

To make war against Muslim rebels was therefore legitimate, and subject to the Muslim rules of war, but it was not *jihād*. Similarly, to make agreements with Muslim rebels was lawful, and such agreements were to be honored, but they were not of the same character as a truce agreed with the rulers of the House of War. This double distinction appears very clearly in the different treatment, by the Ottomans, of the wars which they were conducting on the one hand against the Christian powers of Europe, on the other against their arch rivals, the Shiʿite shahs of Iran, and in the agreements by which hostilities against both kinds of enemy were terminated.

Ottoman collections of treaties (*Muʿāhada*, Turkish *muahede*, from *ʿahd*), both in the archives and in published series, meticulously preserved the texts of the treaties and accords signed between the Ottoman government of the various powers of Europe. They did not include, until early modern times when European practices were adopted, the sometimes far more important peace agreements reached with the shahs of Iran. The Peace of Amasya,[28] agreed in 1555 between Sultan Süleyman the Magnificent of Turkey and Shah Ṭahmāsp of Iran, an event of major importance in the relations between the two countries, does not figure as a bilateral treaty in the annals of either of them, and no document which may be fairly called a treaty survives. What we have is an exchange of letters—or to be more precise, two unilateral statements—in which each of the two sovereigns sets forth the terms which had been agreed, in the form of his own decree. With Muslim rulers, such settlements could only be seen as unilateral, since each Muslim ruler was in his own eyes the legitimate and therefore the sole ruler of Islam. With non-Muslim states, the existence of which is recognized and dealings with which are regulated by Holy Law, bilateral relations, and even contractual agreements, were possible. His Muslim rivals and neighbors could at best be regarded as established rebels.

It was not until the time when European influence was predominant that a Muslim version of multilateralism, or polycentrism, was generally adopted. At no time has it been unchallenged. In 1917, the Grand Vizier of the Ottoman Empire, Said Halim Paşa, declared that "the fatherland of a Muslim is wherever the *sharīʿa* prevails."[29] More recently, the Ayatollah Khomeini has declared that "there are no frontiers in Islam"—though this did not prevent the inclusion in the new Islamic constitution of an article requiring the president of the republic to be of Iranian birth and of Iranian origin.[30]

One particular kind of treaty with non-Muslim states may be mentioned—the so-called capitulations,[31] granting extraterritorial privileges to resident communities of foreigners in the Ottoman and some other Muslim lands. The modern connotation of this term is capitulation in the sense of "surrender," and the capitulations are seen as an example of the unequal treaties imposed by stronger on weaker powers during the imperial expansion of Europe.

The origin of the Middle Eastern capitulations is, however, quite different. The term had nothing to do with surrender, but derives from the Latin *capitula,* referring to the chapter headings into which the texts of these agreements were divided. They date from the time, not of European, but of Muslim predominance, when the Islamic states were at the height of their power, and European merchants and their diplomatic representatives came as humble suppliants. The earliest known examples of such agreements date from the twelfth century, when the Muslims, having defeated and expelled the Crusaders, found it advantageous to allow the European merchants to remain in the Muslim Mediterranean seaports where they had established themselves, and conceded them the facilities which they requested and which they needed in order to carry on their mutually useful activities. Such concessions, perceived by the European trading states as treaties, by the Muslim rulers as edicts, were granted by Muslim sovereigns in North Africa, Egypt, Turkey, Iran, and elsewhere. The capitulations, in Ottoman *ahdname,* "covenant-letter," were granted by the sultans as an act of condescension. The rights and privileges accorded to the foreign merchant communities in the Empire were a logical extension of the autonomy of the *dhimmī* communities and of the medieval Muslim practice of *amān,* conferring the status of *musta'min*. It was not until much later, when the real power relationship between the European states and the Muslim empires changed to the disadvantage of the latter, that the privileges granted in the capitulations were abusively extended, and the resulting extraterritorial rights became vexatious and burdensome.

The fourth category of enemy against whom it is lawful to make war is the apostate—and war against him, unlike the bandit and the rebel and like the unbeliever, can rank as a *jihād*. The unbeliever, *kāfir,* is anyone who has never accepted Islam. The apostate, *murtadd,* is one who had been or had become a Muslim, and then had abandoned Islam and adopted another faith or, more commonly, reverted to his previous or ancestral faith. By so doing, he has renounced his allegiance to the Muslim state, and thus has become an enemy against whom it is legitimate, even obligatory, to wage war. It is in this last sense, commonly used of collectivities more than individuals, that the term acquires political significance.

The question of a war against apostasy arose on the death of the Prophet, when a number of Arabian tribes refused to transfer to the newly appointed caliph the allegiance and tribute which they had agreed to give to the Prophet. From the point of view of the pagans, they had made an agreement with Muḥammad, which was terminated automatically by his death. From the point of view of the Muslims, these tribes had joined the community of Islam, and by refusing to acknowledge the new leader of the Islamic community, they had become apostates and enemies. The ensuing wars, by which they were forcibly brought back to their allegiance, are known in Muslim annals as the Wars of the *Ridda* or Apostasy.[32] These wars, and the actions and rulings of the Muslim authorities which they evoked, provided the proof texts for most subsequent discussions of the legal treatment of apostasy; they also provided the model or paradigm for the treatment of rulers and entities seen as apostate.

The Muslim who abandons his faith is thus not only a renegade; he is a traitor, and the law insists that he must be punished as such. The jurists agreed on the need to execute the apostate individual, and to make war against the apostate state.

The rules of warfare againt the apostate are very much harsher than those governing warfare against the unbeliever. He may not be given quarter or safe conduct, and no truce or agreement with him is permissible. If captured, he is not a prisoner of war. He cannot become a *dhimmī*, nor can he even hope, like other captives of *jihād*, to live on as a slave. The only options before him are recantation or death. He may choose to return to Islam, in which case his offenses committed during his apostasy will be pardoned and his confiscated property—or what remains of it—be returned to him. If he refuses, he must be put to death by the sword. The only belligerent right which he shares with other types of enemy is that of sending ambassadors, whose status and immunity are recognized by the law.

Apostasy is extremely rare in Islamic history, and the apostasy of regimes or countries is even rarer. Accusations of apostasy, however, are not uncommon. As early as the beginning of the ninth century, al-Jāḥiẓ remarks wryly that "the piety of theologians consists of denouncing those who disagree with them as unbelievers."[33] Al-Ghazālī (d. 1111), in an essay on the criteria of distinction between Islam and heterodoxy, speaks with contempt of those "who would constrict the vast mercy of God to his servants and make paradise the preserve of a small clique of theologians."[34] It is a common practice of theologians, he notes, to use *takfīr*—denouncing someone as a *kāfir*—against their rivals and opponents. This he strongly disapproves. A Muslim, he observes, who becomes a *kāfir* is an apostate, and apostasy is a criminal offense under the law, with severe legal consequences. Such charges should not, therefore, be lightly made. They were, in fact, sometimes made by theologians engaged in polemics, but do not seem to have been taken very seriously by the authorities, since the prosecution of dissenting theologians on charges of apostasy is virtually unknown.

Of far greater importance, of course, are the charges of apostasy leveled against regimes and governments. There are two periods in Islamic history when such charges became major political issues. Both of them are periods when the Islamic heartlands of the Middle East were dominated and profoundly influenced by foreign, that is to say, non-Islamic, conquerors, and when a governing class emerged which professed Islam, but which followed many of the ways and customs of the former infidel masters.

The Mongols who conquered the Middle East in the thirteenth century brought with them the *Yasa*,[35] the laws of Jenghiz Khan, and the social and political usages of the steppe peoples. These had a profound effect on all elements of the Middle East. By the end of the century, the Mongol rulers of Iran were converted to Islam, but the Mongol ruling and military classes, even after their conversion, continued to regulate their own affairs by Mongol rather than Islamic law and, in many respects, to follow a Mongol rather than an Islamic way of life. Also in Egypt, which was never conquered by the Mongols, the ruling Mamluks, superficially Islamized newcomers from the Eurasian steppe, introduced elements of Mongol law and custom in the governmental and military apparatus, and adopted some Mongol practices, even in such matters as clothing and hairstyle. The Mongols had been the masters of the world, and Muslim amirs and sultans wore Mongol accoutrements and let their hair flow loose in the Mongol style—just as their modern equivalents, including the most anti-Western, continue to wear European-style fitted tunics, trousers, and visored military caps, in unconscious and continued deference to Western power and prowess.

Between the two groups there is an obvious difference. The Mongols and Mamluks were Islamized pagans; their modern counterparts are denounced as paganized Muslims. The result, however, is the same—a ruling elite of men who bear Muslim names and profess Islam, but who impose and administer non-Muslim laws, and thereby, in the eyes of the faithful, undermine and destroy the fabric of Muslim society, the preservation of which is the principal duty of the Muslims. In the fourteen centuries of Islamic history, few Muslim governments adhered strictly to the *sharīʿa*. But where they failed to conform to the *sharīʿa,* it was by error or avoidance, not by direct challenge, and in certain important areas, such as marriage, divorce, inheritance, and family life, *sharīʿa* law has generally been applied and enforced in Muslim lands. In the Mongol and Mongol-influenced states of the later Middle Ages, and still more in the modernized Muslim states of the nineteenth and twentieth centuries, *sharīʿa* law was not merely neglected or tacitly disregarded; it was, in certain important areas, repealed and replaced by other systems of law, of non-Islamic and therefore, by Muslim definition, nondivine origin.

This, from the traditionalist point of view, is the ultimate betrayal, the worst of all disasters, worse even than infidel conquest and rule, since, under a semblance of Islam, it seeks to subvert the loyalty of the Muslims and destroy the faith and law by which they live. Those who impose infidel laws are infidels; if they are or claim to be Muslims, then they are apostates, and must be treated as such.

The question arose in an acute form in the late thirteenth and early fourteenth centuries. The Muslim sultans of the Syro-Egyptian Empire had for long been at war with the pagan Mongol khans ruling from Iran. Such a war was obviously, from the Muslim point of view, a *jihād.* But the conversion of the Mongol khans to Islam raised a new problem. A war between Muslim states, though it might be legitimate in terms of law, could not be considered a *jihād,* and a Muslim ruler engaged in such a war against other Muslims could not call for the sacrifices of blood, effort, and treasure, which only a *jihād* could summon. The answer was that the Mongol so-called converts were not true Muslims, since they continued to practice and impose the laws of Jenghiz Khan. "Those who follow such laws," says a fourteenth-century jurist, "are infidels, and should be combated until they comply with the laws of God."[36] Such a combat was therefore a *jihād*, with all that that entailed.

To denounce the heathenish practices of an enemy ruler was, for jurists, easy enough. To identify and condemn the heathenish practices of their own lords and masters was more difficult and more dangerous, and in most times and places simply impossible. There is, however, no lack of texts, from the later Middle Ages, in which Muslim jurists and theologians make clear their disapproval of the maintenance in Muslim lands, including their own, of heathen laws and practices, and their desire to return to what they saw as true Islam. In the long run they were successful, and in the Ottoman Empire *sharīʿa* law was not only re-enthroned, but—albeit with some reinterpretations—was more effectively and extensively applied than in any other Muslim state of extensive territory and high civilization.

The question arose again in modern times, with the appearance, first in the Ottoman Empire and then in many other Muslim states, of reformers and modernizers, who tried to introduce Western notions and practices and thereby, intentionally or unintentionally, to transform Muslim government and society. Many of their proposed changes were contrary to the *sharīʿa* as practiced and understood, and were bitterly opposed by sections of the ulema, though sometimes supported by other groups. The reformers tried to deal with this problem in various ways, first by seeking to reinterpret *sharīʿa,* and when this failed to secure acceptance, to circumvent and ultimately to replace it with legal codes copied or adapted from European models.

Some of the ulema, following an old established tradition of pliancy and conformism, were willing to accept and justify the action of sovereigns and ministers in this as in other matters. Other ulema, following an equally ancient tradition of rigorism and dissent, refused, and denounced these reforms as a betrayal of Islam and an attempt to lead the Muslim community from righteousness to sin. Both views won considerable support among the population, the former more especially among the westernized middle and upper classes, the latter among the mass of the population. Clearly, the logical result of such a refusal is to deny the name of Muslim to those who seek to enforce such changes, and to pursue the legal or political consequences of a charge of apostasy against the sovereign.

Two examples may suffice, one from the nineteenth, one from the twentieth, century. The first example comes from the holy city of Mecca, then part of the Ottoman Empire, in April 1855. In that year, reports, only partially accurate, were reaching the holy cities of certain reforms on which the Ottoman government was alleged to be embarking, including such major departures from existing practice as the abolition of black slavery, the granting of equal rights to Christians, and the emancipation of women. The chief of the ulema of Mecca, a certain Sheikh Jamāl, issued a *fatwā,* or "ruling," denouncing all these projected and rumored innovations: "The ban on slaves is contrary to *sharīʿa.* Furthermore . . . permitting women to walk unveiled, giving women the right to initiate divorce, and such like are contrary to the pure divine law. . . . With such proposals the Turks have become infidels. Their blood is forfeit, and it is lawful to make their children slaves." The *fatwā* was followed by a proclamation of *jihād* against the Ottomans, and a revolt against their authority.

By June of the following year, the revolt had been crushed, but the sultan's government had noted the warning, and took steps to forestall a secession of the Ottoman south. Christians were still not admitted to the holy cities; in the Ottoman ban on the trade in black slaves promulgated in 1857, the Hijaz was exempted. The emancipation of women was nothing but a rumor, and no such change had been contemplated either by the Turkish reformers or their European mentors. A letter sent from the chief mufti of Istanbul, to the "kadi, mufti, ulema, sherifs, imams, and preachers of Mecca," tried to dispose of these malicious and false rumors: "It has come to our hearing and has been confirmed to us that certain impudent persons lustful for the goods of this world have fabricated strange lies and invented repulsive vanities to the effect that the lofty Ottoman state was perpetrating—almighty God preserve us—such things as the prohibition of the selling of male and female slaves, the prohibition of the call to prayer from minarets, the prohibition of the veiling of women and the concealment of their private parts, the putting of the right to divorce into the hands of women, the seeking of aid of people who are not of our religion, and the taking of enemies as intimates and friends, all of which is nothing but libelous lies." The careful mixture of the absurd and outrageous with the merely unacceptable no doubt had the desired effect.[37]

The second example is the murder, in 1981, of President Anwar al-Sadat of Egypt, by four members of an Islamic fundamentalist secret group. Their case against Sadat is clearly made in their statements during interrogation and the literature produced by their and other similar groups.[38] Sadat, according to them, was a Muslim only in name. By setting aside the *sharīʿa* and its true exponents, and introducing a Western and therefore infidel system of law and adjudication, society and culture, he had proved himself to be an apostate. The apostate is worse than the usurper, worse than the tyrant, worse even than the infidel ruler, in that there are no circumstances in which his rule may be accepted and his orders obeyed. The penalty for apostasy is death, and the basic Muslim duty of "doing what is right and preventing what is wrong" requires the enforcement of that penalty. Similar arguments were used to justify the overthrow of the Shah of Iran, and are being used against other governments in Muslim countries which do not accept the radicals' interpretation of Islam.

The classical Islamic discussions of the justified war and the laws which regulate its conduct relate almost entirely to struggles against external enemies. The principle of war against the apostate, however, opened the possiblity of legitimate, indeed obligatory, war against an enemy at home, which in modern times has been developed into a doctrine of insurgency and revolutionary war as a religion obligation and a form of *jihād*. This too has its roots deep in the Islamic past.

5

The Limits of Obedience

◆

"Obey God, obey His Prophet, and obey those in authority over you." This verse from the Qur'ān (IV, 59), amplified by exegesis and tradition,[1] has served as the starting point of most Islamic teaching about politics. The message of this teaching is twofold—to the ruler, authoritarian, to the subject, quietist. Ruler and subject alike are bound by certain obligations imposed on them by the Holy Law, both towards God and towards one another, and the primary and essential duty owed by the subject to the ruler is obedience. The consensus of Muslim religious, legal, and political writing is overwhelmingly clear on this point. The duty of obedience to legitimate authority is not merely one of political expediency. It is a religious obligation, defined and imposed by Holy Law and grounded in revelation. Disobedience is therefore a sin as well as a crime.

But neither principle, the authority of the ruler or the obedience of the subject, is absolute or unlimited. Both are subject to the law by which they are imposed, defined, and regulated. The Muslim ruler may be and usually is an autocrat, but he is not a despot. His office, and his tenure of that office, are established and regulated by the law, by which he is bound no less than is the humblest of his slaves. He may not change that law; in principle it is not even his function to interpret it. His task is to maintain and enforce the law and when possible to extend the area in which it prevails. If he fails in these tasks, still more if he violates the law, then he is in breach of his duty and of the contract with the Muslim community by which he was installed as ruler, and certain consequences follow. Among other things, these may affect the duty of obedience of the subject. To be owed this obedience, the ruler must, according to the classical doctors of law, accede legitimately and rule justly. If his rule is illegitimate or unjust, he may forfeit his claim to obedience. Much therefore depends on the definitions of legitimacy and justice.

From the earliest times, the reported events of Islamic history,[2] supported by the precepts of Islamic tradition and law, reflect two distinct and indeed contradictory principles. The one we have called authoritarian and quietist; the other might be called radical and activist. For obvious reasons, the quietist principle was usually dominant, and for that reason among others, it is the best documented and the most studied. But the radical activist tradition is also old and deep-rooted, and is acquiring new significance in our day, with the emergence of the idea of an Islamic revolution, and of leaders and movements devoted to its accomplishment.

In a sense, the advent of Islam was itself a revolution.[3] It began with the Prophet's challenge to the old leadership and the old order in pagan Mecca; it culminated with the overthrow and supplanting of both—the one by the Prophet and his companions, the other by Islam.

While the predominant view among jurists in general supported the authoritarian traditon, there was always another strand in Islamic thought and practice, which was radical and activist, at times even revolutionary. This tradition is as old and as deep-rooted as the first, and its workings can be seen through the centuries, both in Islamic political thought and in the political actions of Muslims. The exponents of both traditions naturally looked to the life and teachings of the Prophet for guidance and inspiration; both concentrated their attention on the political actions which the Prophet found it necessary to undertake in order to accomplish his religious mission. While the authoritarians looked to the Prophet as ruler, as head of the state, exercising sovereign authority over his community in Medina, the radicals looked rather to the earlier career of the prophet, when he was engaged in leading a movement of opposition to the pagan oligarchy of Mecca.

Though this opposition was primarily religious and moral in purpose, it inevitably took the form of political action. In this perception, the Prophet began as an opposition leader against the existing regime in Mecca, found himself obliged to leave his homeland for another place, namely Medina, where in due course he formed what in modern political language might be called a "government in exile," and from there was able to return to Mecca and accomplish his true purposes—the overthrow of paganism and the pagan regime and their replacement by Islam and a new Islamic order. In this, as in all else, the Prophet was seen as a model—the Qurʾanic term is *uswa ḥasana*[4] or in modern sociological language "role model." His career set a pattern which many later political aspirants attempted to follow; some succeeded, others failed. The ʿAbbasids who went to eastern Iran to return to Iraq, the Fatimids who went via Yemen and North Africa to Egypt, were both trying to reproduce the prophetic sequence of opposition, struggle, migration, and return from the periphery to the center. There have been many later leaders, including some very recent ones, who tried to overthrow and supplant their rulers by following a similar route.[5]

The radicals, like the authoritarians, found texts in the Qurʾān and the Traditions to confirm the lessons which they found in the career of the Prophet. There are several passages in the Qurʾān, notably those dealing with Pharaoh of Egypt, in which God commands his people not to follow pagan and wicked rulers. "But fear God and obey me and follow not the bidding of those who are extravagant, who make mischief in the land, and mend not their ways" (XXVI, 150–52). The implication of these and similar verses,[6] that there is no duty of obedience to evil rulers, but on the contrary, a duty of disobedience, is reinforced by several frequently cited traditions.

The radical tradition expressed in the career and teachings of the Prophet continued with what later historians have usually called conquests, but what the Muslim tradition called *futūḥ,* literally "openings." These were not seen as conquests in the vulgar sense of territorial acquisitions, but as the overthrow of impious regimes and illegitimate hierarchies, and the "opening" of their peoples to the new revelation and dispensation. The notion of a superseded old order is vividly expressed in the invocation of an ultimatum said to have been sent by one of the Muslim Arab commanders to the princes of Persia: "Praise be to God who has dissolved your order, frustrated your evil designs and sundered your unity."[7] The use of the root *ftḥ* is thus not unlike the twentieth-century use of the verb "liberate," and is indeed sometimes replaced by the latter verb (*ḥarrara*) in modern Arabic writing on early Islamic history. The Arabic verb *ghalaba,* "conquer," with a connotation of overwhelming by means of superior force, is sometimes used in early accounts of the Muslim conquests, but only in the context of actual military operations. For the conquests as a whole and the establishment of the new order, the normal term is *fatḥ, futūḥ*. On the other hand *ghalaba* is normally used of the conquest or reconquest of Muslim lands by non-Muslim armies.

Underlying this usage, clearly, is a concept of the essential rightfulness or legitimacy of the Muslim advance and the consequent illegitimacy of Muslim retreat before infidel reconquest. This accords with the well-known Muslim doctrine that every infant has an inborn disposition to be a Muslim, but his parents may make him a Jew or a Christian or a Zoroastrian.[8] The advance of Muslim power is thus an opening or a liberation, to give free scope to this divinely implanted propensity.

This spirit of activism is expressed many times in Islamic literature, notably in Qurʾanic injunctions not to obey willful and intemperate rulers who bring corruption to the world, and in traditions to the effect that there must be no obedience in sin—i.e., when the orders of the sovereign conflict with God's commandments.[9] If the first normally refers to non-Muslim rulers, the second would seem to be directed against erring Muslim holders of authority.

To a legitimate ruler, the Muslim subject owes complete and immediate obedience. If that ruler lacks or loses legitimacy, then the duty of obedience lapses, and may even be replaced by a duty of disobedience. The activists and quietists alike did not answer or even ask the crucial question which a modern constitutional lawyer would put: Who is to determine, and by what procedures, whether a ruler is illegitimate or has become sinful, and thereby forfeited the right to govern and to claim obedience?

In fact, of course, the practical issue was normally decided by the arbitrament of political and, where appropriate, other forms of struggle. There is, however, a considerable body of evidence, both theoretical and historical, about how Muslims viewed this question, and what arguments might be put forward to defend a regime or to demand its overthrow. Of particular interest are the solutions propounded by Muslim writers to the common problem of successful revolutionaries: how to justify their disobedience and legitimize their seizure of power, without at the same time opening the way to others who might want to do the same thing to them.

For the Prophet and the first Muslims, there was no problem. The test of legitimacy was God's authorization as vouchsafed by revelation. It was by God's command that the Prophet attacked and overthrew the rulers of Mecca; it was by God's command that he maintained himself in power against any who tried to resist or subvert his authority. Even after the Prophet, there was for a while, for believing Muslims, no real problem. The test of legitimacy was belief in God's faith and the maintenance of God's law. The objective of military and political action was the dethroning of unbelief, which as such could not be legitimate, and its replacement by Islam, through which alone God conferred legitimacy on rulers. The real problem began when the struggle was no longer against pagans and infidels, but against Muslims, i.e., when one Muslim ruler or regime was forcibly overthrown and replaced by another. During the religious and political struggles of the early centuries of Islamic history, legitimacy became a burning issue, and the two concepts, of usurpation and of tyranny, found frequent expression in Islamic political discourse.

Islamic history shows many revolutions, both successful and unsuccessful, but there was no positive term for the violent replacement of one regime by another until modern times, when the influence of the French Revolution, and of other European revolutions that followed it, percolated into Muslim political thought and language.[10]

Classical usage has many terms of disapproval for risings, mutinies, rebellions, subversions, and upheavals of various kinds. The commonest is *fitna,* with the original meaning of "test" or "temptation," often with sexual overtones. The word occurs frequently in the Qur᾿ān, in contexts indicating that the temptation is seen in terms of public policy rather than private belief or conformity—a temptation to disaffection, rather than to dissent. "Expel them [the Meccans] from whence they have expelled you, for *fitna* is worse than killing. Fight them until there is no more *fitna* and the religion of God prevails" (Qur᾿ān II, 191, 193). The "great *fitna*" arose in connection with the murder of the third caliph ʿUthmān in the year 656, followed by a long and bitter civil war between Muslim factions.[11] On the one side were those who saw the caliph as a tyrant and his killing as an execution; on the other, those who saw him as a rightful ruler and his killing as a murder. Thereafter, *fitna* became the commonest term for any serious challenge, whether intellectual or military, to the existing order. Its use is invariably negative—that is to say, it was applied only to movements which were led by others and, in the nature of things, were unsuccessful, since a successful movement, by its success, ceased to be *fitna,* and became a new accession or "opening."[12] *Fitna* was the term used by the first Muslim writers who discussed the French Revolution of 1789, and did not like it. When Muslim writers, in the course of the nineteenth century, began to speak more favorably of revolutions, they coined new words or reconditioned old words to denote them. Ottoman Turkish, followed by Persian, used *inqilāb,* an Arabic verbal noun with the literal meaning of "turning around." In Arabic *inqilāb* acquired a rather negative meaning, with a connotation of coup d'état or putsch, and the positive term for revolution was *thawra,* which in classical usage variously meant "rising," "excitement," "rebellion," or "secession." It is now the universal Arabic term for good or approved revolutions.

The nearest approach, in classical Arabic usage, to a positive term for a violent change of regime was *dawla,* which, as we have seen, has the literal meaning of "rotation" and was applied to the overthrow of the Umayyads and their replacement by the ʿAbbasids in the caliphate. But *dawla* rapidly acquired, and has ever since retained, the meaning of "state," and has entirely lost its previous revolutionary implication.[13]

Muslim political usage, as we have seen, offered a wide range of titles, used at different times by rulers who claimed to be legitimate. There is also an extensive vocabulary to designate those rulers who were seen as being, in varying ways and to varying degrees, illegitimate. The prototype of the illegitimate ruler is, of course, the infidel, particularly—but not exclusively—when he oppresses the apostles of God and the faithful. Such were Pharaoh, Haman and other figures portrayed in the Qurʾān; such too were the pagan chiefs and rulers whom the Prophet Muḥammad ousted or converted in Arabia. The titles used by the tribal chiefs and local rulers of pagan Arabia had no evil connotation in Islamic usage. They were, so to speak, decontaminated and incorporated in the political language of Arabia even after the advent of Islam. The name of Pharaoh has remained to the present day as the model and exemplar of the unjust, evildoing, and anti-Islamic ruler.[14] The Christian kings, whom the early Muslims encountered outside Arabia, being followers of a recognized, revealed religion, were accorded a somewhat better status, and were referred to by neutral or even respectful terms, such as *ṣāḥib* or *ʿaẓīm* or else by their own titles, as for example the "Negus" of Ethiopia and "Caesar" in Constantinople.

The term most commonly applied to non-Muslim rulers, whether before Muḥammad or outside the world of Islam, is *malik,* "king." As we have seen, its connotation in early Islamic times was sufficiently negative for it to be used of non-Muslim rulers. Later, when *malik* acquired a certain legitimacy within the Islamic world, the practice grew of using other, less flattering terms for infidel monarchs. Some of these terms were also to denounce Muslim monarchs who were seen as lacking in legitimacy. One term sometimes used was *ṭāghiya* or *ṭāghūt,* from a root frequently occurring in the Qurʾān, with a connotation of insolence and overweening pride, a disregard for God's law and hostility to God's apostles—in a word, a kind of Muslim equivalent of the Greek notion of hubris. In the Qurʾān it is used of Pharaoh and other pagans who defied the word of God and were duly punished. In Islamic times it was often applied to rulers whose legitimacy was, for one reason or another, not accepted. Thus, in the year 762, in a sermon delivered in Mecca by the ʿAlid pretender Muḥammad al-Nafs al-Zakiyya, he denounced his successful rival the ʿAbbasid caliph al-Manṣūr as *hādhā al-Ṭāghiya ʿaduww Allāh,* "this tyrant and enemy of God."[15] It was frequently used by Shiʿites when speaking of Sunni government, and by many Muslim writers about the Byzantine emperors. Later, it was commonly used in North Africa for the Christian kings of Europe, while eastern Arab writers continued to use the term *malik* for this purpose.

The rulers of the Christian states established by the Crusaders in Muslim territory do not qualify even for this title. They are not *malik,* "king," but *mutamallik,* "pseudo-king." Kings who came from Europe were called *malik,* e.g., Richard Coeur de Lion, but the king of Cyprus, as al-Qalqashandī explains, was called *mutamallik* "because the Muslims had taken [*fataḥa*] Cyprus and then the Christians had conquered [*taghallaba*] the island and ruled it. That is why the one who prevailed over it is called *mutamallik* and is not called *malik*."[16]

Ottoman usage retained the classical Islamic terminology, with some variants. Thus, Christian kings were not called *malik*, but *kıral*, a word of central European origin. The Ottomans were very reluctant to apply any Islamic title, even those of Persian or Turkish origin, to non-Muslims, and only conceded this under pressure. The preferred term was *kıral* (feminine *kiraliçe*), sometimes followed, in accordance with a common Ottoman practice, by an abusive jingle—*kıral bedfial*, "the evildoing king."

There is an interesting contrast in this respect between Ottoman and Persian usage. The rulers of Persia, who called themselves *shāhanshāh*, habitually used what was for them the lesser title *pādishāh* for European monarchs. The Ottomans, who called themselves *pādishāh*, made a point of not using this title when addressing European monarchs. This refusal became a point at issue in Ottoman-European relations. According to French tradition, the title *pādishāh* was first accorded by Sultan Süleyman the Magnificent to the French king Francis I, and this was seen as a triumph of French diplomacy. The evidence for this is, however, flimsy, and there are documents in which the French king is designated, like other European monarchs, as *kıral*, or sometimes with the even lower rank of *bey*.[17] It was formally conceded to the Holy Roman Emperor, previously addressed as the King of Vienna, by the Treaty of Zsitva-Torok of 1606,[18] the first treaty between the Ottomans and a European power which was not imposed by the victorious sultan on a vanquished enemy, but negotiated between equals. It was exacted by the empress Catherine of Russia in the Treaty of Küçük-Kaynarca of 1774,[19] ending a Russo-Turkish war in which the Turks suffered a disastrous defeat. From that time onwards, it was the application of European titles to Muslim rulers, not of Muslim titles to European rulers, that was eagerly sought and reluctantly granted, as a token of independence and equality.

The prototype of the legitimate Muslim ruler is of course the imam or caliph, the lawful head of the *umma*, the Islamic religio-political community. Since the ruler had the right to appoint persons to act in his name, the duty of obedience also extended to those officers and officials who exercised properly delegated authority on his behalf. In earlier times, the jurists insisted strongly on the need for legitimacy and justice. Legitimacy meant that the ruler was qualified and entitled to the office which he held, and that he had acceded to it by lawful means. Justice meant that he ruled in accordance with the Holy Law of Islam. If he failed to meet the first requirement, he was a usurper; if he failed in the second, he was a tyrant.[20]

In the course of the medieval centuries, there were significant changes in the definitions of legitimacy and justice, and consequently also in the definitions of usurpation and tyranny. The first requirement, legitimacy in terms of qualifications and manner of accession, was progressively reduced to the point where, in effect, only two conditions remained—power and Islam. As long as the ruler possessed the necessary armed strength to seize and hold power, and as long as he was a Muslim, however minimal and however nominal, that sufficed.[21] Some were even willing to go a step further and admit the legitimacy of a non-Muslim ruler, provided that he allowed Muslims to live the Muslim life, but this was exceptional, and in classical times was not generally admitted.

As the question of qualification and legitimate accession lost its importance, the attention of the jurists shifted from the manner in which rulership was acquired to the manner in which it was exercised. The hard lessons of a time of upheaval, reinforced by the authoritarian traditions of the older societies which had flourished in the Middle Eastern heartlands of Islam, brought what was in effect a new principle for Muslims—that any authority, however acquired, was legally valid as long as it preserved a basic minimum of legality, i.e., of respect for Islamic legal norms. In this way, even the second qualification, that of ruling justly, was whittled down, though never finally eliminated. It was, in fact, reduced to one basic requirement—public acceptance and maintenance of major Islamic ritual practices and moral principles.

While the limits on the ruler's autocracy were weakened, the subject's duty of obedience was correspondingly strengthened. A tenth-century jurist of the Ḥanbalī school, Ibn Baṭṭa, observed, "You must abstain and refrain from sedition. You must not rise in arms against the Imams, even if they be unjust. The caliph ʿUmar, may God be pleased with him, said: 'If he [the ruler], oppress you, be patient; if he dispossess you, be patient.' The Prophet, may God bless and save him, said to Abū Dharr: 'Be patient, even if he be an Ethiopian slave.'"[22]

The two quotations, the one ascribed to a caliph, the second to the Prophet himself, are undoubtedly false. They are, however, frequently quoted, for obvious purposes—to provide canonical authority for principles expressed with increasing frequency in this period: the need to give unquestioning and unfaltering obedience to the ruler, however oppressive he might be, and to obey the agents of that ruler, however improbable the guise in which they appear.

While writers show keen awareness of the possibility of misrule by sovereigns and misgovernment by officials, they nevertheless insist that obedience, even to a tyrannical ruler, is still due, to avoid the greater evils of sedition and anarchy. They suggest various palliatives by which rulers may be induced, through exhortation and good advice, to govern justly, and are full of pious exhortation on the need for honesty, loyalty, and piety on the part of state officials.[23]

While political writers of a literary or administrative background seem to have no great difficulty with this doctrine of total submission to authority, the jurists and theologians reflect a very different concern. Clearly, they are less willing than the practical men either to relax the limits of authority or to extend the limits of obedience. But even in religious literature, the political necessities of life eventually have their effect. It was not easy for the jurists to accept this doctrine of submission to tyranny, and the terms in which they express their acceptance often indicate great anguish. The great doctors of the Holy Law were men moved by a profound religious conviction and deep moral purpose. Their statement of the need to submit to oppression had its own rationale, different from the flattery of the courtier, the pragmatism of the bureaucrat, or the careerism of the official men of religion. Even oppressive government must be obeyed, say the pious ulema, because the alternatives are worse, and because only in this way can the basic religious and legal prescriptions of Islam be maintained.

The nature of the dilemma, and the reasons for the position adopted, were set forth with remarkable frankness by a succession of jurists and theologians. As early as the tenth century, the point was made very clearly by Ibn Baṭṭa, the author already quoted: "All the ulema have agreed unanimously that the Friday prayers, the two festivals, the ceremonies of Mīnā and of ʿArafāt, warfare against the infidels, the pilgrimage, and the sacrifices are incumbent upon every Amir whether he be upright or an evildoer; that it is lawful to pay them the land tax, the legal alms and the tithe; to pray in the cathedral mosques which they build and to walk on the bridges which they construct. Similarly, buying and selling and other kinds of trade, agriculture and all crafts, in every period and no matter under what amir, are lawful in conformity with the Book and the Sunna. The oppression of the oppressor and the tyranny of the tyrant do not harm a man who preserves his religion and adheres to the Sunna of his prophet, provided that he himself acts in conformity with the Book and the Sunna, in the same way that if a man, under a just imam, makes a sale contrary to the Book and the Sunna, the justice of his imam will be of no avail to him. Similarly, it is lawful to resort to the jurisdiction of their judges, to secure the enforcement of legal punishments and penalties, to seek redress for wrongs from their amir or their police authorities and to obey any officer whom they appoint . . . except in disobedience to Almighty God, for there is no duty of obedience to a creature [against his creator]."[24]

The same basic argument was set forth, with even greater force and passion, by the theologian and philosopher al-Ghazālī, writing towards the end of the eleventh century: "The concessions which we hereby make are not voluntary, but necessity may render lawful even that which is forbidden. We know that it is forbidden to eat carrion, but it would be worse to die of hunger. If anyone does not consent to this, and holds the opinion that the imamate is dead in our time, because the necessary qualifications are lacking, and he persists in this opinion but is not able to replace the imamate, not having at hand anyone who possesses these necessary qualifications, then we would ask him 'Which is the better part, to declare that the qadis are revoked, that all authorizations are invalid, that marriages cannot be legally contracted, that all acts of government everywhere are null and void, and thus to allow that the entire population is living in sin—or is it better to recognize that the imamate exists in fact, and therefore that transactions and administrative actions are valid, given the actual circumstances and the necessities of these times?'"[25] This whole argument is summed up in an aphorism quoted in a variety of forms, to the effect that tyranny is better than anarchy.[26]

In preaching this doctrine of submission, the jurists and theologians made no pretense at either liking or respect for the oppressive government in question, nor did they make any attempt to conceal its oppressiveness. In a passage often quoted by modern scholars, Ibn Jamāʿa, a Syrian jurist of the late thirteenth and early fourteenth centuries, is quite explicit: "At a time when there is no imam and an unqualified person seeks the imamate and compels the people by force and by his armies, without any *bayʿa* or succession, then his *bayʿa* is validly contracted and obedience to him is obligatory, so as to maintain the unity of the Muslims and preserve agreement among them. This is still true, even if he is barbarous or vicious, according to the best opinion. When the imamate is thus contracted by force and violence to one, and then another arises who overcomes the first by his power and his armies, then the first is deposed and the second becomes imam, for the welfare of the Muslims and the preservation of their unity, as we have stated."[27] The desperation felt by an honest and pious observer of the political scene of his time is clearly discernible in these lines.

In principle, a Muslim ruler who does not possess the necessary qualifications or who is not chosen or appointed according to the law, is a usurper. Among the Shīʿa this remained a crucial question, and all Sunni rulers, not being of the line of ʿAlī and not being nominated and appointed by an Alid predecessor, are usurpers. Among Sunni Muslims, as has been noted, effective power became a sufficient qualification. In a phrase used by the Mālikī jurists of North Africa, "whose power prevails must be obeyed."[28] The ruler need no longer be of the Prophet's tribe of Quraysh, as required by most legal formulations. He need no longer possess the legally prescribed qualifications of rectitude, judgment, physical soundness, wisdom, and courage. It is sufficient if he can stay in power and keep order.

Some of the sects, and a minority among Sunni jurists, go a little further, and demand that the ruler be guilty neither of blameful innovation (*bidʿa*), nor of major sin (*fisq*). According to the tenth-century jurist al-Bāqillānī, for example, the ruler forfeits his rulership if he falls into this category and thus ceases to be legally qualified.[29] The same applies if he becomes senile or otherwise physically incompetent. The majority Sunni view was that the ruler, even if he is a sinner, must be obeyed, though some authorities conceded that this might not apply to the ruler's agents who are sinners. In general, however, such limitations were either explicitly dropped or tacitly abandoned. Only one requirement survived the rest—that the ruler rule justly. The notion of usurper had thus lost its meaning; that of tyrant remained. In other words, when a ruler was challenged on religious grounds, the challenge was not based on the manner in which he gained power, but on the manner in which he exercised it—not usurpation, but tyranny.[30]

The rule of an unbeliever is, by definition, illegitimate, since only Islam can confer true legitimacy in government. But with an infidel as with a Muslim ruler, illegitimacy does not necessarily imply injustice. Is it possible then for a non-Muslim ruler, like a Muslim usurper, to compensate for the illegitimacy of his accession to power by the justice with which he exercises it? And, in an age when justice is the sole surviving criterion of acceptable government, may such a non-Muslim ruler claim the obedience, in Muslim law, of Muslim subjects? In the course of the centuries and over the wide extent of the Islamic world, both Muslim theory and practice have given different answers to these questions.

It was not a question to which the early Muslims or the founders of the great juristic and theological schools paid much attention. For the first two centuries, there seemed no good reason for Muslims to doubt that the triumphant progress of Muslim arms would continue until, in a not too distant future, their divinely ordained task was completed. On all three major fronts, in Europe, Asia, and Africa, Islamic power continued to advance. That advance might be halted from time to time by truces, but it was always resumed. Retreats were rare and where they occurred were mostly local and tactical, and involved no more than a temporary loss of recenty acquired infidel territories and populations. For both the jurists and the administrators of the caliphate, the problem of relations between Muslims and non-Muslims arose in two forms—in dealings with the non-Muslim outsider, the denizen of the House of War, and dealings with the non-Muslim subject, the *dhimmī*. The situation in which Muslim populations might find themselves subject to a non-Muslim ruler did not arise, was not conceived, and was not discussed.

The problem first arose in an acute form with the advance of the Christian reconquest in Europe in the eleventh century. When the Normans captured Messina in 1061, much of Sicily had been under Muslim rule for two centuries, and the Norman conquest of the island placed a sophisticated urban Muslim population under Christian rule. The parallel Christian advance in Spain and Portugal subjected even larger and more deeply rooted Muslim populations to Christian domination. The arrival of the Crusaders in the Levant at the end of the century brought the problem to the very heartlands of Islam. Nor was the problem limited to the West, since the growing Muslim weakness of the time allowed the Christian peoples of the Caucasus to recover their independence and even advance into Muslim territory.

As a result of these events, large, settled, and old established Muslim populations suddenly found themselves under the rule of non-Muslim sovereigns and administrators. It was a new and disturbing experience, and one which, in the centuries to come, affected ever greater numbers of Muslims.

The problems of cohabitation posed by the reconquest and the Crusades were both resolved by violent action—the one by the eviction of the remaining Muslims from Spain, Portugal, and Italy, the other by the destruction of the Crusader states and the departure of the Crusaders from the Levant. But in the meantime, other developments were posing the problem of non-Muslim rule over Muslim subjects on a vaster scale and in a more acute form.

The great Mongol conquests of the thirteenth century brought the whole of central Asian and southwest Asian Islam under the domination of an alien, pagan conqueror, and even when, in the course of time, the local Mongol dynasties who replaced the great Khans in the

Middle East were converted to Islams, they retained parts of the Mongol code of law and restricted the operation of the *sharīʿa*. And just when the Muslim lands were beginning to recover from the Mongol invasions and to convert and absorb the surviving Mongol rulers and soldiers, they confronted an even greater danger, this time coming from Europe.

The imperial expansion of Europe at both ends, from Russia across the plains and steppes, from the West across the oceans, in time brought the greater part of the Islamic world under the rule of four major European imperial powers, Russia, Britain, France, and Holland. Only Turkey and Iran managed to preserve an increasingly precarious independence. Elsewhere, the vast Muslim populations of Asia and Africa were subjected to one or another of these four great European empires, and compelled to submit to the rule of a Christian sovereign.

The first legal discussions of the problems posed by these events derive, as one might expect, from the far west of Islam, and deal with the loss to Islam of Sicily and the Iberian peninsula. At a time when the Christian rulers of the reconquered territories had not yet resolved on the expulsion of their Muslim subjects, these confronted a difficult but essential choice—to depart to Muslim lands, or to stay under the new rulers, and if the latter, on what basis?

The answers given by the jurists to these questions differ sharply. According to one school of thought, it was the duty of all Muslims, men, women, and children alike, to leave such territories, for it was against God's law for Muslims to remain under non-Muslim rule. Such rule would make it impossible for them to fulfill their obligations as Muslims under the Holy Law and would moreover subject them and their children to the danger of apostasy. If the infidel ruler was just and tolerant, that danger would be all the greater and the need to depart more urgent.[31]

As is customary, the example of the Prophet was quoted as indicating the course to be followed. The Prophet did not stay under pagan rule in Mecca but, together with his Muslim followers, made a migration, in Arabic *hijra,* to another place, where they could create a Muslim polity and live a Muslim life. The *hijra* was a turning point in the Prophet's mission, and was later adopted as the starting point of the Muslim era. Great stress was laid on its paradigmatic importance. When a Muslim land fell under non-Muslim rule, according to this school, it was the duty of its Muslim people to emulate the example of the Prophet and make a *hijra* to another and better place whence, in God's good time, they or their descendants would return to reconquer the lands which had been lost. Those who accomplished this migration were not called refugees (Arabic *lājiʾ*, Turkish *multeci*),[32] a term which is not part of the classical Islamic vocabulary and was used by the Ottomans of Christian refugees who came to Turkey from Europe, and more particularly of the Hungarian refugees who arrived in some numbers after the suppression of the insurrection of 1848. Muslim refugees from the lands lost to Islam were called *muhājir*, an active participle of the verb from which *hijra* is derived. Many centuries later, when the Ottoman Empire in its decline lost province after province to Russia, Austria, and the Balkan states, some of the Muslim populations elected and were permitted to remain under the new rulers; others left and "returned" to Turkey, where they are still known at the present day as *muhacir*. So too are the Muslims who migrate from secular India to Islamic Pakistan.

Another school of juristic thinking propounded a diametrically opposed solution. It appears to have been first formulated by a twelfth-century Tunisian jurist of Sicilian origin, who, in answer to a question, laid down that Muslims might remain under such a ruler and were obliged to obey his orders, provided only that the conditions existed under his rule for the observance and enforcement of the Muslim law. The jurist, al-Māzarī, goes even further, and allows such a non-Muslim ruler to appoint Muslim qadis, whose judgments and other legal acts would not thereby be invalidated, but would have the same force as if they had been appointed by a Muslim ruler.[33] The justification he gives for this is necessity, *ḍarūra*, a principle often invoked by Muslim jurists to justify the acceptance of situations which are in themselves unacceptable. By basing such recognition on necessity, the jurists were able to compromise on this issue without thereby abandoning the more important principle that territories no longer under Muslim rule have become part of the House of War, subject, when circumstances permit, to *jihād* and reconquest. The acceptance of infidel rule is based, in the last analysis, on the same argument as the acceptance by earlier jurists of Muslim usurpers and tyrants—the need to preserve the social fabric of Muslim life, and prevent anarchy.

An Iraqi historian, writing about half a century after the Mongol conquest of Baghdad, depicts the Mongol conqueror as knowing this trend in Muslim political thought and exploiting it to his own advantage. "In the year 656 A.H.," he says, "when Hulagu conquered Baghdad, he gave orders that the ulema be asked for a *fatwā* stating which is preferable, a just infidel sultan or an unjust Muslim sultan. He assembled the ulema in the Mustanṣiriyya college for this purpose, and when they became aware of the proposed *fatwā,* they held back from giving an answer. Now Raḍī al-Dīn ibn ʿAlī ibn Ṭāʾūs was present at this meeting, and he was preeminent and respected. When he saw how they held back, he took the *fatwā* and wrote his reply on it, preferring the just infidel to the unjust Muslim, and the others wrote after him."[34]

This narrative is not confirmed by other Arabic or Persian chroniclers of the time, and it may well represent a familiar feature of medieval historiography—the dramatic concentration of a long-term development into a single incident. It is clear, however, that Muslim jurists and theologians found ways—of necessity—to legitimize obedience to heathen Mongol authority, and that the Mongols, with the help of Muslim advisers, were able to make good use of such arguments.

The problem of heathen Mongol domination was, in any case, of brief duration, and ended with the conversion of the Mongol rulers of central and southwest Asia to Islam. That of European rule lasted somewhat longer.

The growth of the European empires brought vast territories and immense populations under infidel rule, far too great for migration or withdrawal to be a practical possibility. The basic argument of al-Māzarī—accommodation to necessity, so as to preserve the Muslim social and religious order—found many supporters among the jurists of the colonized countries. At the same time, the principle was maintained that such a rule was inherently illegitimate, and that it was the duty of Muslims to seek its overthrow when there was a reasonable prospect of success in the undertaking—but only then.

The earliest Muslim resistance movements against European imperial penetration and expansion, in Russian Caucasia, French North Africa, British India, and the Dutch East Indies, were entirely religious in their inspiration, their ideology, and their forms of expression. It was not until after at least a generation of imperial rule that another perception of the struggle began to appear among the Muslim subjects of empire—a perception of foreign rule as "imperialism" and of resistance to it as a struggle for national freedom and independence. These were new ideas and a new vocabulary was needed to express them. Some indeed, in Muslim countries, have seen in the acceptance of these ideas and use of this vocabulary the signs of an even deeper enslavement to an alien and infidel domination.

During the age of imperial expansion, and for a while, even after the withdrawal of the Western empires, such ideas exercised an enormous influence among the political class in Muslim lands, and brought a transformation in the concepts and hence also in the language of politics. The regimes against which the struggle was directed were no longer defined in traditional terms as infidel or tyrannical, but rather as alien and colonial. So far-reaching was this change and so profound its effects that even the Islamic past was rewritten in accordance with the new perception. The Ottoman sultan, accepted at the time by the overwhelming majority of his Arab, as of his other, Muslim subjects, as the legitimate Muslim sovereign of a universal Islamic state, was now redefined as a foreign imperialist, and the rule of the Ottomans, and indeed of other Turkish dynasties before them, was described and condemned as a domination of Turks over Arabs, and as such, evil and unacceptable. At the same time, in a new mythology, this domination was held responsible for everything that had gone wrong in the Arab world for the last thousand years.

The struggle against imperialism was waged in the name of nationalism, and its object was the ending of imperial domination and its replacement by freedom and independence. In the countries under imperial rule, these two words were treated as more or less synonymous, and were defined in national terms. This habit persisted for a while, even after independence was achieved. In those countries which, though threatened by the imperial powers, were never entirely taken over, independence as such was not a major issue, and the discussion of freedom was concerned primarily not with the rights of the group against other groups or of the state against other states, but rather with the rights of the individual against the group or the state. Its first exponents were liberal patriots rather than nationalists, inspired by west European rather than middle European examples, and their main aim was to limit the autocracy of their sovereigns by means of constitutional and representative government.

The new ideologies required a new vocabulary, to denote both the aims and the targets. Empire and imperialism were visibly alien and could be denoted with loanwords. *Imbīriyāliyya* in Arabic, *emperyalizm* in Turkish, brought an appropriately foreign sound to the discussion of this foreign intrusion. And an empire—even the Ottoman Empire—was reclassified in both languages as an *imbarāṭūriyya* or an *imparatorluk*.

Freedom and independence were a different matter, and could hardly be offered or sought under foreign labels. The terms "free" and "independent" made their first official and political appearance in the Russo-Ottoman Treaty of Küçük Kaynarca of 1774, in which the Tatars of the Crimea were declared to be "free and entirely independent of any foreign power." The freedom and independence of the Crimean Tatars was a sham and a subterfuge, and merely an intermediate stage between the ending of Ottoman suzerainty and the absorption of the Crimea into the Russian empire in 1783. But while the clause was no more than a face-saving device for the Ottoman sultan, it is of some interest as marking a stage in the development of Islamic political language. By the terms of the treaty, both the czar and the sultan agreed to recognize freedom and independence of the Crimean Tatars. The Tatars were to recognize the sultan as "grand caliph of Muhammadanism," but this recognition was to be purely religious, and was agreed "without thereby compromising their political and civil liberty as established."[35]

The choices made by the Ottoman dragoman who prepared the Turkish text of the treaty, in finding Turkish equivalents for such terms as "political freedom" and "independence," are interesting and significant. It is noteworthy that he did not use the terms *hür* and *hürriyet*, which mean "free" and "freedom" in the technical language of Islamic law, and thus denote free as opposed to slave. Instead he chose the word *serbest*[36], which, with its derivatives, became the common Turkish term for "freedom" during the momentous events of the French Revolutionary wars and the nineteenth-century Ottoman reforms. *Serbest* is a Persian word and means, among other things, "exempt," "untrammeled," "unrestricted." In Persian it could be used of an individual acting independently, but did not normally have a political connotation. Persian preferred *āzād* and its derivatives in this sense. In classical Ottoman texts and documents its normal meaning was neither legal nor political, but administrative and fiscal. Its commonest use is to indicate the absence or removal of normal limitations and restrictions. It appears most frequently in connection with grants of revenues assigned to the "feudal" cavalry. Normally, while most revenues were allocated to the recipient of such a grant, certain revenues such as, for example, the poll tax on non-Muslims, were reserved to the imperial treasury. A *serbest* grant was one untrammeled by any such restrictions or limitations in which, therefore, all the revenues went to the assignee.

The use of the term in political contexts seems to date from the early eighteenth century, and to judge from the earliest examples that have so far come to light, was due to external influences. A Turkish ambassador who went to France in 1720 noted, in the course of his itinerary, visits to the "free cities" (*serbest şehir*) of Toulouse and Bordeaux. Not content with merely using this term, he provided the explanation which he obviously felt his readers needed. Each city was the seat of a *parlement* and *président*. Both words are given in French, transcribed into the Turko-Arabic script, and explained. The ambassador noted that these cities had the valuable privilege of being garrisoned only by their own levies and not having royal troops stationed in them.[37] Another early eighteenth-century Turkish text describes the free city of Danzig in similar terms.[38] The first internal use, also in the eighteenth century, occurs in relation to the limited autonomy of the two Danubian principalities under Ottoman rule.

By the late eighteenth and early nineteenth centuries, the abstract noun *serbestiyet,* "freedom," appears to have been in common use. Thus, the Ottoman ambassador Azmi Efendi, who passed through Hungary in 1790 on his way to Berlin, noted that the previous emperor Joseph had deprived the Hungarians of their "ancient liberties" (*kadimi serbestiyetler*) but that the reigning emperor Leopold had restored them.[39] The Ottoman ambassador in Paris under the Directoire, Morali Esseyid Ali Efendi, speaks of French *serbestiyet* in his report,[40] while the chief secretary in Istanbul, Atif Efendi, in his important memorandum written in 1798 to examine the political situation created by the revolution in France and the activities of the revolutionary government, uses the word several times—first to describe the basic ideas of the French revolutionaries and their commitment to equality and freedom (*müsavat ve serbestiyet*) and then, in the context of more immediate Ottoman concern, in describing French propaganda among the Greeks and their attempt to install "a form of liberty" in the Greek islands and mainland towns which they had occupied.[41]

By the early nineteenth century the word was already in use in Turkey in domestic contexts. Thus, the historian Şanizade, who died in 1826, gives a description of the principles of consultation and the way in which such consultations should be conducted. A point to which he attaches obvious importance is that the discussion in these assemblies should be free (*ber vech-i serbestiyet*).[42] In the period that followed, the ideology and vocabulary of political freedom became familiar, more especially through the discussions of European affairs and the translations of European writings.

The first occurrence so far recorded of the use of the term *ḥurriyya* in the sense of "political freedom" dates from the year 1798, when General Bonaparte, arriving in Egypt, issued a declaration in Arabic addressing the Egyptians on behalf of the French Republic "founded on the basis of freedom and equality."[43] The choice of *ḥurriyya* for freedom was presumably made by the Arabic translators employed by the French. In classical usage *ḥurr* and its Persian equivalent *āzād* were primarily legal terms, but did at certain times and in certain places also have a social content, being applied to social groups enjoying privileges and exemptions. Thus, the Arabic-Spanish word list published in Granada in 1505 translates *ḥurr* as "franco, privilegiado." The political connotation of freedom, though new and previously unknown, was rapidly adopted and assimilated in the course of the nineteenth century, and became common usage in Arabic and other Islamic languages, including Turkish.

The commonest term for independence is *istiqlāl* (Turkish *istiklâl*) which, though of Arabic etymology, also derives ultimately from Ottoman administrative usage. The primary meaning of the verb is "to act alone," i.e., independently of others. In classical Ottoman administrative parlance it was applied to a high official such as the governor of a province, the commander of an army, or some other high functionary, who was given discretionary or even unlimited powers.[44] Such powers were normally granted only in serious emergencies. As late as 1834, in a Turkish translation of an Italian history of the Napoleonic period, it is still used in the context of unrestricted or unlimited rule. Thus, in one passage "autocratic" and "aristocratic" rule (*ber vech-i istiklâl*) is contrasted with the rule of liberty (*ber vech-i serbesti*).[45] By the midcentury, however, there are indications that the new meaning of sovereign independence was becoming known, and it is specifically cited in a British consular dispatch of 1858 from Jerusalem.[46] By the late nineteenth century, the use of *istiqlāl* in the sense of political sovereignty or independence was general in both Turkish and Arabic. Together with freedom, it came to express the ultimate objective of political struggle against oppressive rule in the period of European imperial domination, and the somewhat longer period of European intellectual influence. In times of Islamic resurgence, both notions have undergone some changes.

The notion of limited government has been fundamental to Islamic political thought since the earliest times. Indeed, in principle the Muslim ruler was more limited than Christian monarchs, since unlike them he did not possess the right to legislate, to make or change the law. In fact, however, the limitation on the power of the sovereign in traditional society was itself of limited effect, and rarely went beyond imposing a respect for the basic religious and social norms accepted in Muslim societies. Where entrenched intermediate groups existed, such as the Janissaries, the notables, and the ulema of the late Ottoman Empire, these could exercise a considerable limiting effect on the autocratic power of the state. But such intermediate powers were of rare occurrence, and the advance of modernization, bringing a rapid improvement in the means of surveillance and enforcement at the disposal of government, substantially increased the autocratic power of the ruler.

The effectiveness of the Holy Law as a limitation on the power of the sovereign was flawed in two important respects. One was that the law itself gave the ruler extensive autocratic powers. The second was that while the law prescribed limitations both on the authority of the ruler and the duty of obedience of the subject, it established no apparatus and laid down no procedures for enforcing these limitations, and no device for preventing or challenging a violation of the law by the ruler, other than force.

The optimism of the nineteenth century and what seemed at the time to be the successful example of the European powers suggested how this problem might be resolved. The answer, so it seemed at the time, was constitutional government, in which many Middle Eastern and other Muslims saw the secret of Western freedom, prosperity, and power. The first constitution in a Muslim country was proclaimed in Tunisia, in January 1861, and many others followed, notably in Turkey and Persia, when the sultan and the shah, in response to powerful pressure from below, granted constitutions to their peoples. The new states established after the First World War and, in greater numbers, after the Second, were almost all equipped with written constitutions, providing for representative institutions and limited sovereignty on the west European model.[47] Subsequent events have imposed some reassessment, at least in part of the Islamic world.

From the first, Muslim constitutionalists, like other reformers, tried to find a basis for their new prescriptions in Islamic law and tradition. There was no lack of suitable material. The classical doctrine of limited authority and limited obedience, under law; the contractual and, according to the Sunnis, elective character of the imamate; the insistence of the classical tradition on justice as the main object of government and on consultation as a means of ensuring justice were all cited in support of constitutionalism. By 1909, the fusion of Islamic and constitutional notions had been carried so far that in the speech from the throne, read by the sultan to parliament and written for him by the Young Turk government, he began with a reference to constitutional and consultative government as "prescribed by the *sharīʿa*."[48] The Young Turks were, of course, secular modernists, but even the radical fundamentalists of the Iranian Revolution found it necessary, after establishing themselves in power, to draft a new constitution for their Islamic republic, setting forth what they perceived to be an Islamic doctrine of government.

The insistence of both theorists and politicians on linking constitutional government to *sharīʿa* origins makes it all the more remarkable that the vocabulary of constitutional government, in Arabic, Persian, and Turkish alike, owes nothing to the technical language of the *sharīʿa,* but on the contrary, draws from quite different sources. The Arabic word for constitution has, since the first Tunisian constitution of 1861, been *dustūr.* This word, of Persian origin, was adopted by both Arabic and Turkish. It occurs in all three languages in the sense of "counselor," and even appears as one of the honorific titles of the Grand Vizier of the Ottoman Empire. In Arabic it had a variety of meanings, including "model" or "formulary," "tax-list," "register" or "record book," and, colloquially, "leave" or "permission." The commonest meaning was "rule" or "regulation," and in particular the codes of rules and conduct of the guilds. In Ottoman bureaucratic language, in the form *destur ul-ʿamel,* it was often applied to the rule book or manual of practice of an administrative department. It was no doubt in this sense that it was adopted when an equivalent was needed for the European term "constitution." The parallel with other modern political terms, adapted from the Ottoman language of bureaucracy rather than from the Arabic language of law, will be obvious.

In Ottoman and later in Persian usage, the term for constitution is *kanun-i esasi,* a literal translation of "fundamental law." Here again, the choice of the term used to translate "law" is significant. The technical language of the *sharīʿa* has many words for law, and for different kinds of law and ruling. It has no word for "enactment," since according to *sharīʿa,* this is not a human activity and is accomplished by God alone through revelation.

The word *kanun* (Arabic *qānūn*) has a long and interesting history. Derived ultimately from an ancient Semitic root meaning "a reed," and possibly connected with the English word "cane," it reached Turkish via Greek and Arabic. In medieval usage, *qānūn* sometimes appears as a synonym of *dustūr* in the sense of a "list or register of taxes or revenues." In Ottoman times, it was customarily used for the rules and regulations or manuals of procedure of a variety of organizations such as the craft guilds, tax offices, and other administrative departments. There were *kanuns* of an office, *kanuns* of a province, and even *kanuns* of the empire. *Kanun* was also used in the sense of "code of behavior or conduct," setting forth general principles. In earlier Ottoman times, a *kanun* might be composed of diverse elements, including local custom and the will of the ruler as well as principles of *sharīʿa* law. In later times, the term *kanun* is often used to indicate state-made, i.e., nonreligious law, as contrasted with *sharīʿa*. In the course of the nineteenth century, when the reformers enacted new codes of law and set up new judiciaries to administer them, *kanun* was the term applied to all these codes. It was no doubt in this sense of state-made, secular law, that it was applied to constitutions. The choice of an Ottoman administrative term, and in particular of one indicating a contrast from *sharīʿa* law, is surely significant.

The second half of the twentieth century brought great disappointment and much soul searching. The talismans from the mysterious Occident worked no magic; the nostrums offered by various foreign hucksters brought no cure to the ills of the Islamic lands and peoples. Constitutional government, contrary to expectation, did not make them healthy, wealthy, and strong. Independence solved few problems and brought many more, while freedom—now meaning the freedom of the individual against his own compatriots and coreligionists—seemed further away than ever. Many imported remedies were tried—from eastern as well as western Europe, from South as well as North America. None of them have worked very well, and increasing numbers of Muslims have begun to look to their own past, or what they perceive as their own past, to find a diagnosis for their present ills and a prescription for their future well-being. The revolution in Iran has shown one way, and there are men and women in every Muslim country today who seek either to follow the Iranian way, or to find a better alternative, in order to return to the true, original, and authentic Islam of the Prophet and his companions. The political language of Islam is acquiring a new relevance and a new significance.

It is also acquiring a new content. A revised or reconstructed past is never the same as the past as it was, and the Ayatollah Khomeini's revolution owes more to the outside world than just guns, direct dialing, and cassettes, important as these were in his seizure of power. Among fundamentalist circles in Iran, Egypt, and elsewhere, a new Islamic political language is emerging, which owes an unacknowledged debt to the westernizers and secularists of the past century and their foreign sources, as well as to prophetic and classical Islam. Much will depend on their ability to harmonize these different traditions.

Notes

♦

Chapter 1

1. In 1968, the federal government of Yugoslavia allowed Muslims in Bosnia-Herzegovina to register as a "nationality." Later, persons in other republics professing the muslim faith were allowed to opt for this "nationality" if they wished. Muslims with a small *m* were followers of a religion; Muslims with a capital *M* constituted one of the nationalities of which the Yugoslav population is composed. This term is not territorial, since the Muslim nationality has no defined territory, and Muslims live in several of the constituent republics of the Yugoslav federation. They are not merely a religious community, since religion as such has no place in the constitutional structure or legal apparatus of a communist state. Nor are they definable as an ethnic or linguistic group, since Yugoslav Muslims, in different parts of the country, speak Serbo-Croat, Albanian, Macedonian, or Turkish. See Alexandre Popovic, *L'Islam balkanique: Les Musulmans du sud-est européen dans la période post-ottomane* (Berlin, 1986), pp. 343ff.

2. The Turkish word was a neologism, *ladini,* with the literal meaning of "nonreligious." This term, coined by the famous sociologist and nationalist theoretician Ziya Gökalp, was often taken to mean "irreligious" or even "antireligious," and these interpretations further increased the hostility with which the notion was received. Later it was replaced by *lâyik,* a loanword from the French. Arabic adopted a term from the usage of the Christian Arabs, who needed to express this notion long before it aroused the interest or concern of the Muslims. The word they created was *ʿālamānī,* from *ʿālam,* "world," thus meaning worldly, as opposed to other-worldly or spiritual. In modern times, it has been revocalized and is pronounced *ʿilmānī,* and it is taken to mean scientific, from *ʿilm,* "knowledge" or "science," as opposed to religious. This is an entirely mistaken etymology and interpretation. See Niyazi Berkes, *The Development of Secularism in Turkey* (Montreal, 1964); Bassam Tibi, "Islam and Secularization," in *Proceedings of the First International Islamic Philosophy Conference 19–22 November 1979: Cairo (Egypt)* (Cairo, 1982), pp. 65–79.

3. It is now common usage to apply the term "fundamentalist" to a number of Islamic radical and militant groups. The use of this term is established

and must be accepted, but it remains unfortunate and can be misleading. "Fundamentalist" is a Christian term. It seems to have come into use in the early years of this century, and denotes certain Protestant churches and organizations, more particularly those which maintain the literal divine origin and inerrancy of the Bible. In this they oppose the liberal and modernist theologians, who tend to a more critical, historical view of Scripture. Among Muslim theologians there is as yet no such liberal or modernist approach to the Qur᾽ān, and all Muslims, in their attitude to the text of the Qur᾽ān, are in principle at least fundamentalists. Where the so-called Muslim fundamentalists differ from other Muslims and indeed from Christian fundamentalists is in their scholasticism and their legalism. They base themselves not only on the Qur᾽ān, but also on the Traditions of the Prophet, and on the corpus of transmitted theological and legal learning. Their aim is nothing less than to abrogate all the imported and modernized legal codes and social norms, and in their place to install and enforce the full panoply of the *sharīʿa*—its rules and penalties, its jurisdiction, and its prescribed form of government.

4. On the place of Islam in the constitutions of Arab states, see Monika Tworuschka, *Die Rolle des Islam in den arabischen Staatsverfassungen* (Walldorf-Hessen, 1976); on Muslim constitutions in general, *Dustūr: A Survey of the Constitutions of the Arab and Muslim States* (Leiden, 1966), reprinted, with additional material, from the *Encyclopaedia of Islam,* 2d ed. (hereafter cited as *EI*²).

5. Many terms are used to denote outsiders. Thus, Arab is contrasted with *ʿAjam,* which originally simply meant non-Arab and was then often specialized to mean the Persians, who were, so to speak, the non-Arabs par excellence on the horizon of ancient Arabia. In later Arabic usage, *ʿAjam* is used almost exclusively in the sense of "Persian." In Turkish, by a development of the earlier usage, the adjectival form *ʿajemī* (modern Turkish *acemi*) sometimes has the sense of "clumsy" or "inept." The classical Arabic term *ʿilj,* plural *ʿulūj,* with the meaning, among others, of "gross, "coarse," is sometimes contrasted with *ʿArab,* and has the sense, more or less, of "barbarian." It does not necessarily have a religious connotation, as is shown by the fact that a Syrian Christian author like Ibn al-ʿIbri uses it when speaking of the Franks. It has disappeared from modern usage. The Arabic term *Barbar* or *Barbarī,* akin to the Greek *Barbaros,* is normally limited to the pre-Arab inhabitants of North Africa and, in Egyptian usage, to the black peoples of the upper Nile. It is sometimes given to other unfamiliar neighbors, e.g., the Mongol-descended Hazāra in Afghanistan, but it does not carry a connotation of barbarism.

6. Arabic is a Semitic language, of the same family as Hebrew, Aramaic, and Ethiopic. Persian is Indo-European, and thus is related to the major languages of India and Europe. Turkish is one of the Altaic group of languages, distantly related, according to a generally accepted view, to Finnish, Estonian, and Hungarian.

7. On these books see *Encyclopaedia Iranica,* s.v. "Āʾīn-Nāma" (by A. Tafazzoli); Arthur Christensen, *L'Iran sous les Sassanides* (Copenhagen, 1944), pp. 62–64, 72, 217–18, 318, 402; M. Inostranzev, *Iranian Influence on Moslem Literature,* part 1 (Bombay, 1918), with supplementary appendices from Arabic sources by G. K. Nariman; Jan Rypka, *Iranische Literaturgeschichte* (Leipzig, 1959), p. 46. One of the earliest to translate and cite Persian books on statescraft was the Persian convert to Islam Ibn al-Muqaffaʿ (720?–756?), who wrote or adapted a number of important political treatises in Arabic. On him and his work see *EI*², s.v. "Ibn al-Muḳaffaʿ" (by F. Gabrieli), where further bibliography is given.

8. On the reception of Greek thought in the medieval Islamic world see A. R. Badawi, *La transmission de la philosophie grecque au monde arabe* (Paris, 1968); Franz Rosenthal, *Das Fortleben der Antike im Islam* (Zurich and Stuttgart, 1965), especially pp. 153ff. (on politics); for English translations, see Ralph Lerner and Muhsin Mahdi, eds., *Medieval Political Philosophy* (Ithaca, N.Y., 1963). There is an extensive literature on Muslim political philosophy of the Hellenistic school. For introductory accounts, see E. I. J. Rosenthal, *Political Thought in Medieval Islam: An Introductory Outline* (Cambridge, 1958), and F. Gabrieli's contribution on Muslim political thought, "Pensiero politico," in *Storia delle idee politiche, economiche e sociali,* ed. Luigi Firpo (Turin, 1971).

9. Another Latin loanword in the Qurʾān is *qaṣr,* "castle," from *castrum.* This word returned from Arabic to Europe via the Spanish Alcazar, al-Qaṣr. On loanwords in Arabic, reference may be made to Siegmund Fraenkel, *Die aramäischen Fremdwörter im Arabischen* (Leiden, 1886); Arthur Jeffery, *The Foreign Vocabulary of the Qur'an* (Baroda, 1938); Muḥammad ʿAlī Emām Shushtarī, *Farhang-i Vāžehā-i Fārsī dar zabān-i ʿArabī* (Tehran, 1347 s.); A. Siddiqi, *Studien über die persischen Fremdwörter im klassischen Arabisch* (Göttingen, 1919); Murad Kamil, "Persian Words in Ancient Arabic," *Bulletin of the Faculty of Arts* (Cairo University) xix/i (1957), pp. 55–67. For a remarkable discussion of these loanwords, by a tenth century Ismāʿīlī theologian, see Abū Ḥātim Aḥmad ibn Ḥamdān al-Rāzī, *Al-Zīna fī'l-muṣṭalaḥāt al-Islāmiyya al-ʿArabiyya,* ed. Ḥusayn al-Hamdānī (Cairo, 1956–58), vol. 1, pp. 81ff.

10. Various etymologies, both Arabic and Persian, have been suggested for *dīwān.* The two most commonly cited in classical sources derive it from the Arabic verb *dawwana,* "to collect" or "to register," or from the Persian *dīvāne,* "mad," i.e., possessed by a *dēv,* or "devil." The latter is usually accompanied by a story telling how the Persian Emperor Khusru entered one of his government offices and, astonished by the demented-seeming noise and demeanor of the secretaries, exclaimed "*Dīvāne,*" "mad," whence the office took its name. The latter version is obviously a humorous popular etymology; the former relies on what is almost certainly a denominative verb, formed in Arabic from a borrowed Persian substantive. Another explanation

relates *dīwān* to the Iranian root *dipi,* "to write," whence also *dabīr,* "a scribe," and *defter,* "a register," "record," or "account book," from the Greek *diphthera,* "a hide prepared for writing"—itself a loanword from Old Persian. In Arabic and Islamic Persian *dīwān* normally means "a government department or office." Later meanings are the ruler's court or council; the collected poems of a poet (i.e., ordered and classified); a senior government minister or official (India only); a board, a public session (Ottoman), and hence an audience, a levee, a court (of justice); a sofa or couch (Ottoman). In the forms *aduana, douane,* etc., it passed into the Romance languages with the meaning of "customs," or "custom-duties." See *EI*[2], s.vv. "Dīwān" (by A. A. Duri, H. L. Gottschalk, G. S. Colin, A. K. S. Lambton, and A. S. Bazmee Ansaree), and "Dīwān-i Humāyūn" (by B. Lewis); Ḥasan al-Bāshā, *Al-Funūn al-Islāmiyya wa'l-Waẓā'if ʿala al-Āthār al-ʿArabiyya* (Cairo, 1966), pp. 537–48; idem, *Al-Alqāb al-Islāmiyya fi'l-ta'rīkh wa'l-wathā'iq wa'l-Āthār* (Cairo, 1957), pp. 292–93.

11. On the origin and development of the term *wazīr,* and the office which it denoted, see S. D. Goitein, "The Origin of the Vizierate and Its True Character," *Islamic Culture* xvi (1942), pp. 255–63, 380–92, reprinted with appendix in idem, *Studies in Islamic History and Institutions* (Leiden, 1966), pp. 168–96; Dominique Sourdel, *Le vizirat ʿabbaside de 749 à 936,* 2 vols. (Damascus, 1959–60); ʿAbd al-ʿAzīz al-Dūrī, *Al-Nuẓum al-Islāmiyya* (Baghdad, 1950), pp. 210–37; Adam Mez, *The Renaissance of Islam,* trans. Salahuddin Khuda Bukhsh and D. S. Margoliouth (London, 1937), pp. 89–106 (German original, *Die Renaissance des Islam* [Heidelberg, 1922]); ʿAṭiyya Muṣṭafā Musharrafa, *Nuẓum al-Ḥukm bi-Miṣr fi ʿAṣr al-Fāṭimiyyin* (Cairo, 1948), pp. 116–42; ʿAbbās Eghbāl, *Vezārat dar ʿahd-i salāṭīn-i buzurg-i Saljūqī* (Tehran, 1338s); al-Bāshā, *Funūn,* pp. 1322–42 (particularly valuable for epigraphic material). For contrasting views on the Persian origins of the vizierate see Christensen, *L'Iran sous les Sassanides,* pp. 109, 113ff.; W. Barthold, "Die Persische Šuʿubija und die moderne Wissenschaft," *Zeitschrift für Assyriologie* xxvi (1912), pp. 249–66 (Russian text in V. V. Bartold, *Sočineniya,* vol. 7 [Moscow, 1971], pp. 359–70). On the Ottoman vizierate, see H. A. R. Gibb and Harold Bowen, *Islamic Society and the West,* vol. 1, part 1 (London, 1950), pp. 107–17, 363–64; Mehmet Zeki Pakalın, *Osmanlı Tarih Deyimleri ve Terimleri Sözlüğü,* vol. 3 (Istanbul, 1946–54), pp. 81–88, 590–95. Under the classical caliphate there was one wazir only, who was chief of the entire administrative apparatus and was the nearest and most powerful helper of the sovereign. He was a civilian, and his emblem of office was an inkpot. Under the later medieval rulers and the early Ottomans, the vizierate underwent a number of changes and was at times militarized, at times multiplied, with a group of wazirs serving under a chief. This was, for a while, the Ottoman practice and gave rise to the conventional Western rendering "Grand Vizier," by which the Ottoman chief minister was known in Europe. His title in Turkish—and that of his analog in Iran—was

Sadrıazam (Perso-Arabic *Ṣadr-i Aʿẓam*). The form "vizier" derives from the Turkish pronunciation of the Arabic *wazīr.*

In modern Arabic and Persian, but not Turkish, *wazīr* is used as the equivalent of minister, in the sense both of diplomatic representative and political head of a government department.

12. On this transformation, see B. Lewis, "The Mongols, the Turks and the Muslim Polity," in *Transactions of the Royal Historical Society,* 5th ser., no. 18 (London, 1968), pp. 49–68, reprinted in idem, *Islam in History* (London, 1973), pp. 179–98.

13. On this point, see the interesting observations of David Ayalon, "The European-Asiatic Steppe: A Major Reservoir of Power for the Islamic World," in *Proceedings of the Twenty-fifth Congress of Orientalists (Moscow 1960),* vol. 2 (Moscow, 1963), pp. 47–52, reprinted in idem, *The Mamluk Military Society: Collected Studies* (London, 1979).

14. On the effects of westernization on Arabic political language, see Charles Issawi, "European Loan-Words in Contemporary Arabic Writing: A Case-Study in Modernization," *Middle Eastern Studies* iii (1967), pp. 110–33; B. Lewis, "On Some Modern Arabic Political Terms," in *Orientalia Hispanica sive studia F. M. Pareja Octogenario dicata,* ed. J. M. Barral, vol. 1, part 1 (Leiden, 1974), pp. 465–71, reprinted in idem, *Islam in History,* pp. 282–88; and especially, Ami Ayalon, *Language and Change in the Arab Middle East* (New York, 1987).

15. Karl Lokotsch, *Etymologisches Wörterbuch der europäischen . . . Wörter orientalischen Ursprungs* (Heidelberg, 1927); A. Steiger, *Origin and Spread of Oriental Words in European Languages* (New York, 1963); E. Littmann, *Morgenländische Wörter im Deutschen,* 2d rev. ed. (Tübingen, 1924).

16. Thus, for example, a series of Iranian offensives against the Iraqi forces was code-named Karbalāʾ, after a battle that was fought in A.D. 680. This was the occasion when the grandson and family of the Prophet, along with their faithful Shiʿite supporters, were massacred in a hopeless fight against the armies of the Umayyad caliph Yazīd. At the same time, Iranian war propaganda denounces the Iraqi leader Ṣaddām Ḥusayn as the Yazīd of our time. The Iraqis, on their side, call the Iranians *Furs,* a somewhat derogatory term in medieval times, with a suggestion that the Persians were the heirs of the Zoroastrians defeated at the battle of Qādisiyya in A.D. 637. This battle, which shattered the military power of the Iranian emperors and led to the incorporation of all their lands and peoples in the Muslim Arab Empire, is claimed with pride by both sides. For the Iraqis, it was a victory of Arabs over Persians, and the first decisive step in the conquest of Iran. For the soldiers of the Islamic Republic, it was a victory of Muslims over heathens, and a blessed beginning of the Islamization of the peoples of Iran.

This kind of historic allusion is by no means limited to Iraq and Iran. The Egyptian assault on the Israeli Bar Lev Line in October 1973 was code-named Badr, the name of a military victory won by the prophet Muḥammad over the pagan Arabs of Mecca. The formations of the Palestine Liberation Army are named after major victories won by Muslims against non-Muslims in medieval times—the battle of the Yarmūk against the Byzantine Christians (A.D. 636), the battle of Qādisiyya against the Zoroastrian Persians, the battle of Ḥaṭṭīn against the Crusaders (A.D. 1187), and the battle of ʿAyn Jālūt, against the heathen Mongols (A.D.1260).

17. On the function of eulogy and satire in propaganda and polemic, see Régis Blachère, *Histoire de la littérature arabe,* 3 parts (Paris, 1952–66), pp. 434ff., 544ff., 580ff., 599ff., 686ff. For examples of political poetry, see E. García Gómez, "Poésie politique à Cordoue," *Revue des Études Islamiques* (1949), pp. 5–11; Marius Canard, "L'impérialisme des Fatimides et leur propagande," *Annales de l'Institut d'Études Orientales,* vol. 6 (Algiers, 1942–47), pp. 156–93. According to medieval Egyptian encyclopedists, the Fatimid caliphs had large numbers of official poets attached to their office of chancery (*dīwān al-inshā*ʾ), including both Sunni poets who refrained from excessive, i.e., heretical, panegyric and Shiʿite poets who indulged in it (al-Qalqashandī, *Ṣubḥ al-Aʿshā,* vol. 3 [Cairo, 1914], p. 497). The Prophet himself took political poetry very seriously, as can be seen from the fate of poets who attacked him. See W. Montgomery Watt, *Muhammad at Medina* (Oxford, 1956), p. 15; Maxime Rodinson, *Mohammed,* translated from the French (London, 1971), pp. 157–58, 171–72.

18. See for example Isa. 8:19 and the rabbinic commentaries on this verse.

19. On *siyāsa* see B. Lewis, "Translation from Arabic," *Proceedings of the American Philosophical Society* cxxiv (1980), pp. 41–47; idem, "Siyāsa," in *In Quest of an Islamic Humanism: Arabic and Islamic Studies in Memory of Mohamed al-Nowaihi,* ed. A. H. Green (Cairo, 1984), pp. 3–14; Fauzi M. Najjar, "Siyasa in Islamic Political Philosophy," in *Islamic Theology and Philosophy: Studies in Honor of George F. Hourani,* ed. Michael E. Marmura (Albany, 1984), pp. 92–111, 295–97; David Ayalon, "The Great *Yasa* of Chingiz Khan: A Reexamination (C_2)," *Studia Islamica* xxxviii (1973), pp. 115ff.; Aḥmad ʿAbd al-Salām, *Dirāsāt fi Muṣṭalaḥ al-Siyāsa ʿind al-ʿArab* (Tunis, 1978).

20. Ibn Qutayba, *ʿUyūn al-Akhbār,* vol. 1 (Cairo, 1962), p. 43. Cf. a similar usage in an anti-Jewish poem, composed in Granada, Spain, in the eleventh century. The poet, addressing a king whom he accuses of showing undue favor to the Jews, exclaims, "Why should you alone be different and bring them near when in all the land they are kept afar?" (English translation in Lewis, *Islam in History,* p. 160; Arabic text in E. García Gómez, *Un alfaquì espanol: Abū Isḥāq de Elvira* [Madrid and Granada, 1944], pp. 149ff.)

21. Maimonides, in his *Guide of the Perplexed* (Arabic *Dalālat al-Ḥāʾirīn*), discusses the significance of nearness and remoteness in some detail (I, 10, 18, 20; III, 51). My thanks are due to Professor Ralph Lerner for drawing my attention to this passage.

22. *Vali* and *vilâyet* are the Turkish pronunciation of the active participle and verbal noun of the Arabic root *w-l-y,* "to be near" and hence "to take charge of"; they mean, respectively, governor and governorship or province. *Mollah* (also *mullah, moollah*), comes into English via Urdu and Persian, and derives from the Arabic passive participle *mawlā,* which among other things means "one to whom clientage is due" and hence, more generally, "patron," "master," "protector." In Iran and India it is commonly applied to men learned in religion. *Mawlānā,* "our master," is used to address divines in the Islamic East and monarchs in the Islamic West. (See al-Bāshā, *Alqāb,* pp. 516–22; idem, *Funūn,* pp. 1169–74.)

23. See al-Qalqashandī, *Ṣubḥ al-Aʿshā,* vol. 5, pp. 449–52.

24. Pakalın, *Osmanlı Tarih Deyimleri,* vol. 2, pp. 375–77. Gibb and Bowen, *Islamic Society and the West,* vol. 1, part 1, pp. 72, 80, 342–46.

25. Two frequently quoted traditions of the Prophet make the point clear: "Whoever removes himself from the [Islamic] Community by a single span, withdraws his neck from the halter of Islam"; and "If anyone dies after being separated from the Community, it is as if he had died in the Time of Ignorance" (i.e., before the advent of Islam]. See EI^2, s.v. "Djamāʿa" (by L. Gardet). Another Arabic noun, *ḥizb,* "party," is conventionally derived from a verb meaning "to befall," used of an event, more especially a painful or distressful event. Most probably, *ḥizb* is a loanword from Ethiopic (Jeffery, *Foreign Vocabulary of the Qur'an,* pp. 108–9). The expression *ḥizb Allāh,* "the party, or adherents, of God," occurs twice in the Qurʾān (V, 61/56; LVIII, 22), in an obviously favorable sense. Most commonly, however, in the Qurʾān and in early traditional and historical narratives, *ḥizb* has a rather negative connotation, and is used of a variety of ancient factions (EI^2, s.v. "Ḥizb," by D. B. MacDonald). In the early twentieth century it became the common Arabic term for political parties, in the Western sense.

26. See Meir (= Martin) Plessner, "Hadashim gam yeshanim la-sugiya 'Yemin-Smol,'" in *Meḥqare ha-Merkaz le-ḥeqer ha-Folklor,* vol. 1 (Jerusalem, 5730j), pp. 260–74.

27. On some uses of *raʾīs,* see al-Bāshā, *Alqāb,* pp. 308–9; on *raʾs,* idem, *Funūn,* pp. 545–51; on *baş,* Pakalın, *Osmanlı Tarih Deyimleri,* vol. 1, pp. 160–69.

28. Examples in al-Bāshā, *Alqāb,* pp. 403–4.

29. Even in modern Arabic, *ḍaʿīf* is often linked with *miskīn,* "poor," "wretched," to denote artisans and peasants (R. B. Serjeant, "Professor A. Guillaume's translation of the Sirah," *Bulletin of the School of Oriental and African Studies* [hereafter cited as *BSOAS*] xxi [1958], p. 11). In classical usage, it is sometimes used as the converse of *sharīf,* "noble," "wellborn," and commonly to denote the non-arms-bearing orders of society. Thus, *ḍaʿīf* sometimes connotes one who lacks *manʿa,* i.e., the ability to defend himself against attack, whether with arms, armed retainers, or fortified places. This ability clearly indicates a certain social status, as does also the lack of it.

In a *ḥadīth* frequently cited in political writings, the Prophet is asked by the ascetic Abū Dharr to appoint him to a position of command and replies, "You are weak [*ḍaʿīf*] and this is a trust which, on the Day of Judgment, will bring shame and regret, save only to him who took it rightly and discharged the duties it imposed on him" (English translation in Lewis, ed. and trans., *Islam from the Prophet Muḥammad to the Capture of Constantinople,* vol. 1 (New York, 1974), p. 159; Arabic text in Muslim, *Ṣaḥīḥ,* vol. 6, *K. al-Imāra* [Cairo, *A. H.* 1283], p. 706; Abū Yūsuf, *Kitāb al-Kharāj,* 3d ed.; [Cairo, 1962–63], pp. 3–17). The defense of the weak against their oppressors figures prominently in the appeals of Muslim rebels, from early times. For examples from the seventh and eighth centuries, see Lewis, *Islam,* vol. 2, pp. 53–55. *Ḍaʿīf* is frequently linked with *dhalīl,* "humble," as in the saying cited by al-Jāhiz, *Al-Bayān wa'l-Tabyīn,* ed. ʿAbd al-Salām Muḥammad Hārūn, vol. 3 (Cairo, 1960), p. 368.

30. A Qur'anic term, meaning "those who are seen as weak," and hence despised and downtrodden. It occurs notably in IV, 75, 97–98, 127, and VIII, 26. The first of these reads, "And why should you not fight in the cause of God, and of those men, women and children who are downtrodden [*mustaḍʿaf*], and who cry out: Our Lord, take us out of this city whose people are oppressors, and appoint for us a protector [*wali*] and a helper [*nāṣir*] from you." This passage, which refers to the fate of the Muslims in pagan Mecca, became a proof text for Muslim revolutionaries.

31. *Shaykh* has many derivatives, denoting various types of authority, and may sometimes be replaced by native words of similar meaning in Persian, Turkish, and other Islamic languages. One such, widely used in the Turkish languages, is *aksakal,* literally "white beard" and contextually usually something like "elder." The Persian word *pīr,* the lexical equivalent of the Arabic *shaykh,* is commonly used in a religious sense, to denote saints, heads of Dervish orders, etc. It does not normally carry a connotation of political seniority or authority. The modern Turkish word for an old man is *ihtiyar,* from an Arabic word meaning "choice"—an interesting example of how metaphor can affect even basic usage. The old men are those who have the right to make decisions, and the capacity to make the right choice—and so choice means "an old man." On modern Arabic usage, see Ami Ayalon, *Language and Change,* pp. 58ff, 97ff, and index s.v. *shaykh.*

32. On these terms, see EI^2, s.vv. "Ghulām" (by D. Sourdel, C. E. Bosworth, P. Hardy, and Halil Inalcık); "Aḥdāth" (by Cl. Cahen), and "Futuwwa" (by Cl. Cahen and Fr. Taeschner).

33. A group called "Young Egypt" (*Miṣr al-Fatāt*) existed in Alexandria in 1879–80. It seems to have had little effect and quickly disappeared. A number of its active members were Christians and Jews (J. M. Landau, *Parliaments and Parties in Egypt* [Tel Aviv, 1953], pp. 101–3). There seems to be no connection between this group and the ultranationalist organization of the same name which flourished in Egypt in the 1930s.

The first occurrence in Turkey, in a quasi-political context, of a Turkish adjective with an unequivocal connotation of youth was the *Genç Kalemler,* "Young Pens," the name of a literary review founded in Salonica in 1911. Articles in this review laid stress on Turkish, rather than on Ottoman or Islamic, identity and loyalty.

34. See EI^2, "Atabak" (by Cl. Cahen); al-Bāshā, *Alqāb,* pp. 122–25; idem, *Funūn,* pp. 3–24.

35. See EI^2, "Baba" (by Fr. Taeschner); al-Bāshā, *Alqāb,* p. 220; idem, *Funūn,* pp. 291–92. Among Christian Arabs, as among other Christians, priests are called father.

36. Cf. Hebrew *umma,* Aramaic *ummetha,* South Arabian *lumiya.*

37. See EI^2, s.v. "Agha" (by H. Bowen).

38. See EI^2, s.v. "Abnāʾ" (by K. V. Zettersteen and B. Lewis).

39. See al-Bāshā, *Alqāb,* pp. 367–76; idem, *Funūn,* pp. 651–89; Henry Yule and A. C. Burnell, *Hobson-Jobson: A Glossary of Colloquial Anglo-Indian Words and Phrases,* 2d ed. revised by William Crooke (London, Boston, and Madras, 1985), pp. 781–82. *Ṣāḥib* was used, from early times, for the ruler of a foreign people or country (e.g., Ṣāḥib al-Rūm for the Byzantine emperor, Ṣāḥib al-Zanj for the leader of the black slaves who revolted in ninth-century Iraq); the commandant of a city, a citadel, a garrison, and more generally, a military force; the governor or independent ruler of a province; the chief of police; the head of a department or an office, especially in government; the person in charge of a task or duty or a service. Under the Buyids, it served as a title of the wazir, and under most dynasties it figures prominently in royal titulature. In British India, it came to be used more particularly as a respectful form of address to Europeans.

40. Abū Yūsuf, *Kitāb al-Kharāj,* English translation of the introduction in Lewis, *Islam,* vol. 1, pp. 151–70.

41. For example, *shādhdh,* "deviant," used especially of deviant religious doctrines; *ḍalāla,* "going astray," hence "false or erroneous belief or practice," and *taḍlīl,* "misleading," "misguidance"; *murūq,* "deviation," hence "disloyalty," "defection," "apostasy," and *māriq,* "astray," hence "renegade" or "heretic"; *zāgha,* "to swerve," hence "to deviate from truth," "to deceive or swindle." Another root, *ghalā,* meaning "to go too far," "to overshoot," is used to convey the notion of excess, of extremism. But *ghālī* (plural *ghulāt*), "extremist," and *ghuluww,* "extremism," are used only of religious movements, and have political significance only in the sense that all Islamic religious movements have political implications.

42. See EI^2, s.v. "Furūsiyya" (by G. Douillet and D. Ayalon).

43. The root *rashada* means "to follow the right path," "to be rightly guided," and is thus the converse, figuratively as well as literally, of the various terms denoting deviation and error. It is used especially of God's guidance, i.e., to Islam. Derivatives include *rashīd,* "rightly guided" (e.g., in the regnal title of the caliph Hārūn), *murshid,* "guide," *irshād,* "guidance," all of

which figure frequently in religio-political language. The passive sense, "to be rightly (i.e., divinely) guided" is denoted by the root *hadā,* whence *hudā,* "guidance," and *mahdī,* "the one guided" (by God).

44. London, Public Record Office (PRO), S.P.102/61/14.

45. London, PRO, S.P.102/62.

46. See *EI²,* s.v. "Ḥādjib," (by D. Sourdel, C. E. Bosworth, and A. K. S. Lambton). According to an early Ottoman account of the capture of Constantinople, Sultan Mehmed II, contemplating the captured and ruined city, mused on the transience of worldly power, and uttered these verses:

The spider is curtain-bearer in the Palace of Chosroes,
The owl sounds the relief in the castle of Afrasiyab.

(*Tarih-i Ebu'l-Fetih* [Istanbul, 1330 s.], p. 57.) (Chosroes and Afrasiyab are figures from ancient Iranian history and myth.)

47. See *EI²,* s.vv. "ʿAnaza" (by G. C. Miles), "ʿAṣā" (by A. Jeffery), "Dūrbāsh" (by J. Burton-Page), and "Ḳaḍīb" (by D. Sourdel). Cf. the interesting reflections of C. H. Becker, *Islamstudien,* vol. 1 (Leipzig, 1924), pp. 469–71.

48. On this dictum, see I. Goldziher, *Muslim Studies,* trans. C. R. Barber and S. M. Stern, vol. 2 (London, 1971), pp. 67–68; idem, "Du sens propre des expressions Ombre de Dieu, Khalife de Dieu, pour designer les chefs dans l'Islam," *Revue de l'Histoire des Religions* xxxv (1897), pp. 133–40; Fārūq ʿUmar, "Min alqāb al-Khulafāʾ al-ʿAbbāsiyyīn khalīfat Allāh wa-ẓill Allāh," *Majallat al-Jāmiʿa al-Mustanṣiriyya* 2 (1971), pp. 3–19.

49. Known in Arabic as *shamsa, shamsiyya, miẓalla,* or *jitr* (from the Indian *čatr*?), the ceremonial parasol dates back to remote antiquity. For discussions, see Mez, *Renaissance of Islam,* pp. 133–34; Marius Canard, "Le cérémonial fatimite et le cérémonial byzantin: Essai de comparaison," *Byzantion* xxi (1951), p. 389 n. 3; Émile Tyan, *Institutions du droit public musulman,* vol. 2, *Sultanat et califat* (Paris, 1956), pp. 31, 155.

50. On the *tāj,* see *Encyclopaedia of Islam,* 1st ed. (hereafter cited as *EI¹*) s.v. "Tādj" (by W. Bjorkman); R. Dozy, *Dictionnaire détaillé des noms de vêtements chez les Arabes* (Amsterdam, 1845, reprinted Beirut, n.d.), pp. 100–4; Canard, "Le cérémonial fatimite," pp. 389–92; Dominique Sourdel, "Cérémonial abbaside," *Revue des Études Islamiques,* 1960, p. 134; Tyan, *Institutions,* vol. 1 (Paris, 1953), p. 490; Shaul Shaked, "From Iran to Islam: On Some Symbols of Royalty," *Jerusalem Studies in Arabic and Islam* vii (1986), pp. 75–76.

51. On the *sarīr,* see Shaked, "From Iran to Islam," pp. 79–82; Tyan, *Institutions,* vol. 1, pp. 488–90, vol. 2, p. 89; Sourdel, "Cérémonial abbaside," pp. 130–31; Becker, *Islamstudien,* vol. 1, pp. 468–69. Other terms for throne include Arabic *kursī* and *arīka,* Persian *takht* and *dast* (literally "hand"), Turkish *sandali* (literally "made of sandalwood," but cf. *sandalye,* "chair"). In Persian- and Turkish-speaking dynasties the usual term for

throne was *takht,* whence *pāy-i takht,* "foot of the throne," the capital city. For a discussion of the Arabic terms for throne, by an Ismāʿīlī theologian, see Abū Ḥātim al-Rāzī, *Kitāb al-Zīna fi'l-kalimāt al-Islāmiyya al-ʿArabiyya,* ed. Ḥusayn al-Hamdānī, vol. 2 (Cairo, 1950), pp. 150–59.

In addition to the mace, the sword, the parasol, the crown, and the throne, there are other insignia and rituals of sovereignty, notably the mantle of the Prophet (*burda*), flags and banners, and the ceremonial drums (*nawba, ṭablkhāna*). The two most basic tokens of sovereign power in Islamic history are practical and direct, rather than symbols or metaphors. They are the right to be named on the coinage (*sikka*) and in the bidding prayer recited at public worship in the mosques on Friday (*khuṭba*). These were the most universally accepted expressions of independent sovereignty. The omission of a sovereign's name from these two—especially from the *khuṭba,* which had more immediate impact—was the recognized way of announcing a bid for independence. On these, see Tyan, *Institutions,* vol. 1, pp. 474–83, vol. 2, pp. 28–30, 228–30; Norman Calder, "Friday Prayer and the Juristic Theory of Government: Sarakhsi, Shirazi, Mawardi," *BSOAS* xlix (1986), pp. 35–47.

52. Al-Yaʿqūbī, *Kitāb al-Buldān,* 2d ed., ed. M. J. de Goeje, (Leiden, 1892), p. 238. Al-Yaʿqūbī and other Arabic historians and geographers were, however, mistaken in thinking that Baghdad was the first and only round city in the world. The circular plan was familiar in the Middle East since ancient times. See K. A. C. Creswell, *A Short Account of Early Muslim Architecture* (London, 1958), pp. 170–73; *EI*[2], s.v. "Baghdād" (by A. A. Duri), p. 896, where further references are given.

53. Al-Khaṭīb al-Baghdādī, *Taʾrīkh Baghdād* (Cairo, 1931), p. 72, English translation in Jacob Lassner, *The Topography of Bagdad in the Early Middle Ages* (Detroit, 1970), p. 52.

54. The image of "the navel of the world" is widely used and appears in Jewish and Indian, as well as Islamic, writings. See A. J. Wensinck, *The Ideas of the Western Semites concerning the Navel of the Earth,* in *Verhandlingen der Koninglijke Akademie van Wetenschappen te Amsterdam, Afdeeling Letterkunde, nieuwe Reeks, Deel* xvii, no. 1 (Amsterdam, 1916).

Chapter 2

1. On Kâtib Çelebi (a pseudonym of Ḥājjī Khalīfa, Turkish Hacı Halife), see *EI*[2], s.v. (by Orhan Şaik Gökyay). His booklet, entitled *Destur ul-Amel li-Islah il-Halel* (the manual of procedure for the correction of defects) was published in Istanbul in A.H. 1280, as an appendix to *Kavanin-i Al-i Osman* of Ayn-i Ali. A German translation, made from a manuscript, by W. F. A. Behrnauer, had already been published in the *Zeitschrift der deutschen morgenländischen Gesellschaft* xi (1857), pp. 110–132. An English summary, from the German, is appended to E. I. J. Rosenthal, *Political Thought,* pp. 228–33. The events which led to the writing of this booklet are described

by the Ottoman historian Naima, in the year A.H. 1063 (Naima, *Tarih,* 4th ed., vol. 5 [Istanbul, n.d.], pp. 281–83).

The use of the human organism as a metaphor for the polity has been familiar since antiquity. The Latin historian Florus, allegedly inspired by Seneca the Elder, wrote a history of Rome divided into four periods—infancy, youth, manhood, and old age. This book was widely read in the Middle Ages. The comparison between the city or household and the human body, in coordination, in health, and in sickness, is drawn in some detail by the philosopher al-Fārābī (d. 950), e.g., in his *Risāla fī ārā' ahl al-Madīna al-Fāḍila,* ed. F. Dieterici (Leiden, 1895) pp. 54ff., German trans. F. Dieterici, *Der Musterstaat von Alfarabi* (Leiden, 1900), pp. 85ff., and in his *The Fusūl al-Madanī, Aphorisms of the Statesman,* ed. and trans. D. M. Dunlop (Cambridge, 1961), pp. 37–39. Al-Fārābī does not, however, pursue the metaphor to the point of decline and death. This image was given its classical formulation by Ibn Khaldūn (1332–1406), who, in his famous *Al-Muqaddima* (English trans. Franz Rosenthal, *The Muqaddimah,* 3 vols. [New York, 1958]), made it the framework of a sociology and philosophy of history. See Mohammed Talbi, "Ibn Haldun et le sens de l'histoire," *Studia Islamica* xxvi (1967), pp. 73–148. While Ibn Khaldūn's influence on his contemporaries and compatriots was limited, he seems to have made a considerable impression in Ottoman Turkey (see B. Lewis, "Ibn Khaldun in Turkey," in *Studies in Islamic History and Civilization in Honour of Professor David Ayalon* [Jerusalem and Leiden, 1986], pp. 527–30).

2. See A. J. Wensinck, "The Refused Dignity," in *A Volume of Oriental Studies Presented to Edward G. Browne,* ed. T. W. Arnold and Reynold A. Nicholson (Cambridge, 1922), pp. 491–99; A. K. S. Lambton, *State and Government in Medieval Islam* (Oxford, 1981), pp. 190–91, 242ff.; Goitein, *Studies in Islamic History,* pp. 205–8.

3. For introductory accounts, see E. I. J. Rosenthal, *Political Thought;* Gabrieli, "Pensiero politico," and Lerner and Mahdi, *Medieval Political Philosophy.* For a very useful collection of relevant articles, see Joel L. Kraemer and Ilai Alon, eds., *Religion and Government in the World of Islam* (Tel-Aviv, 1983), = *Israel Oriental Studies* x (1980).

4. On *adab* see *EI²,* s.v. (by F. Gabrieli); Carlo Alfonso Nallino, *Raccolta di Scritti,* vol. 6 (Rome, 1948), pp. 1–20.

5. For a listing of books on *adab al-kātib, adab al-muftī, adab al-qāḍī, adab al-wazīr,* etc., see Carl Brockelmann, *Geschichte der arabischen Litteratur,* supp. 3 (Leiden, 1942), pp. 790–91.

6. Rūḥullāh Mūsavī Khomeinī, *Vilāyat-i Faqīh* (Najaf, 1971), Arabic version, *Al-Ḥukūma al-Islāmiyya* (reprinted Beirut, 1979), English translation in *Islam and Revolution,* trans. and annotated by Hamid Algar (Berkeley, 1981).

7. By far the best-known and most frequently cited of these is the treatise of Abu'l-Ḥasan ʿAlī ibn Muḥammad al-Māwardī (d. 1058), *Al-Aḥkām al-*

Sulṭāniyya (Cairo, n.d.), excerpts in English translation in Lewis, *Islam,* vol. 1, pp. 171–79. For a complete, but somewhat outdated, French translation, see Mawerdi, *Les statuts gouvernementaux,* trans. E. Fagnan (Algiers, 1915). For comprehensive studies of the juristic literature on politics, see Lambton, *State and Government,* and Tilman Nagel, *Staat und Glaubensgemeinschaft im Islam* (Zurich and Munich, 1981). Important earlier studies by H. A. R. Gibb and others are listed by Lambton. For a classical statement of the Islamic legal position, by an orientalist and jurist, see David Santillana, *Istituzioni di diritto musulmano malichita con riguardo anche al sistema sciafiita,* vol. 1 (Rome, 1926), pp. 1–24. Santillana's formulation has never been improved or replaced. For a brief account, by the same author, in English and without documentation, see his chapter "Law and Society" in *The Legacy of Islam,* ed. Sir Thomas W. Arnold and Alfred Guillaume (Oxford, 1931), pp. 284–310. The new edition of *The Legacy of Islam,* ed. Joseph Schacht and C. E. Bosworth (Oxford, 1974), contains chapters on "Politics and War" (B. Lewis, pp. 156–209) and "Islamic Political Thought" (A. K. S. Lambton, pp. 404–24).

8. The phrase occurs frequently in the Qur'ān (III, 104, 110, 114; VII, 157; IX, 67, 71, 112; XXII, 41; XXXI, 17) and is much used in later writings.

9. See *EI*[2], s.v. "Idjmāʿ" (by M. Bernand); George Hourani, "The Basis of Authority and Consensus in Sunnite Islam," *Studia Islamica* xxi (1964), pp. 13–60.

10. On the mufti, see Émile Tyan, *Histoire de l'organisation judiciaire en pays d'Islam,* 2d ed. (Leiden, 1960), pp. 219–30; Joseph Schacht, *An Introduction to Islamic Law* (Oxford, 1964), passim; al-Bāshā, *Funūn,* pp. 1116–20 (on mentions in inscriptions). On the Ottoman mufti, see Gibb and Bowen, *Islamic Society and the West,* vol. 1, part 2, pp. 133–38, and Pakalın, *Osmanlı Tarih Deyimleri,* vol. 2, pp. 599–601.

11. *Mujtahid* is the active participle (verbal noun *ijtihād*) of a verb meaning, literally, "to exert oneself." In the technical language of Muslim jurisprudence, *ijtihād* means "the exercise of independent judgment," whether on a specific case or on a rule of law, where the Qur'ān and the Traditions of the Prophet do not give explicit directions. By the beginning of the fourth century of the *hijra,* ca. A.D. 900, Sunni jurists agreed that all such uncertainties had been resolved by consensus, and that "the door of *ijtihād* was closed." Independent reasoning was no longer necessary or therefore permitted, and henceforth the tasks of theologians and jurists were to explain and interpret the eternal truths and apply the eternal laws. In modern times the "door of *ijtihād*" has been reopened by some Sunni theologians and jurists, struggling to confront the complexities of modern life. The closing was never recognized by the Shīʿa, whose ulema called themselves *mujtahid,* "one who practices *ijtihād,*" to assert this right. They did not, however, exercise it very often. In practice, Sunni jurists, especially in the Ottoman Empire, were more innovative, and Shiʿite *mujtahids* less innovative, than their

theoretical positions would imply. For several interesting historical discussions of these matters, see R. Brunschvig and G. E. von Grunebaum, eds., *Classicisme et déclin culturel dans l'histoire de l'Islam* (Paris, 1957), especially the chapter by Joseph Schacht (pp. 141–66); George Makdisi, "Freedom in Islamic Jurisprudence: *Ijtihad, Taqlid* and Academic Freedom," in *La notion de liberté au Moyen Âge: Islam, Byzance, Occident,* published under the joint auspices of the University of Paris-Sorbonne and the University of Pennsylvania (Paris, 1985), pp. 79–88.

12. See *EI²*, supp., s.v. "Āyatullāh" (by J. Calmard); Hamid Algar, *Religion and State in Iran 1785–1966* (Berkeley, 1969).

13. It was in this sense that the word was coined by Josephus (*Contra Apionem,* II, 165) to describe the polity of the ancient Israelites.

14. See Sir Thomas W. Arnold, *The Caliphate* (Oxford, 1924), new edition with a concluding chapter by Sylvia G. Haim (London, 1965). *EI²* contains two articles, on "Imāma" and "Khalīfa." The first (by Wilferd Madelung) deals with the theoretical formulations of the theologians and jurists, the latter with the development of the caliphate as a historical institution (by D. Sourdel) and in political theory (by A. K. S. Lambton).

15. On the term *umma,* see Louis Massignon, "L'*umma* et ses synonymes: Notion de 'communauté sociale' en Islam," *Revue des Études Islamiques,* 1941–46, pp. 151–57; C. A. O. van Nieuwenhuijze, "The Umma—An Analytic Approach," *Studia Islamica* x (1959), pp. 5–22; Louis Gardet, *La cité musulmane: Vie sociale et politique* (Paris, 1954), pp. 193–221; W. Montgomery Watt, *Islamic Political Thought* (Edinburgh, 1968), pp. 9–14 and passim; *EI¹*, s.v. "Umma" (by R. Paret), where Qur'ān references are enumerated and discussed; A. J. Wensinck, J. P. Mensing, and J. Brugman, eds., *Concordance de la tradition musulmane* (Leiden, 1936–69), s.v. "umma" for references in *ḥadīth.* On modern Arabic usage, see Ami Ayalon, *Language and Change,* pp. 21ff, 50ff, 131ff.

16. Fraenkel, *Die aramäischen Fremdwörter,* pp. 280–81. The fullest discussion of the various types of city will be found in al-Fārābī's *Kitāb al-Siyāsāt al-Madaniyya* (Hyderabad, A.H. 1346), pp. 57–76, German version by Paul Brönnle, *Die Staatsleitung vor Alfarabi* (Leiden, 1904), pp. 71–91. They include the *madīna fāḍila* (excellent or ideal city); *jāhila* (ignorant city), also the *fāsiqa* (sinful), *mubaddala* (perverted), and *ḍālla* (erring) cities; *madīnat nadhāla* (vile city, probably corresponding to the Platonic oligarchy); *madīnat karāma* (timocracy); *madīna mutaghalliba* (tyranny); *madīna jamāʿiyya* (democracy). It will be noted that this classification is based on that of the Greeks, with Islamic modifications and additions. See E. I. J. Rosenthal, *Political Thought,* pp. 125–42; Lambton, *State and Government,* pp. 316–25; Muhsin Mahdi, "Alfarabi ca. 870–950," in *History of Philosophy,* ed. L. Strauss and J. Cropsey (New York, 1963), pp. 161ff.

17. Arabic *amīr* is often shortened to *mīr* in Persian. Turkish uses both forms, as well as the Turkish equivalent *bey.* Thus, the governor-general of a

province, in the Ottoman Empire, may be referred to in documents as *beylerbey, mīr-i mīrān,* and *amīr al-umarāʾ,* interchangeably.

18. Ibn al-Muqaffaʿ, *Al-Adab al-Ṣaghīr* (Beirut, 1956), p. 121; = *Rasāʾil al-Bulaghāʾ,* 4th ed., ed. Muḥammad Kurd ʿAlī (Cairo, 1954), p. 14.

19. Al-Ghazālī, *Iḥyāʾ ʿUlūm al-Dīn,* vol. 2 (Cairo, 1933), p. 124, English translation in H. A. R. Gibb, "Constitutional Organization," in *Law in the Middle East,* ed. Majid Khadduri and Herbert J. Liebesny (Washington, D.C., 1955), p. 19. Cf. al-Ghazālī, *Kitāb al-Iqtiṣād* (Cairo, A.H. 1320), p. 107, English translation in Gibb, "Constitutional Organization," p. 19; see also Lambton, *State and Government,* pp. 110–11; Santillana, *Istituzioni,* vol. 1, pp. 22–23.

20. Al-Ṭabarī, *Taʾrīkh,* ed. M. J. de Goeje et al. (Leiden, 1879–1901), vol. 2, p. 75. Cf. Tyan, *Institutions,* vol. 1, p. 448.

21. ʿAbd al-Ḥamīd, "Risāla ilāʾl-kuttāb," in *Rasāʾil al-Bulaghāʾ,* pp. 222ff., English translation in Lewis, *Islam,* vol. 1, pp. 186ff.

22. Examples in al-Bāshā, *Alqāb,* pp. 323ff. For examples from Fatimid Egypt, see S. D. Goitein, *A Mediterranean Society: The Jewish Communities of the Arab World as Portrayed in the Documents of the Cairo Geniza,* vol. 1, *Economic Foundations* (Berkeley and Los Angeles, 1967), p. 267, p. 467 nn. 5, 6. Cf. Arnold, *Caliphate,* pp. 202ff.

23. Ibn al-Muqaffaʿ, *Al-Adab al-Ṣaghīr,* p. 124, in *Rasāʾil al-Bulaghāʾ,* p. 17.

24. See B. Lewis, "Hukûmet and Devlet," *Belleten* x/vi (1982), pp. 415–21, where further references are given. On modern terms for government, see Ami Ayalon, *Language and Change,* pp. 97ff.

25. Al-Ghazālī, *Iḥyāʾ ʾUlūm al-Dīn,* vol. 2, p. 130; cf. I. Goldziher, *Streitscrift des Gazali gegen die Batinijja-Sekte* (Leiden, 1916), pp. 82–83; Lambton, *State and Government,* p. 116; Henri Laoust, *La politique de Gazali* (Paris, 1970), pp. 40, 127, 194–96, 247–51. On the *Dhu Shawka* as de facto ruler, see Santillana, *Istituzioni,* vol. 1, p. 70.

26. See al-Bāshā, *Alqāb,* pp. 260–64; Armand Abel, "Le Khalife, présence sacrée," *Studia Islamica* vii (1957), pp. 29–45.

27. On *milla,* see Jeffery, *Foreign Vocabulary of the Qurʾan,* pp. 268–69; *EI*[1], s.v. "Milla" (by F. Buhl). On the Ottoman *millet* see Gibb and Bowen, *Islamic Society and the West,* vol. 1, part 2, pp. 212ff.; B. Lewis, *The Emergence of Modern Turkey,* 2d ed. (London, 1968), pp. 229ff.; B. Braude and B. Lewis, eds., *Christians and Jews in the Ottoman Empire* (New York, 1982). For this and some other terms, a useful guide to Ottoman usage, at least as perceived and understood by European visitors, may be found in the lexicographic and related writings of European Ottomanists from the sixteenth-century onwards. On *millet,* for example, see the dictionaries of Giovanni Molino, *Dittionario della lingua Italiana Turchesca* (Rome, 1641), p. 161; Joh. Christian Clodius, *Compendiosum Lexicon Latino-Turcicum Germanicum* (Leipzig, 1730), pp. 249, 444, 567, 631; and the dialogues of the seven-

teenth-century Hungarian Jakab Nagy de Harsany, ed. G. Hazai, *Das Osmanisch-Türkische im XVII. Jahrhundert* (The Hague–Paris, 1973), index s.v., especially pp. 162ff. In classical Ottoman usage *millet* is used of groups which are defined entirely (Muslims, Christians, Lutherans) or primarily (Greeks, Armenians, Jews) in religious terms. The change to a partly, and then primarily, national application occurred during the nineteenth century. As early as 1826, an addendum to the Akkerman Convention signed in that year spoke of the "Serb Millet" (Turkish text in *Mecmua-i Muahedat* [Istanbul, A.H. 1294–98], vol. 4, p. 69). On modern Arabic usage, see Ami Ayalon, *Language and Change,* pp. 19ff, 26ff.

28. For an example of these letters, translated from one of the many preserved in the Public Record Office in London, see B. Lewis, "The Ottoman Archives," in *Report on Current Research, Spring 1956* (Middle East Institute, Washington, D.C.).

29. In classical Ottoman geographical and other writings, when a precise territorial definition of the Ottoman realms was required, the term most commonly used was *Rūm,* inherited from Rome via Byzantium. The terms *Rūm* and *Rūmī* remained in use in some quarters into the twentieth century to distinguish the Ottoman state, lands, and peoples from other Muslims and other Turks. As these terms were also used of the Greek Orthodox *millet,* there was some danger of confusion.

30. On *waṭan,* see B. Lewis, *The Middle East and the West* (Bloomington, Ind., 1964, reprinted New York, 1966), pp. 75–77; idem, *Emergence of Modern Turkey,* pp. 334–40, 358–59; Ami Ayalon, *Language and Change,* pp. 52–53. On earlier Ottoman usage, see Franciscus Mesgnien-Meninski, *Lexicon Arabico-Persico-Turcicum,* rev. ed. (Vienna, 1780), p. 5387; Clodius, p. 520.

31. Lewis, *Emergence of Modern Turkey,* p. 336.

Chapter 3

1. Ibn al-Athīr, *Usd al-Ghāba,* vol. 5 (Cairo, 1869–71), p. 155. The remainder of the tradition foretells the coming of a messianic figure, of the family of the Prophet, who will fill the world with justice.

2. On *khalīfa,* see al-Bāshā, *Alqāb,* pp. 275–79; and *Funūn,* pp. 489–99; *EI²,* s.v. "Khalīfa" (by D. Sourdel, A.K.S. Lambton, F. de Jong, and P. M. Holt); D. S. Margoliouth, "The Sense of the Title *Khalifa,*" in *A Volume of Oriental Studies Presented to Edward G. Browne* (Cambridge, 1922), pp. 322–28; cf. W. Montgomery Watt, "God's Caliph: Qur'anic Interpretations and Umayyad Claims," in *Iran and Islam: In Memory of V. Minorsky,* ed. C. E. Bosworth (Edinburgh, 1977), pp. 565–74; Rudi Paret, "Signification Coranique de *Ḫalīfa* et d'autres dérivés de la racine *ḫalafa,*" in *Studia Islamica,* xxxi (1970), pp. 212–17; idem, Ḫalīfat Allah—Vicarius Dei," in *Melanges d'Islamologie; volume dédié à la mémoire de Armand Abel,* ed. Pierre Salmon

(Leiden, 1974), pp. 224–32. Tyan, *Institutions,* passim. For a juridical and historical discussion of the caliphate by a major Muslim historian, see Ibn Khaldūn, *Al-Muqaddima,* ed. E. Quatremère, vol. 1 (Paris, 1858), pp. 342ff.; English trans. F. Rosenthal, *The Muqaddimah* vol. 1, pp. 385ff.

In recent years, critical scholarship has called into question a very large part of the previously accepted record of early Islamic history, as transmitted by the Muslim tradition. This questioning will certainly change our modern perception of the early Islamic past. It has not as yet produced a generally accepted alternative, nor is there adequate contemporary documentation of the use of political terms in the early Islamic centuries. All this does not affect the way in which Muslim thinkers and writers, in the classical period, understood and used the record of the past as transmitted to them.

3. Margoliouth, "Sense of the Title *Khalīfa,*" p. 322, citing an inscription (Glaser 618) of the year A.D. 543.

4. Qur'ān VI, 165; VII, 67; VII, 67, 72; X, 15, 74; XXXV, 37. Cf. the use of *mustakhlaf* in LVII, 7.

5. Badīʿ al-Zamān al-Hamadhānī, *Rasāʾil* (Beirut, 1890), p. 289, translation in Margoliouth, "Sense of the Title *Khalifa,*" pp. 323–24. Other versions in al-Ṭabarī, *Taʾrīkh,* vol. 1, pp. 2748–49, translation in *Islam,* Lewis, vol. 1, p. 17.

6. The title *khalīfat Allāh* appears on coins of ʿAbd al-Malik (John Walker, *A Catalogue of the Arab-Sassanian Coins* [London, 1941], p. 25; idem, *A Catalogue of the Arab-Byzantine and Post-Reform Umaiyad Coins* (London, 1956), pp. 30–31; idem, "Some New Arab-Sassanian Coins," *The Numismatic Chronicle,* 6th ser., xii [1952], p. 110; Raoul Curiel, "Monnaies arabosasanides," *Revue Numismatique,* vii [1965], p. 328) and on an embroidery, probably of the same period (al-Bāshā, *Alqāb,* p. 276, n. 1). The coins are described in George C. Miles, "Miḥrāb and ʿAnazah: A Study in early Islamic Iconography," in *Archaeologia Orientalia in Memoriam Ernst Herzfeld,* ed. G. C. Miles (Locust Valley, N.Y., 1952), pp. 158, 168, 171; and idem, "Some Arab-Sasanian and Related Coins," in *The American Museum Society Museum Notes,* vii (New York, 1957), p. 192. On the use of the title in coins of al-Maʾmūn, dated A.H. 202–4 (A.D. 817–20), and an inscription of al-Nāṣir in Mecca, dated A.H. 584 (A.D. 1188), see al-Bāshā, *Alqāb,* pp. 276–78; George C. Miles, *The Numismatic History of Rayy* (New York, 1938), pp. 103–7; cf. Johannes Østrup, *Catalogue des monnaies arabes et turques du Cabinet Royal des médailles du Musée National de Copenhague* (Copenhagen, 1938), p. 37, n. 425. The inscription is published in the *Répertoire chronologique de l'épigraphie arabe,* vol. 9 (Cairo, 1937), pp. 165–66, previously published by Rifʿat Pasha, *Mirʾāt al-Ḥaramayn* (Cairo, 1925), vol. 1, p. 214. On the use of the title, see Margoliouth, "Sense of the Title *Khalifa,*" Tyan, *Institutions,* and the studies by Goldziher and Fārūq ʿUmar, cited above, chap. 1, n. 48. On the policies and activities of the caliph al-Nāṣir, see An-

gelika Hartmann, *An-Nāṣir li-Dīn Allāh (1180–1225)* (Berlin, 1975), especially pp. 109–22. For a strongly divergent interpretation of the title, see Patricia Crone and Martin Hinds, *God's Caliph: Religious Authority in the First Centuries of Islam* (Cambridge, 1986), received when this book was already in proof.

7. On the Fatimid-Ismāʿīlī political conception of imamate and caliphate, see P. J. Vatikiotis, *The Fatimid Theory of State* (London, 1957); Sami Nasib Makarem, *The Political Doctrine of the Ismaʿilis* (New York, 1977), an edition and translation of an Ismāʿīlī treatise on imamate. On Fatimid politico-religious propaganda, see W. Ivanow, "The Organization of the Fatimid Propaganda," *Journal of the Bombay Branch of the Royal Asiatic Society* xv (1939), pp. 1–35, and Canard, "L'impérialisme des Fatimides."

8. W. Barthold, *Turkestan down to the Mongol Invasion,* translated from the Russian, 3d rev. ed. (London, 1968), pp. 346–47, citing both the Turkish and Persian versions, which differ slightly. Cf. Persian text in al-Rāwandī, *The Rāhat-uṣ-Ṣudūr,* ed. Muḥammad Iqbāl (London, 1921), p. 334. A slightly earlier Persian historian, Abu'l-Faḍl Bayhaqī (995–1077), expresses the same idea in a slightly earlier form: "Know that the Lord Most High has given one power to the prophets and another power to kings; and He has made it incumbent upon the people of the earth that they should submit themselves to the two powers and should acknowledge the true way laid down by God" (*Ta'rīkh-i Masʿūdī,* ed. Q. Ghanī and ʿA. A. Fayyāḍ [Tehran, 1324 (A.D. 1945)], p. 99, English version in C. E. Bosworth, *The Ghaznavids: Their Empire in Afghanistan and Eastern Iran* [Edinburgh, 1963], p. 63, Arabic translation by Yaḥyā al-Khashshāb and Ṣādiq Nash'at, *Ta'rīkh al-Bayhaqī* [Cairo, n.d., preface dated 1956], pp. 102–3). See further George Makdisi, "Les rapports entre calife et sultan a l'époque saljuqide," *International Journal of Middle Eastern Studies* vi (1975), pp. 228–36.

Two texts may suffice to illustrate the change which had occurred in the meaning of *khalīfa*. The first is by Ibn al-Athīr, writing in the early thirteenth century. When dealing with events of earlier times, he quotes more or less verbatim from earlier sources. But when his source says the caliph took some action, Ibn al-Athīr substitutes "the sultan," knowing that, to the readers of his time, "caliph" would convey a wrong impression, since it no longer carried a connotation of effective sovereign power (e.g., in his account of the wars against the Carmathians, based mainly on Thābit ibn Sinān, *Ta'rīkh Akhbār al-Qarāmiṭa,* ed. Suhayl Zakkār [Beirut, 1971]). A second and even more vivid example comes from the second quarter of the fifteenth century, from the Turkish historian Yazıcıoğlu Âli, who, describing the position of the Greek Orthodox patriarch of the court of the Byzantine emperor, says that "he is, among the unbelievers, much the same as the caliph is among the Muslims." Yazıcıoğlu Âli was, of course, referring not to the caliph of classical times, but to the caliph kept as a sort of court functionary by the Mamluk sultans in Cairo. The Turkish historian had not quite understood the nature of the Greek Orthodox patriarchate, but his comparison is a much better one than the wholly inaccurate comparison which is sometimes made between the caliphate and the papacy. See Paul Wittek, "Yazijioghlu ʿÂli on the Christian Turks of the Dobruja," *BSOAS* xiv (1952), pp. 649–50; idem, "Islam und Kalifat," *Archiv für Sozialwissenschaften und Sozialpolitik* liii (1925), p. 412.

9. On the Cairo caliphate, see David Ayalon, "Studies on the Transfer of the Abbasid Caliphate from Baghdad to Cairo," *Arabica* vii (1960), pp. 41–59; P. M. Holt, "Some Observations on the ʿAbbasid Caliphate of Cairo," *BSOAS* x/vii (1984), pp. 501–7; R. Hartmann, *Zur Vorgeschichte des ʿabbasidischen Schein-Chaliphates von Cairo, Abhandlungen der deutschen Akademie der Wissenschaften zu Berlin,* Phil.-hist. Kl. 1947, no. 9 (Berlin 1950); Annemarie Schimmel, "Kalif und Kadi im spätmittelalterlichen Ägypten, *Welt des Islam,* 1943, p. 3–27; Arnold, *Caliphate,* pp. 89–106.

10. On the Ottoman caliphate, see Arnold, *Caliphate,* pp. 129–58, 163–83; Nallino, *Raccolta di Scritti,* vol. 3 (Rome, 1941), pp. 234–83; Gibb and Bowen, *Islamic Society and the West,* vol. 1, part 1, pp. 26–38.

11. Article 3 of the treaty. The Italian original has "Supremo Califfo Maomettano," which in the Turkish version becomes *Imām al-Muʾminīn ve khalīfat al-Muwaḥḥidīn.* Italian text in G. F. de Martens, *Recueil des traités . . .,* vol. 4 (Göttingen, 1795), pp. 610–12; Turkish text in Cevdet, *Tarih,* 2d ed., vol. 1 (Istanbul, A.H. 1309), pp. 358–59, and *Mecmua-i Muahedat,* vol. 3, pp. 254–73.

The idea of some kind of Ottoman caliphate seems to have been in circulation somewhat earlier. Thus, the English traveler J. Hanway, in his book *The Revolutions of Persia,* vol. 2 (London, 1762), p. 253, says of the Ottoman-Persian agreement of 1727 that by its terms "the Grand Signior shall be acknowledged head of the Musselmen and the true successor of the Caliphs." There is, however, no such clause in the Turkish text of the Treaty of A.H. 1140 (A.D. 1727), published in the *Mecmua-i Muahedat,* vol. 2, pp. 312–13, and it is unlikely that any such proviso was agreed. Caliphal titles were sometimes used by Ottoman sultans, and accorded to them by others, even before the conquest of Egypt, and mean no more than a recognition of the growing Ottoman preeminence among Muslim states, especially by the crucial test of the conduct of *jihād.* This gave the Ottoman sultans considerable prestige, which was, of course, greatly increased when they extended their rule to the old caliphal capitals in Damascus, Baghdad, and Cairo, and to the two holy cities of Mecca and Medina.

12. Roderic H. Davison, "'Russian Skill and Turkish Imbecility': The Treaty of Kuchuk Kainardji Reconsidered," *Slavic Review* 35 (1976), pp. 463–83.

13. On an ironic attempt, by a Turkish official, to exercise this right, see

Cevdet, *Tezakir,* ed. Cavid Baysun, vol. 3 (Ankara, 1963), pp. 236–37; cf. B. Lewis, "The Ottoman Empire in the Mid-Nineteenth Century," *Middle Eastern Studies* 1 (1965), p. 292.

14. Mouradgea d'Ohsson, *Tableau général de l'empire ottoman,* vol. 1 (Paris, 1787), p. 89; cf. Arnold, *Caliphate,* pp. 146–47.

15. Thomas Hope, *Anastasius,* vol. 1 (London, 1819, reprinted Paris, 1831), p. 257. In another place, speaking of some tactless German tourists who asked awkward and dangerous questions, the narrator remarks that "they would scarcely have neglected the opportunity, had it been offered, of inquiring of the Sultan himself whether he was legitimate heir to the caliphate, as he asserted" (vol. 1, p. 110). Clearly, when Hope visited the Middle East, the claim was perceived as new and dubious.

16. Article 3 of the constitution. The claim was also supported with appropriate rituals. In 1808 Mahmud II, like many of his predecessors, was girded with two swords, said to be those of the Prophet and of Osman, the founders of the faith and of the dynasty. In 1839 his successor Abdülmecid was girded with only one sword, said to be that of the caliph ʿUmar, and the imperial historiographer of the day, Lûtfi, makes the significant and demonstrably false statement that this was "ancient Ottoman practice" (Lûtfi, *Tarih,* vol. 6 [Istanbul, A.H. 1302 (A.D. 1885)], p. 51). The same sword was used again in 1861, at the accession of Abdülaziz, and the historian Cevdet explains why: "This was the blessed sword of the caliph ʿUmar . . . which was in the possession of that ʿAbbasid who fled to Egypt at the time when Hulegu occupied Baghdad. It was used to consecrate the Abbasid caliphs in Egypt. When Sultan Selim the Grim conquered Egypt and brought the Abbasid caliph to Istanbul, the Abbasid caliph girded Sultan Selim with this sword and thus transferred the Islamic caliphate to the house of Osman" (*Tezakir,* vol. 2 [Ankara, 1960], p. 152). The myth was now fully accepted, and remained until the abolition of the Ottoman caliphate by Kemal (Atatürk) in 1924.

17. This form of title is widely used in Islamic protocol. Thus, the chief qadi is the *qāḍī'l-quḍāt;* the chief chamberlain is the *ḥājib al-ḥujjāb,* etc. The pattern has antecedents both in pre-Islamic Iran (*shāhanshāh,* "king of kings," *mōbedhān mōbēdh,* "priest of priests," i.e., high priest), and in Europe, where the Bishop of Rome asserted his primacy over other bishops with the title *Servus Servorum Dei,* "servant of the servants of God."

18. On *sulṭān,* see al-Bāshā, *Alqāb,* pp. 323–39; *EI*[1], s.v. "*Sulṭān*" (by J. H. Kramers); C. E. Bosworth, "The Titulature of the Early Ghaznavids," *Oriens* xv (1962), pp. 222–25; Arnold, *Caliphate,* pp. 202–3; Tyan, *Institutions,* vol. 2; Barthold, *Turkestan,* p. 271; idem, "Caliph and Sultan," trans. N. S. Doniach, *Islamic Quarterly* vii (1963), pp. 117–35; cf. C. H. Becker in *Der Islam,* vol. 6 (1915–16), pp. 350–412. On imperial titles in modern Arabic usage, see Ami Ayalon, *Language and Change,* pp. 29ff.

19. See above, pp. 47ff.

20. See A. D. Alderson, *The Structure of the Ottoman Dynasty* (Oxford, 1956), pp. 77ff.; Leslie Peirce, "Topkapi," *FMR* xv (1985), pp. 67–87; *EI*[1], s.v. "Wālide Sultan" (by J. Deny).

21. In Arabic *khidewi*. According to J. H. Kramers (*EI*[1], s.v. "Khediw"), the Persian title *khedive,* meaning, approximately, "lord," "was occasionally given to Muhammadan rulers since the Middle Ages." No examples are, however, cited by al-Bāshā, though it is mentioned in the survey of titles by the sixteenth-century Ottoman historian Âli (*Künh ül-Ahbar,* vol. 5 [Istanbul, n.d.], pp. 14ff.). In the Ottoman Empire it was sometimes used as an honorific title for the Grand Vizier. It was used unofficially by Muḥammad ʿAlī Pasha, whose department of internal affairs was called *Dīwān al-Khidewi,* and by his successors in Egypt in 1867. The sultan formally conferred this title, by imperial *ferman,* on Ismāʿīl Pasha, and it was retained by his successors until 1914 when, after the outbreak of war between Britain and Turkey, the British formally ended Ottoman suzerainty and proclaimed a British protectorate in Egypt. The last khedive, ʿAbbās II, was deposed, and Ḥusayn Kāmil replaced him with the title Sultan of Egypt. According to a story occurring in both Turkish and Western sources, Ismāʿīl Pasha had originally asked for the Qurʿanic title of the ruler of Egypt, *ʿAzīz Miṣr,* "the Mighty One of Egypt," (Qurʿān XII, 30, 51), but was refused by the Sultan Abdülaziz, literally "Slave of the Mighty One," i.e., God, since it clashed with his own name (Memduh Paşa, *Mirʾat-i Şuʿunat* [Izmir, A.H. 1328], pp. 34–35; E. Dicey, *The Story of the Khedivate* [London, 1902], p. 60). A likelier reason for the refusal, if indeed such a request was ever made, was the fact that the title *ʿAzīz Miṣr* had in earlier times been used, in Ottoman texts, of the Mamluk sultans of Egypt (e.g., in the headings in Feridun, *Munşeʾat-i Selatin,* two editions, Istanbul, 1848–49 and 1858).

22. See *EI*[2], s.v. "Khādim al-Ḥaramayn" (by B. Lewis).

23. On this title, see B. Lewis, "Malik," in *Mélanges Charles Pellat* (in press), and Ami Ayalon, "*Malik* in Modern Middle Eastern Titulature," *Die Welt des Islams,* n.s., xxiii–xxiv (1984), pp. 306–19; idem, *Language and Change,* pp. 30ff, al-Bāshā, *Alqāb,* pp. 496–506; idem, *Funūn,* vol. 3, pp. 1139–42; Aḥmad ʿAbd al-Salām, *Dirāsāt,* pp. 41ff; Abū Ḥātim, *Kitāb al-Zīna,* vol. 2, pp. 99–102.

24. Text in *Répertoire chronologique de l'épigraphie arabe,* vol. 1 (Cairo, 1931), no. 1, pp. 1–2 (where earlier publications are listed).

25. See Gunnar Olinder, *The Kings of Kinda* (Lund, 1927); Irfan Kawar (= Shahid), "Byzantium and Kinda," *Byzantinische Zeitschrift* iii (1960), pp. 57–73; idem, *EI*[2], s.v. "Kinda."

26. In one passage (XVIII, 78–79), the Qurʾān speaks of a "king who confiscates every good ship," while in another (XXVII, 34), the Queen of Sheba, in conversation with Solomon, remarks that "when kings enter a city,

they pillage it and make its nobles destitute. Thus, know kings." It is noteworthy that David and Solomon, both very positive figures in the Qur'ān, though depicted in monarchical splendor, are not actually designated by the word *malik*. The only one of the ancient Israelite kings expressly designated as such in the Qur'ān is the somewhat equivocal figure of Saul. In another passage (V, 23) the Qur'ān, reproaching the Jews of Medina with their ingratitude, reminds them of God's benefactions to them in the past: "He gave you prophets and made you kings, and gave you what He gave to no others in the world." Here again, the reference to kings, though not hostile, is not exactly favorable.

27. Al-Ṭabarī, *Ta'rīkh*, vol. 1, p. 2754.

28. *"Mulkan kasrawiyyan . . . ghasban qayṣariyyan"* (ʿAmr ibn Baḥr al-Jāḥiẓ, *Rasā'il*, ed. Ḥasan al-Sandūbī [Cairo, 1933], p. 117, French trans. Charles Pellat in *Annales de l'Institut d'Études Orientales*, vol. 10 [Algiers, 1952], p. 314).

29. See Wilferd Madelung, "The Assumption of the Title Shahanshah by the Buyids and 'The Reign of the Daylam' (Dawlat al-Daylam)," *Journal of Near Eastern Studies* xxxiii (1969), pp. 84–183; Bosworth, "Titulature of the Early Ghaznavids," pp. 214ff.; R. P. Mottahedeh, "Some Attitudes towards Monarchy and Absolutism in the Eastern Islamic World of the Eleventh and Twelfth Centuries A.D.," in Kraemer and Alon, *Religion and Government*, pp. 86–91; al-Bāshā, *Alqāb*, pp. 352–54.

30. For a thorough examination of the use and development of this title in the Ottoman Empire, see Halil Inalcık, "Padişah," in *Islam Ansiklopedisi* (*IA*), vol. 9, pp. 491–95. Earlier discussion in Gibb and Bowen, *Islamic Society and the West*, vol. 1, part 1, pp. 30–31; *EI*[1], s.v. "Pādishāh" (by F. Babinger). In India, where the form *pādishāh* could have indecent associations, Muslim rulers were called *badishah*.

31. On *khan* and *khaqan*, see Gerhard Doerfer, *Türkische und mongolische Elemente im Neupersischen*, vol. 3 (Wiesbaden, 1967), pp. 141–79; H. H. Zarinezade, *Fars dilinde Azerbaycan Sözleri* (Baku, 1962), pp. 289–92; al-Bāshā, *Alqāb*, pp. 271–74; *EI*[2], s.vv. "Khāḳān" and "Khān" (both by J. A. Boyle). On the earlier Turkish use of *khan*, see Sir Gerard Clauson, *An Etymological Dictionary of Pre-Thirteenth Century Turkish* (Oxford, 1972), p. 630. On the political concepts of the steppe peoples, see Bahaeddin Ögel, *Türklerde Devlet Anlayışı: 13 yüzyıl sonlarına kadar* (Ankara, 1982); P. B. Golden, "Imperial Ideology and the Sources of Political Unity amongst the Pre-Cinggisid Nomads of Western Eurasia," *Archivum Eurasiae Medii Aevi* ii (1982), pp. 37–97. For a persuasive explanation of the adoption of *khan* by the Ottoman sultans see Paul Wittek, "Notes sur la tughra ottomane," *Byzantion* xviii (1948), pp. 329–34, xx (1950), pp. 279–82. On *kürgän*, see Doerfer, *Türkishe und mongolische Elemente*, vol. 1, pp. 475–77.

32. On the use of ceremonial, see Inostranzev, *Iranian Influence on Mos-*

lem Literature; Sourdel, "Cérémonial abbaside"; Canard, "Le cérémonial fatimite"; and Paula Sanders, "Ceremonial as Polemic: The Fatimid Celebration of Ghadir Khumm" (in press).

33. See Tyan, *Institutions,* vol. 1, pp. 315–57, vol. 2, pp. 344–55; idem, *EI²,* s.v. "Bayʿa"; Lambton, *State and Government,* pp. 18–19 and passim.

34. On *raʾīs* in medieval times, see E. Ashtor, "L'administration urbaine en Syrie médiévale," *Rivista degli Studi Orientali* 31 (1956), pp. 92–111; Claude Cahen, "Mouvements populaires et autonomisme urbain dans l'Asie musulmane du Moyen Âge," *Arabica* v (1958), pp. 236–50, vi (1959), pp. 8–9, 11ff., 253; al-Bāshā, *Alqāb,* pp. 308–9; Nikita Elisseeff, *Nūr al-Dīn: Un grand prince musulman de Syrie au temps des Croisades (511–569 H/1118–1174)* (Damascus, 1967), pp. 830–32; Roy P. Mottahedeh, *Loyalty and Leadership in an Early Islamic Society* (Princeton, 1980), pp. 129–35.

35. Notably the Jewish Exilarch, in Aramaic *Rēsh Galūtā,* a title and office dating back to pre-Islamic Iran. For a critical bibliography, see Mark R. Cohen, "The Jews under Islam: From the Rise of Islam to Sabbetai Zevi," in *Bibliographical Essays in Medieval Jewish Studies* (New York, 1976), especially pp. 183ff. On the *Raʾīs al-Yahūd* in Egypt, idem, *Jewish Self-Government in Medieval Egypt: The Origins of the Office of Head of the Jews, ca. 1065–1126* (Princeton, 1980).

36. The Ottomans retained the classical Islamic practice of calling heads of departments or services by the Arabic term *raʾīs,* or by its Persian (*sar*) and Turkish (*baş*) equivalents. The best known of these in the outside world was the Reis ul-Küttab, the chief secretary, often known as the Reis Efendi. He was in charge of the department in the office of the Grand Vizier which dealt, among other things, with relations with foreign countries.

37. On *zaʿīm,* see Lewis, *Islam in History,* pp. 287–88; al-Bāshā, *Alqāb,* pp. 310–11.

38. Abū Shāma, *Tarājim rijāl al-qarnayn al-sādis waʾl-sābiʿ,* ed. Muḥammad Zāhid al-Kawtharī (Cairo, 1947), p. 81; Kamāl al-Dīn ibn al-ʿAdīm, "Biography of Rāshid al-Dīn Sinān," ed. B. Lewis, *Arabica* xiii (1966), p. 266.

39. Al-Qalqashandī, *Ṣubḥ al-Aʿshā,* vol. II, p. 51.

40. Ibid.

41. Ibn al-Fuwaṭī, *Al-Ḥawādith al-Jāmiʿa,* ed. Muṣṭafā Jawād (Baghdad, A.H. 1351), p. 218. Walter J. Fischel, *Jews in the Economic and Political Life of Medieval Islam* (London, 1937), p. 131, simply translates *zaʿīm* as "leader," thereby missing the point of the use of *zaʿīm* instead of the customary *raʾīs.*

42. Pedro de Alcalá, *Vocabulista aravigo en letra castellana* (Granada, 1505). The anonymous *Vocabulista in Arabico,* ed. C. Schiaparelli (Florence, 1871), p. 112, translates *zaʿim* as "Baro."

43. For examples of Mamluk usage see al-Bāshā, *Alqāb,* pp. 310–11, to which one may add *RCEA,* vol. 3, pp. 53–55, and al-Qalqashandī, *Ṣubḥ al-*

A'shā, vol. 6, pp. 15, 51, 76, 110, 131. In Ottoman Egypt the title was sometimes used of a city police chief (Stanford J. Shaw, *Ottoman Egypt in the Age of the French Revolution* [Cambridge, 1964], p. 92, n. 86]. In the Ottoman Empire generally the term *zaim* usually denoted the holder of a *zeamet,* a category of quasi-feudal grant, with an income assessed at between 20,000 and 100,000 aspers. To complicate matters further, *za'īm* is sometimes used in the sense of "guarantor" or "surety" (e.g., Qur'ān XII, 72; LXVIII, 40).

44. Some other terms are also used. Al-Fārābī speaks of the *mar'ūs,* literally "headed," as the antonym of the *ra'īs,* "the head," but this term for "subject" rarely occurs outside the philosophical literature. *Ahl* is the universal term for "people," "population," "inhabitants," also "kinsfolk" (cf. the Hebrew cognate *ohel,* "tent"), and the membership or followers of a group, whether religious, ethnic, local, occupational, or other. The term *sūqa* is derogatory, and it may be translated as "mob" or "rabble." Its most probable derivation is not, as has been suggested, from *sūq,* "market," but rather from the verb *sāqa,* "to drive or herd" (cattle, prisoners, etc.).

45. Ibn al-Muqaffa' uses it commonly (e.g., *Al-Adab al-Kabīr* (Beirut, 1956), pp. 22, 31, 38, = *Rasā'il al-Bulaghā',* pp. 46, 52, 56. *Ra'iyya* does not occur in the Qur'ān, and its appearances in the Traditions are few and problematic. For Ottoman usage see Molino, pp. 440, 473 ("vassallo," "suddito"); Meninski, pp. 2330–31 ("subditi," "coloni," "Unterthanen," "contadini," "paysans"); and Clodius, p. 856 ("Unterthan"). Later, it becomes the standard term to denote subjects outside as well as inside the Islamic oecumene. Thus, an eighteenth-century Moroccan ambassador to Spain, in what must be the first Arabic account of the American Revolution, remarks that "the people [*ahl*] of America were the *ra'iyya* of the English" (Muḥammad ibn 'Uthmān al-Miknāsī, *Al-Iksīr fi fikāk al-asīr,* ed. Muḥammad al-Fāsī [Rabat, 1965], p. 97). On modern usage, see Ami Ayalon, *Language and Change,* pp. 44ff., 52–53, 73–74.

46. Abū Yūsuf, *Kitāb al-Kharāj,* pp. 3–17, English translation in Lewis, *Islam,* vol. 1, pp. 151–70.

47. In Ottoman usage it appears to denote status rather than function. It included retired or unemployed askeris, their wives and children, manumitted slaves of the sultan and of the askeris, and, in addition, the families of the holders of religious public offices in attendance on the sultan. It included both the slave and military establishments and the quasi-feudal levies. It was further recruited from the military landed gentry of the newly acquired European territories. All those who did not belong to this group, the subject population including both Muslims and non-Muslims, were collectively known as the *reaya.* Sometimes this term is extended to the whole subject population, in both town and countryside; sometimes—with increasing frequency—it is restricted to the peasantry. Thus, a late sixteenth-century Ottoman author speaks of "the people of ploughing and planting, who in our time are called *re'āyā*" (Ḥasan Kāfī, *Uṣūl al-ḥikam fi niẓām al-'ālam,* ed.

N. R. al-Hmoud [Amman, 1986], p. 20). Kāfī puts the peasantry in third place among the four orders of society, below (1) rulers and soldiers and (2) the ulema and scholars, and above (4) the merchants and artisans. This is significantly different from the early Persian classification, which put the learned first, the soldiers second, the merchants third, and the peasants last. See for example the widely circulated treatises of Jalāl al-Dīn Davānī and Naṣīr al-Dīn Ṭūsī, both available in English translation: W. F. Thompson, *Practical Philosophy of the Muhammadan People* (London, 1839), p. 388; G. M. Wickens, *The Nasirean Ethics* (London, 1964), p. 230. In this as in some other respects, Ottoman writers show a sharper awareness of political realities than do some of their predecessors.

The Ottoman askeris were, in theory, not a privileged feudal aristocracy. They had no prescriptive or hereditary right to any office, status, or grant, all of which could be conferred or withdrawn at the will of the sultan. In fact, however, the sultan normally gave these grants and offices only to the members of the askeri class, who were still considered as such even when deprived of any office or grant. Indeed, it was regarded as contrary to the basic laws of the Ottoman Empire to appoint men of peasant stock (that is, of course, apart from the famous levy of boys) to askeri positions. The Ottoman memorialists of the seventeenth century, discussing the causes of the decline of Ottoman power, adduce as one of them the violation of the rule by the sultans. An askeri could, by decree, be demoted to the *reaya* class or a *raiyya* be promoted as a reward for exceptional services to be an askeri. Both were infrequent in the early period. By the early sixteenth century, however, Sultan Süleyman the Magnificent found it necessary to issue a decree confirming holders of military grants who were of peasant descent in their holdings and protecting them from dispossession on the grounds of their peasant origin. In the period of decline, the dilution of the military caste by the intrusion of peasants and townspeople became a common complaint, and by the eighteenth century the status of askeri was so widely distributed as to have no real meaning.

48. A classification much used by medieval Muslim writers on politics divides the wielders and servants of authority into two groups, the men of the sword (*sayf*) and the men of the pen (*qalam,* from the Greek *kalamos,* "a reed," "a reed-pen," hence "a pen"). The latter at first included both scribal and religious civilians. By Ottoman times they were subdivided into these two categories, the latter known as *ilmiye,* from *ʿilm,* "knowledge," more specifically the religious knowledge possessed by the *ʿālim,* plural *ʿulamāʾ*.

49. The first use of *tābiʿ* as a technical term dates from early Islamic times, where it was applied to the second generation of companions of the Prophet. A companion *stricto sensu* (*ṣāḥib*) was one who had known the Prophet personally; a *tābiʿ* was one who had known a companion personally (see Miklos Muranyi, *Die Prophetengenossen in der frühislamischen Geschichte* (Bonn, 1973), pp. 29–32). *Tābiʿ* was also used in the general senses of "fol-

lower," "disciple," "adherent." In the geographical literature, a feminine plural form, *tawābiʿ*, denotes the dependencies and outlying areas of a city or province. The technical administrative usage dates from the late Middle Ages, and is amply documented from early Ottoman times. Its use in the context of nationality and citizenship would seem to date from the nineteenth century. See Ami Ayalon, *Language and Change*, p. 141 n. 4. The Egyptian historian al-Jabartī, who wrote a contemporary account of the French occupation of his country, sometimes prefixes French names with the word *sītūyān*, an Arabic transcription of *citoyen*, which he obviously regarded as a title.

50. See for example al-Fārābī's *Fuṣūl al-Madanī*, passim. In Persian and Turkish *madanī/medeni* meant "city dweller" and hence, probably by calque, acquired the meanings of "urbane" in Persian and "civilized" in Turkish.

51. On the use of *waṭan*, see above, pp. 40–41, and chap. 2, n. 30. On *muwāṭin*, see Ami Ayalon, *Language and Change*, pp. 44, 52–53, 131.

52. On the institution and vocabulary of slavery, see *EI*², s.vv. "ʿAbd" (by R. Brunschvig), "Ghulām" (by D. Sourdel, C. E. Bosworth, P. Hardy, and Halil Inalcık), "Kul" (by C. E. Bosworth), "Mamlūk" (by D. Ayalon), etc.

53. On the terms for "free" and "freedom," see Franz Rosenthal, *The Muslim Concept of Freedom* (Leiden, 1960); François de Blois, "'Freemen' and 'Nobles' in Iranian and Semitic Languages," *Journal of the Royal Asiatic Society*, 1985, pp. 5–15; Lewis, *Islam in History*, pp. 267–81; idem, "Serbestiyet," *Istanbul Universitesi Iktisat Fakültesi Mecmuası* x/1 (1984), pp. 47–52; Dominique Sourdel, "Peut-on parler de liberté dans la société de l'Islam médiéval?" in *La notion de liberté*, pp. 119–33. On Ottoman usage, see Molino, p. 234; Meninski, pp. 1738–39 (*ḥur* = "non servus," "ingenuus") and p. 2583 (*serbest* = exempt, tax-free); Clodius, pp. 341–42. On modern Arabic usage, see Ami Ayalon, *Language and Change*, pp. 47, 52–53, 105–6, 125.

54. See above pp. 4–5.

55. Examples in Lewis, *Islam*, vol. 2, pp. 224ff.

56. For some examples, see Bahriye Üçok, *Femmes turques souveraines et régents dans les états islamiques* (n.p., n.d., [Ankara? 1985?]).

57. On the *mawālī*, see Ignaz Goldziher, *Muslim Studies*, vol. 1 (London, 1967), pp. 101ff. (German original, *Muhammedanische Studien*, vol. 1 [Halle, 1889], pp. 104ff.). On the *dhimmī* and the *mustaʾmin*, see pp. 77–78. On eunuchs, see David Ayalon, "On the Eunuchs in Islam," *Jerusalem Studies in Arabic and Islam* i (1979), pp. 67–124.

58. See *EI*², s.v. "Al-Khāṣṣa waʾl-ʿĀmma" (by M. A. J. Beg); Mez, *Renaissance of Islam*, pp. 74, 147ff.; Ira M. Lapidus, *Muslim Cities in the Later Middle Ages* (Cambridge, Mass., 1967), pp. 79ff.; Mottahedeh, *Loyalty and Leadership*, pp. 115–29 and passim.

59. For examples of the use of *ḍaʿīf* in classical texts, see al-Jāḥiẓ, *Al-Bayān waʾl-Tabyīn*, vol. 3, p. 368; Muslim, *Ṣaḥīḥ*, vol. 6, *K. al-Imāra*, p. 706, English translation in Lewis, *Islam*, vol. 1, p. 159. For a modern ex-

ample, from southern Arabia, where *ḍaʿīf* is linked with *miskīn* to describe peasants and artisans, see Serjeant in *BSOAS,* xxi (1958), p. 11.

60. The word *ʿadl,* from a root with the connotation of "straight," "even," "balanced," early acquired the meaning of "justice." It occurs frequently in the Qurʾān (cf. Toshihiko Izutsu, *Ethico-Religious Concepts in the Qurʿān* [Montreal, 1966], pp. 91, 209–11, 234) and in the Traditions (Wensinck et al., *Concordance,* s.v. "ʿAdl"). According to one tradition, frequently quoted with minor variants, the Prophet said that "an hour of justice is better than sixty years of worship." According to another, "the most beloved of God's creatures and the nearest to Him is a just imam; the most hateful and the most severely punished on the Day of Judgment is an oppressive imam" (al-Ghazālī, *Faḍāʾiḥ al-Bāṭiniyya,* ed. ʿAbd al-Raḥmān Badawī [Cairo, 1964], p. 204); cf. Abū Yūsuf, trans. Lewis, *Islam,* vol. 1, p. 159.

There is an extensive literature on the definition and significance of justice. The classical view is magisterially stated by al-Ghazālī, in the course of an early discussion of justice: "Justice is distinguished from tyranny [*ẓulm*] only by law [*sharʿ*]; the religion [*dīn*] of God and the law [*sharʿ*] of His Prophet are the goal and sanctuary of every departure and every arrival" (*Faḍāʾiḥ al-Bāṭiniyya,* p. 205; cf. Goldziher, *Streitschrift des Gazali,* p. 94). In later medieval and early modern times *ʿadl* was used in a sense closer to its original meaning of "balance," "equilibrium," and denoted a situation in which each order of society kept its proper place and function. See A. K. S. Lambton, "Justice in the Medieval Persian Theory of Kingship," *Studia Islamica* xvii (1962), pp. 91–119; Franz Rosenthal, "Political Justice and the Just Ruler," in Kraemer and Alon, *Religion and Government,* pp. 92–101; Mottahedeh, *Leadership,* p. 179; and Majid Khadduri, *The Islamic Conception of Justice* (Baltimore and London, 1984).

In Ottoman times it became a common practice for sultans, especially at their accessions, to publish and circulate a special kind of *ferman* called *adaletname,* literally "justice letter," expressing the sultan's wish to ensure that justice is done to all his subjects, especially the poor and weak, and to prevent oppression by government officials. See Uriel Heyd, *Studies in Old Ottoman Criminal Law,* ed. V. L. Menage (Oxford, 1973), p. 150, n. 4. A number of *adaletnames* were edited by Halil Inalcık in *Belgeler* ii (1965), pp. 49–145. On the notion of *ẓulm* as Ottoman law, see Ahmet Mumcu, *Osmanlı Hukûkunda Zulüm Kavramı* (Ankara, 1972).

By the early nineteenth century, an Egyptian sheikh in Paris, confronted with the unfamiliar French notion of (political) freedom, explains to his readers that what the French call freedom (*ḥurriyya*) is the same as what the Muslims call justice and equity (Shaykh Rifāʿa Rāfiʿ al-Ṭahṭāwı, *Takhlīṣ al-Ibrīz fī talkhīs Bārīz,* ed. Mahdī ʿAllām, Aḥmad Badawī, and Anwar Lūqā [Cairo, n.d. (1958?)], p. 148. Cf. L. Zolondek, "Al-Tahtāwī and Political Freedom," *Muslim World* liv [1964], pp. 90–97).

61. A number of medieval texts, particularly from the period of radical

ferment in the eighth and ninth centuries, give some indication of what was perceived as bad government, calling for action against it. Thus Zayd ibn ʿAlī, who led a rebellion in 738, is quoted as follows: "We summon you to the Book of God, to the Sunna of His Prophet, may God bless and save him, to wage Holy War against oppressors and defend those who have been abased, to give pay to those who are deprived of it and to share the booty equally among those who are entitled to it, to make good the wrongs done by the oppressors, to recall those who have been kept too long on campaigns, and to aid the House of the Prophet against those who obstruct us and disregard our rights" (al-Ṭabarī, *Taʾrīkh,* vol. 2, pp. 1687–88). Another text, frequently repeated by medieval Arab authors, quotes the complaint of a disappointed revolutionary, one who had supported the ʿAbbasid revolution against the Umayyads, in the hope of achieving better things, and was greatly dissatisfied with the results: "By God, our booty, which was shared, has become a perquisite of the rich; our leadership, which was consultative, has become arbitrary; our succession, which was by the choice of the community, is now by inheritance. Pleasures and musical instruments are bought with the portion of the orphan and the widow. The *dhimmis* [non-Muslims] lord it over the persons of the Muslims, and evildoers everywhere govern their affairs" (Ibn Qutayba, *ʿUyūn al-akhbār,* ed. Aḥmad Zakī al-ʿAdawī, vol. 2 [Cairo, A.H. 1343–48 (A.D. 1925–30)], p. 115). In about 840, al-Jāḥiẓ, one of the greatest writers in Arabic literature, in the course of a lengthy discussion of tyranny and revolt, offers his own definition of bad government: "These [bad] rulers take . . . hostages . . . [taking] a friend for a friend, and a kinsman for a kinsman; they terrorize the good and encourage the wicked, and rule by favoritism and caprice, the flaunting of power, contempt for the people, repression of the subjects, and accusations without restraint or discretion" (al-Jāḥiẓ, *Rasāʾil,* pp. 295ff.). On the whole question of ʿAbbasid revolutionary propaganda, see now Jacob Lassner, *Islamic Revolution and Historical Memory: An Enquiry into the Art of ʿAbbasid Apologetics* (New Haven, 1986).

Chapter 4

1. See J. Chelhod, *Les structures du sacré chez les Arabes* (Paris, 1964); R. B. Serjeant, "Haram and Hawtah, the Sacred Enclave in Arabia," in *Mélanges Taha Husayn* (Cairo, 1962), pp. 41–58. For modern examples see Wilfred Thesiger, *Arabian Sands* (London, 1959).

2. Thus, the two holy cities of Mecca and Medina are commonly known as *al-Ḥaramayn*. The title *Khādim al-Ḥaramayn,* "servant or custodian of the two holy cities," was apparently first adopted by Saladin. It was used occasionally by the Mamluk sultans of Egypt, and became part of the regular titulature of the Ottoman sultans after the extension of Ottoman power to

the Hijaz. It disappeared with the Ottoman dynasty, but has recently been revived by the Saudi monarchy.

Other derivatives from *ḥrm,* with approximate meanings, include *ḥarīm* (Turkish, *harem*), the closed, inner part of a house; *ḥarām,* unlawful, sacrosanct, taboo; *ḥurma,* reverence, veneration, sanctity; *muḥtaram,* honored, revered; *iḥrām,* the state of ritual consecration of a pilgrim in Mecca; *taḥrīm,* ban, interdiction; *Muḥarram,* the name of the first month, during which warfare was forbidden in ancient Arabia.

Other holy places, in Arabia and elsewhere, are also usually called *Ḥaram.* One of the best known is the enclosure containing the Aqsa Mosque and the Dome of the Rock in Jerusalem. The Arabic name of the city of Jerusalem, *al-Quds,* is of comparatively late appearance. In the earliest Arabic references, from the time of the Prophet and shortly after, Jerusalem is normally called *Iliyāʾ,* from *Aelia,* the name which the Romans gave to the city in the second century, or, in full, as *Iliyāʾ madīnat bayt al-maqdis,* "Aelia, the city of the temple." Later, the city is referred to as *Bayt al-Maqdis,* and then simply as *al-Quds.* The resemblance to the ancient Hebrew *Bayt ha-Miqdash* and [*Ir ha-*]*Qodesh* will be obvious. On this see further *EI*², "Ḳuds" (by S. D. Goitein).

3. See above, p. 12 and p. 123, n. 22.

4. The law relating to *jihād* is discussed at length in the classical treatises and in the modern studies based on them. See for example Santillana, *Istituzioni,* vol. 1, pp. 68–75, for an excellent and fully documented summary of Mālikī law, with some reference also to Shāfiʿī law, on the subject. The laws relating to war and peace are discussed at greater length in two books: Majid Khadduri, *War and Peace in the Law of Islam* (Baltimore, 1955); and Muhammad Hamidullah, *Muslim Conduct of State,* 7th ed. (Lahore, n.d. [1977?]). Some modern developments of the concept and regulation of *jihād* are discussed by Rudolph Peters, *Islam and Colonialism: The Doctrine of Jihad in Modern History* (The Hague, 1979), and A. K. S. Lambton, "A Nineteenth-Century View of Jihad," *Studia Islamica* xxxii (1970), pp. 181–92. For comparisons of Muslim and Christian notions of holy war, see Marius Canard, "La guerre sainte dans le monde islamique et dans le monde chrétien," *Revue Africaine* 79, no. 2 (1936), pp. 605–23, and Albrecht Noth, *Heiliger Krieg und heiliger Kampf im Islam und Christentum: Beiträge zur Vorgeschichte und Geschichte der Kreuzzüge* (Bonn, 1966). For sample translations of relevant Islamic texts see Lewis, *Islam,* vol. 1, pp. 209–12 (excerpts from Qurʾān and *ḥadīth*); O. Rescher, *Beiträge zur Dschihad-Literatur,* 3 parts (Stuttgart, 1920–21) (translations from the *Kanz al-ʿUmmāl* of al-Muttaqī and the *Ṣaḥīḥ* of Muslim); R. Peters, *Jihad in Mediaeval and Modern Islam: The Chapter on Jihad from Averroës' Legal Handbook 'Bidāyat al-Mudjtahid' and the Treatise 'Koran and Fighting' by the Late Shaykh al-*

Azhar Maḥmūd Shaltūt (Leiden, 1977); Majid Khadduri, *The Islamic Law of Nations: Shaybani's Siyar* (Baltimore, 1966). The last is a translation of an important treatise by the Ḥanbalī jurist Abū ʿAbdallāh Muḥammad al-Shaybānī (750–805), published with a commentary by al-Sarakhsī (d. 1090), *Sharḥ al-Siyar al-Kabīr,* 4 vols. (Hyderabad, Deccan, A.H. 1335–36). For a brief account by a lawyer, see *EI*², s.v. "Djihād" (by E. Tyan), and for a more extensive historical treatment, *IA,* s.v. "Cihad" (by Halim Sabit Sibay).

During the nineteenth century, under the influence of the westernizing reforms, there seems to have been a certain change of attitude with regard to the conduct of war. But the older concepts and practices still survived in the remoter areas of Islam, as for example in Afghanistan, where as late as 1896 a *jihād* was launched by the amir ʿAbd al-Raḥmān against the non-Muslim population of the province until then known as Kāfiristān, "the land of unbelievers." Its people were conquered and forcibly converted to Islam, and their province was renamed Nūristān, "The land of light." The resistance to European colonial expansion in the nineteenth century often took a religious form, as for example after the French conquest of Algeria, the Russian conquest of Daghistan and the Caucasus, and the British conquest of northwest India, all of which were resisted by religious leaders proclaiming *jihād.* Even more striking examples may be found in Muslim Africa in the holy wars proclaimed by such religious leaders as the *Mahdī* of the Sudan and the so-called Mad Mullah of Somaliland. On the latter, see the remarkable study of Said S. Samatar, *Oral Poetry and Somali Nationalism: The Case of Sayyid Mahammad ʿAbdille Hasan* (Cambridge, 1982). In 1912 the Sanūsī leader in Cyrenaica proclaimed a *jihād* in due form against the Italians. Somewhat more sordid examples may be found in the recurring practice of proclaiming *jihād* against unconverted blacks in Africa in order to legalize their capture and sale as slaves. In Muslim law, no Muslim, even no non-Muslim living under the protection of the Muslim state, can legally be enslaved, but only an infidel captured in the holy war. Since the *jihād* was thus the sole source of legally valid slaves, every slave raid had to be dignified with this title. This practice was the subject of repeated protests by Muslim jurists, especially black jurists. See for example Mahmoud A. Zouber, *Ahmad Baba de Tombouctou (1556–1627), sa vie et son oeuvre* (Paris, 1977), especially pp. 129ff, and *Slaves and Slavery in Muslim Africa,* vol. 1, *Islam and the Ideology of Enslavement,* ed. J. R. Willis (London, 1984).

The end of this phase came with the abortive Ottoman *jihād* proclaimed in 1914 against the Allied and Associated powers. This *jihād*—contemptuously styled "the holy war made in Germany" by the Dutch Islamicist Snouck Hurgronje (reprinted in his *Verspreide Geschriften,* vol. 3 [Bonn and Leipzig, 1923], pp. 257ff.; cf. the comments of Becker, *Islamstudien,* vol. 2, 281ff.)—failed utterly in its purpose of arousing the Muslim soldiers in the British, French, and Russian imperial armies against their European masters.

Thereafter the older concept fell into disuse and for a while into disrepute. In the meantime, Muslim scholars had been defining and refining a new concept of *jihād*, primarily peaceful and concerned with striving for the propagation of the Islamic faith and the conversion of the infidel. Its military aspect was downplayed and presented as essentially defensive. On the revival and reinterpretation of *jihād* as combat, this time in the sense of revolutionary struggle, see above, pp. 90, 92–93, 95–96.

5. See *EI*², s.vv. "Dār al-Islām" and "Dār al-Ḥarb" (by A. Abel).

6. Al-Muttaqī, *Kanz al-ʿUmmāl*, vol. 2 (Hyderabad, A.H. 1312), p. 252, English translation in Lewis, *Islam*, vol. 1, p. 210.

7. Classical Arabic usage has a number of terms for the frontier zones and those who live and fight in them. The frontier area between the Byzantine and the caliphal empires, in northern Syria and Iraq and southern Turkey, was known as *al-ʿAwāṣim*, plural of *al-ʿāṣima*, literally "the protectress." In modern Arabic *al-ʿāṣima* denotes the capital of a country. The advanced fortresses of the zone were called *al-thughūr*, literally the "clefts" or "openings." These terms were later also applied to other frontier zones, and even to certain coastal areas, called *thughūr baḥriyya*, "maritime openings." See *EI*², s.v. "Al-ʿAwāṣim" (by M. Canard), and *EI*¹, s.v. "al-Thughūr" (by E. Honigmann). The term *ribāṭ*, from a root meaning "to bind or attach," is used extensively but not exclusively in North Africa, for a kind of fortified convent manned by members of a militant and more or less military order. These members are called by the active participle *murābiṭ*, whence the French word *marabout* and the dynastic name of the Almoravids, a dynasty which began as a religiously inspired order of Berber frontier fighters and ruled over much of Morocco and Muslim Spain in the late eleventh and early twelfth centuries. The military monastery has obvious parallels in the history of both Eastern and Western Christendom. The pre-Islamic Persian terms *marz*, "border," and *marzbān*, "warden of the borders," "marquis," survive in Persian usage, but for the most part without a specifically Islamic content (Christensen, *L'Iran sous les sassanides*, index).

The Turkish word *uj* (modern orthography *uc*) appears in early Ottoman usage, as for example in the titles of the first Ottoman rulers, who described themselves as *uj begi*, "march lord." By far the commonest term for the march warriors was *gazi*, on which see below.

8. The sacralization of the root *ghzy* seems to date from the time of the Prophet, when it was used of the raids and other military expeditions undertaken by the community of Medina under his leadership. Later, *ghāzī* became the common term for the frontier fighters, zealots and soldiers of fortune alike, who fought to extend the Islamic frontiers in Anatolia, Mesopotamia, Central Asia, India, and elsewhere. By early Ottoman times it had become a title of honor and a claim to leadership. In an inscription of 1337, Orhan, the second ruler of the Ottoman line, describes himself as "Sultan, son of the Sultan of the Gazis, Gazi son of Gazi . . . march lord of the hori-

zons." The Ottoman poet Ahmedi, writing ca. 1402, defines a *gazi* as "the instrument of God's religion, a servant of God who cleanses the earth from the filth of polytheism . . . the sword of God." See Paul Wittek, "Deux chapitres de l'histoire des Turcs de Roum," *Byzantion* xi (1936), pp. 285–319; idem, *The Rise of the Ottoman Empire* (London, 1938). Rudi Paul Lindner's findings, *Nomads and Ottomans in Medieval Anatolia* (Bloomington, Ind., 1983), while rejecting Paul Wittek's theory on the *ghāzī* origin of the Ottoman state, do not affect the significance of the term and notion of *ghāzī* as such.

9. See B. Lewis, *The Assassins: A Radical Sect in Islam* (London, 1967, rev. ed. New York, 1987). On the group of Turkish conspirators in 1859, who called themselves *fidāʾī*, see Uluğ Iğdemir, *Kuleli Vakası hakkında bir araştırma* (Ankara, 1933), and Lewis, *Emergence of Modern Turkey,* pp. 151–52.

10. See Marius Canard, "Les expéditions des Arabes contre Constantinople dans l'histoire et dans la légende," *Journal Asiatique* ccvii (1926), pp. 105–6, citing al-Muttaqī, *Muntakhab Kanz al-ʿUmmāl,* vol. 6, p. 12, and Ibn ʿAbd al-Ḥakam, *Futūḥ Miṣr,* ed. C. C. Torrey (New Haven, 1922), p. 257.

11. Al-Ṭabarī, *Taʾrīkh,* vol. 1, p. 1850, English translation in Lewis, *Islam,* vol. 1, p. 213.

12. Hamidullah, *Muslim Conduct of State,* pp. 149–52; Khadduri, *War and Peace,* pp. 239–50. For discussions of various aspects of diplomatic practice in medieval Islamic states, see the notes and commentary of Ṣalāḥ al-Dīn al-Munajjid in his edition of Ibn al-Farrāʾ, *Kitāb Rusul al-Mulūk waman yaṣluḥu biʾl-risāla waʾl-safāra* (Cairo, 1947).

13. In Ottoman and other Turkish usage, *safīr* is often replaced by its Turkish equivalent *elçi,* from *el* or *il,* a word meaning "country," "people," or "state," with the occupational suffix *ci* (=*ji*). On this term, see Clauson, *Etymological Dictionary,* pp. 121ff. Other terms for ambassador include Arabic *qāṣid* and Turkish *yalavaç*.

14. Ibn Shāhīn al-Ẓāhirī, *Zubdat Kashf al-Mamālik,* ed. P. Ravaisse (Paris, 1894), p. 40, French translation J. Gaulmier, *La Zubda kachf al-mamālik* (Beirut, 1950), p. 60. On the law relating to the giving and taking of hostages, see al-Sarakhsī, *Sharḥ al-Siyar al-Kabīr,* vol. 4 (Hyderabad, Deccan, n.d.), pp. 41–60.

15. Hamidullah, *Muslim Conduct of State,* pp. 173ff.; Khadduri, *War and Peace,* pp. 74ff. For a somewhat different presentation, see J. L. Kraemer, "Apostates, Rebels and Brigands," in Kraemer and Alon, *Religion and Government,* pp. 34–73.

16. Willi Heffening, *Das islamische Fremdenrecht bis zu den islamisch-fränkischen Staatsvertragen* (Hanover, 1925); N. Kruse, *Islamische Völkerrechtslehre* (Göttingen, 1953), not seen; Hamidullah *Muslim Conduct of State,* pp. 76–79; Khadduri, *War and Peace,* pp. 162–69, 245–46, 243–44; Khadduri-Shaybānī, *Islamic Law of Nations,* pp. 158–79; Julius Hatschek,

Der Musta'min (Berlin and Leipzig, 1919); *EI*[2], s.v. "*Amān*" (by J. Schacht).

17. For an examination of early Arabic historical accounts of armistices and truces under the first caliphs, see Donald R. Hill, *The Termination of Hostilities in the Early Arab Conquests A.D. 634–656* (London, 1971). On the law regarding the termination of hostilities, see Hamidullah, *Muslim Conduct of State,* pp. 263–74; Khadduri, *War and Peace,* pp. 133–37; Khadduri-Shaybāni, *Islamic Law of Nations,* pp. 142–57.

18. See Santillana, *Istituzioni,* vol. 1, pp. 80–81, 292–93; Hamidullah, *Muslim Conduct of State,* pp. 99ff. See further the collection of studies by Tilman Nagel, Gerd-R. Puin, Christa-U. Spuler, Werner Schmucker, and Albrecht Noth, *Studien zum Minderheitenproblem im Islam,* vol. 1 (Bonn, 1973); Albrecht Noth, "Zum Verhältnis von kalifaler Zentralgewalt und Provinzen in umayyadischer Zeit: Die 'Sulh-ʿAnwa' Traditionen für Ägypten und der Iraq," *Welt des Islam* xiv (1973), pp. 150–62; shortened version in idem, "Some Remarks on the 'Nationalization' of Conquered Lands at the Time of the Umayyads," in *Land Tenure and Social Transformation in the Middle East,* ed. Tarif Khalidi (Beirut, 1984), pp. 223–28.

19. See *EI*[1], s.v. "Salām" (by C. van Arendonk). For Biblical examples of the Hebrew analog, see Gen. 43:23; Judg. 6:23, 19:20. Rabbinical examples in E. Ben-Yehudah, *Thesaurus Totius Hebraitatis . . .,* s.v. "Shalom." For an early Ismāʿīlī discussion of the significance of *Salām,* see Abū Ḥātim al-Rāzī, *Kitāb al-Zīna fi'l-Kalimāt al-Islāmiyya al-ʿArabiyya,* ed. Ḥusayn al-Hamdānī, vol. 2 (Cairo, 1958), pp. 63–69. In Ottoman usage *selam* appears only in the sense of greeting (cf. Clodius, pp. 661, 851, "salutatio"). On *sulh* see Meninski, pp. 2980–81.

20. Cited in Ibn Saʿd, *Ṭabaqāt al-Ṭabaqāt al-Kubrā,* ed. Eduard Sachau et al. (Leiden, 1904–40), 1/II, pp. 28–29. Examples of other letters in Muḥammad Ḥamīdullāh al-Haydarabādī, *Majmūʿat al-Wathā'iq al-Islāmiyya li'l-ʿahd al-nabawī wa'l-khilāfa al-Rāshida* (Cairo, 1958).

21. See for example the increasingly hostile messages exchanged between Ibn Saʿūd and the Imam Yaḥyā of the Yemen, culminating in the outbreak of war between them in 1934. The texts of these messages were published in a Saudi Arabian Green Book, *Bayān ʿan al-ʿIlāqāt bayn al-Mamlaka al-ʿArabiyya al-Suʿūdiyya wa'l-Imām Yaḥyā Ḥamīd al-Dīn ʿāmm 1353* (Mecca, A.H. 1353).

22. Adolf Grohmann, *Arabic Papyri in the Egyptian Library,* vol. 3 (Cairo, 1938), pp. 5, 8, 13, etc.; B. Lewis, *Muslim Discovery of Europe* (New York, 1982), p. 204.

23. A comparison between royal letters sent from Muslim to Christian monarchs, and the contemporary translations, shows a recurring tendency to tone down the always haughty and sometimes offensive language of the originals. Thus, the term "infidel," for the recipient and his allies, may be replaced by "Christian"; and an injunction to be loyal and submissive may become an appeal for friendship and good relations. For some examples, see

Susan A. Skilliter, *William Harborne and the Trade with Turkey 1578–1582* (London, 1977).

24. In several independent Arabic translations, the title of Tolstoy's *War and Peace* is rendered *Al-Ḥarb wa'l-Salām*. My thanks are due to Professor Sasson Somekh for drawing my attention to this.

25. See *EI*², s.vv. "Dār al-ʿAhd" (by Halil Inalcık) and "Dār al-Ṣulḥ" (by Armand Abel).

26. For a translation and discussion of the *baqṭ*, see Yūsuf Fadl Ḥasan, *The Arabs and the Sudan, from the Seventh to the Early Sixteenth Century* (Edinburgh, 1967). For a critical examination of the history and prehistory of the agreement, in the light of newly discovered documentary evidence, see Martin Hinds and Hamdi Sakkout, "A Letter from the Governor of Egypt to the King of Nubia and Muqurra concerning Egyptian-Nubian Relations in 141/758," in *Studia Arabica et Islamica, Festschrift for Ihsan ʿAbbas on His Sixtieth Birthday* (Beirut, 1981), pp. 209–30.

27. Al-Māwardī, *Al-Aḥkām al-Sulṭāniyya* pp. 51–61, French translation Fagnan, pp. 109ff.; cf. Khadduri, *Islamic Law of Nations,* passim; Hamidullah, *Muslim Conduct of State,* pp. 180ff.; Kraemer, "Apostates, Rebels and Brigands."

28. On the treaty of Amasya, see Peçevi, *Tarih* (Istanbul, A.H. 1283) pp. 336ff.; Hammer, *Hist. Emp. Ott.*, vol. 6 (Istanbul, A.H. 1264), p. 48; text in Feridun, *Munşe'at-i Selatin,* vol. 1, pp. 507–12, citing the shah's "letter of supplication" and the sultan's response.

29. Cited in Mahmud Kemal Inal, *Osmanlı Devrinde son Sadrıazamlar* (Istanbul, 1940–53), p. 1892.

30. Chapter 9 of the constitution (articles 113–32) deals with the presidency of the republic. Article 115 lays down the conditions of eligibility, the first of which is "Iranian origin and Iranian nationality."

31. There is an extensive literature on the capitulations. For a discussion of how they were perceived from the Muslim side, see *EI*², s.v. "Imtiyāzāt" (by J. Wansbrough, Halil Inalcık, A. K. S. Lambton, and G. Baer).

32. The first modern critical study of the *ridda* wars and the literature relating to them was the epoch-making work of Leone Caetani, *Studi di storia orientale,* vol. 3 (Milan, 1914). The most recent is that of Fred McGraw Donner, *The Early Islamic Conquests* (Princeton, 1981). See also Elias S. Shoufani, *Al-Riddah and the Muslim Conquest of Arabia* (Toronto, 1973); Ella Landau-Tasseron, "The Participation of Ṭayyi in the *Ridda,*" *Jerusalem Studies in Arabic and Islam* v (1984), pp. 53–71; and, on the law relating to wars against apostates, Hamidullah, *Muslim Conduct of State,* pp. 174–77; Khadduri, *War and Peace,* pp. 149–52; Khadduri, *Islamic Law of Nations,* pp. 195–229.

33. Al-Jāḥiẓ, *Al-Ḥayawān,* 2d ed., vol. 1 (Cairo, 1938), p. 174.

34. Al-Ghazālī, *Fayṣal al-Tafriqa bayn al-Islām wa'l-Zandaqa* (Cairo, 1901), p. 68.

35. For a masterly study of the sources, literature, and issues, see Ayalon, "The great *Yasa* of Chingiz Khan," *Studia Islamica* xxiii–xxxiv (1971), pp. 97–180, xxxvi (1972), pp. 113–58, xxxviii (1973), pp. 107–56.

36. Ibn Taymiyya, *Fatāwā,* vol. 4 (Cairo, 1909), pp. 198, 280–81; cited by Emmanuel Sivan, in *Radical Islam: Medieval Theology and Modern Politics* (New Haven, 1985), p. 98.

37. On this incident, see B. Lewis, "The Tanzimat and Social Equality," in *Économies et sociétés dans l'empire ottoman,* ed. Jean-Louis Bacqué-Grammont and Paul Dumont (Paris, 1983), pp. 52–53; Ehud Toledano, *The Ottoman Slave Trade and Its Suppression* (Princeton, 1983), pp. 129–35; William Ochsenwald, "Muslim European Conflict in the Hijaz: The Slave Trade Controversy, 1840–1859," *Middle Eastern Studies* xvi (1980), pp. 115–26. The major published source, from which the above citations are taken, is Cevdet, *Tezakir 1–12,* ed. Cavid Baysun (Ankara, 1953), pp. 101–52. An interesting account of these events may also be found in the reports of Stephen Page, the acting British Vice Consul in Jedda, PRO, F.O.195/375, letters of 4 August, 13 November, and 23 November 1855.

38. See Johannes J. G. Jansen, *The Neglected Duty: The Creed of Sadat's Assassins and Islamic Resurgence in the Middle East* (New York, 1986); Gilles Kepel, *Muslim Extremism in Egypt: The Prophet and Pharaoh* (Berkeley and Los Angeles, 1986); Sivan, *Radical Islam.*

Chapter 5

1. See for example the traditions in al-Muttaqī, *Kanz al-ʿUmmāl,* vol. 3, 197ff., English translation in Lewis, *Islam,* vol. 1, pp. 150–51; other traditions in Wensinck et al., *Concordance,* s.vv. "Amīr," "Imām," "Wali," etc.

2. For this purpose, what matters is that they were reported, and that the reports were universally accepted and believed in the Islamic world. Recent questioning of the historicity of these reports has no relevance to their acceptance in the past, and is unlikely to have much effect on their acceptance in the present.

3. For a fuller discussion of this theme, see B. Lewis, "On the Revolutions in Early Islam," *Studia Islamica* xxxii (1970), pp. 215–31, reprinted in idem, *Islam in History,* pp. 237–52.

4. Qur'ān XXXIII, 21. Cf. LX, 446, where the same phrase is used of Abraham and his companions. The phrase occurs frequently in later Islamic writings, especially among the Shiʿa.

5. The Ayatollah Khomeini has successfully followed the same pattern, returning to Iran via Iraq and Neauphle-le-Château.

6. For example XVIII, 28; cf. XXVIII, 3–5, XXXIV, 33–37, LIX, 7. See further B. Lewis, "On the Quietist and Activist Traditions in Islamic Political Writing," *BSOAS* x/ix (1986), pp. 141–47.

7. Al-Ṭabarī, *Ta'rīkh,* vol. 1, p. 2053; cf. ibid., p. 2020; Abū Yūsuf,

Kitāb al-Kharāj, p. 85; Abū ʿUbayd al-Qāsim ibn Sallām, *Kitāb al-Amwāl,* ed. Muḥammad al-Fiqi (Cairo, 1934), p. 34. Similar expressions occur in other early letters ascribed to Muslim commanders and governors. See for example the texts collected by Ḥamīdullāh, *Majmūʿat al-Wathāʾiq,* especially pp. 295ff.

8. See D. B. MacDonald, *The Religious Attitude and Life in Islam* (Chicago, 1909), pp. 243–44; idem, *EI²,* s.v. "Fiṭra." According to a much-cited *ḥadīth,* "Every child is born according to God's plan [*ʿalaʾl-fiṭra*]; then his parents make him a Jew or a Christian or a Magian." References in A. J. Wensinck, *A Handbook of Early Muhammadan Tradition* (Leiden, 1921), p. 43, and Wensinck et al., *Concordance,* vol. 5, pp. 179–80.

9. *Maʿṣiya,* literally "disobedience" (i.e., of God) is one of the terms for sin. Two frequently cited traditions are "there is no [duty of] obedience in disobedience [to God]" and "there is no [duty of] obedience to a creature against his Creator." Others are even more explicit. According to one, the Prophet told his followers, "If any of your rulers [*amīr*] orders you to do anything in disobedience to God, do not obey him." The first caliph, Abū Bakr, is quoted as saying, "Obey us as long as we obey God and his Prophet. If we disobey God and his Prophet we have no claim to your obedience" (al-Ghazālī, *Faḍāʾiḥ al-Bāṭiniyya,* pp. 206–8). From these and other traditions, al-Ghazālī concludes, "Obedience to the Imams is obligatory, but only in obedience to God and not in disobedience to Him."

For a modern study of the Islamic principle of limited conditional obedience, see Hādi al-ʿAlawī, "Naqd al-Sulṭa wa-mabdaʾ al-ṭāʿa al-mashrūṭa fīʾl-Islām," *Al-Nahj* ix (1985), pp. 74–84, x (1985), pp. 80–92.

Traditions cited in Wensinck et al., *Concordance,* s.vv. "Maʿsiya," "Ẓulm," etc.

10. See Raʾif Khuri, *Modern Arab Thought: Channels of the French Revolution to the Arab East,* trans. Ihsan Abbas (Princeton, 1983); Berkes, *Development of Secularism in Turkey;* B. Lewis, "The Impact of the French Revolution on Turkey: Some Notes on the Transmission of Ideas," *Journal of World History* i (1953), pp. 105–25. On the discussion of the French Revolution, in Arabic, see Ami Ayalon, *Language and Change,* especially pp. 43–44, 98–100, 107–8.

11. The precedent set by the ideological murder of ʿUthmān (the earlier murder of his predecessor ʿUmar seems to have been purely personal) was followed by many later dissidents and sectaries, who saw in the removal of the ruler a quick and simple way to change the world or at least to terrorize those who ruled it. The word "assassin," though of Arabic etymology, from *ḥashīshiyya,* does not mean "murderer" in Arabic. Two terms are commonly used for political or religious murders. One of them, *ightāla,* from a root meaning "to destroy," indicates disapproval. The other, *zakkā,* "purify," was used by pious assassins to ennoble their work.

12. Thus, the more or less official account of the successful revolution which established the Fatimid caliphate is called *Iftitāḥ al-Daʿwa,* "the opening (or conquest) of the mission." There are two editions—by Widād al-Qāḍī (Beirut, 1970) and by Farhāt al-Dashrāwī (Tunis, 1975). The author, Nuʿman ibn Muḥammad, was the chief qadi of the fourth Fatimid caliph. On the *daʿwa,* the preaching or summoning which prepared the way for both the ʿAbbasid and Fatimid revolutions, see *EI²,* s.vv. "Dāʿī" (summoner) (by M. G. S. Hodgson) and "Daʿwa" (by M. Canard).

13. See above, pp. 35–36.

14. In the few moments that passed between the murder of President Sadat and the arrest of his murderers, their leader proudly proclaimed that "I have killed Pharaoh." In the Qurʾān, as in the book of Exodus, Pharaoh is the villain of a story in which Moses and the children of Israel are the heroes, and there are several passages in which Pharaoh appears as the ultimate example of the irreligious and oppressive ruler whom it is the believer's duty to disobey and if possible to overthrow. Notably, he is punished in the Qurʾān as an oppressor, not as an appeaser, of the children of Israel. But for a long time now, Egyptians have been taught in their schools to regard Pharaoh, not as a tyrant or an evildoer, but rather as a symbol of the greatest and most glorious age of Egypt's past, a source of national pride rather than an oppressor of God's servants. It is, therefore, the more remarkable that in the moment of truth, the leader of a group of Islamic radical militants in Egypt should have chosen Pharaoh as the prototype of tyranny. By doing so, he rejected the nationalist rewriting of the remote and recent past, and expressed a Muslim religious perception of the offense, the judgment, and the punishment executed.

15. Al-Ṭabarī, *Taʾrīkh,* vol. 3, p. 197.

16. Al-Qalqashandī, *Ṣubḥ al-Aʿshā,* vol. 7, pp. 29, 51–52. Cf. al-ʿUmarī, *Al-Taʿrīf biʾl-Muṣṭalaḥ al-sharīf* (Cairo, 1912), pp. 55–56. Al-Maqrīzī, in his *Khiṭaṭ* (ed. Gaston Wiet [Cairo, 1911–27], vol. 3, p. 297) refers to the Christian ruler of Nubia as a *mutamallik,* but elsewhere (e.g., *Sulūk,* vol. 1, p. 611), discussing the same episode, conforms to the common practice of according this ruler the title *malik,* with the implied recognition as an old established state outside the House of Islam. In contrast, the Armenian king of Sīs, a Christian ruler of a city which had been conquered (*ftḥ*) by the Muslims and then reconquered (*ghlb*) by the Christians, was called *mutamallik,* and al-Qalqashandī was of the opinion that the Christian Georgian king of Tiflis, which had similarly been won and lost, should be addressed in the same way (*Ṣubḥ al-Aʿshā,* vol. 7, pp. 29–30).

17. See J. L. Bacqué-Grammont, "Deux lettres de Soliman le Magnifique à François Premier," in *Actes du Vingt-neuvième Congrès International des Orientalistes, Études Turques,* vol. 1 (Paris, 1976), pp. 18–19; idem, "Une lettre d'Ibrahim Paşa à Charles-Quint," in J. L. Bacqué-Grammont and

E. van Donzel, *Comité International d'Études pre-ottomanes et ottomanes, VI Symposium Cambridge 1–4 July 1984* (Istanbul, Paris, and Leiden, 1986), pp. 77, 86–87.

18. Turkish text in *Mecmua-i Muahedat,* vol. 3, pp. 69–72; Latin text in G. Noradounghian, *Recueil d'Actes internationaux de l'Empire Ottoman . . .* (n.p., 1892–1903), vol. 1, pp. 103ff. In subsequent treaties, however, the emperor is designated by a modified Turkish rendering of his own title, as *Roma Imperatoru,* "Emperor of Rome," but without the adjective "holy."

19. Article 13 of the treaty states, "The Sublime Porte promises to employ the sacred title of the Empress of all the Russias in all public acts and letters, as well as in all other cases, in the Turkish language that is to say "Temamen Roussielerin Padischag" (English text cited from J. C. Hurewitz, *The Middle East and North Africa in World Politics: A Documentary Record,* vol. 1 [New Haven, 1975], p. 96). For references to Italian and Turkish texts, see above, p. 134, n. 11. It will be noted that the European text includes the Turkish words on which the Russians insisted, and that this phrase was drafted in Russian, as is indicated by the use of *g* for *h* in *pādishāh.*

20. According to a tradition often cited by writers of politics, the Prophet said, "Rule [*imāra*] is the best of things for one who acquired it lawfully and licitly, and the worst of things for one who acquired it unlawfully, and will be an affliction to him on the Day of Judgment." On this al-Ghazālī comments, "Any ruler who deviates from the Sharīʿa in his judgments has acquired his rulership unlawfully" (*Faḍāʾiḥ al-Bāṭiniyya,* p. 208). See further B. Lewis, "Usurpers and Tyrants: Notes on Some Islamic Political Terms," in *Logos Islamikos: Studia Islamica in Honorem Georgii Michaelis Wickens,* ed. Roger M Savory and Dionisius A. Agius (Toronto, 1984), pp. 259–67; M. Sharon, "Notes on the Question of Legitimacy in Government in Islam," in Kraemer and Alon, *Religion and Government,* pp. 116–27.

21. This development was first traced and analyzed by A. von Kremer (*Geschichte der herrschenden Ideen des Islams* [Leipzig, 1868], pp. 413ff., and *Culturgeschichte des Orients unter der Chalifen,* vol. 1 [Vienna, 1875], 380ff.) and presented in exemplary form by Santillana (*Istituzioni* vol. 1, especially pp. 12–24, where the major Arabic sources are cited). See further H. A. R. Gibb, *Studies on the Civilization of Islam* (London, 1962), pp. 141ff.; idem, "Constitutional Organization," pp. 3–27. The whole question has recently been thoroughly and comprehensively reexamined by Lambton in *State and Government.*

22. Abū ʿAbdallah ʿUbaydallah ibn Muḥammad Ibn Baṭṭa, *Kitāb al-Sharḥ waʾl-Ibāna ʿalā uṣūl al-Sunna waʾl-Diyāna,* ed. Henri Laoust (Damascus, 1958), pp. 66–67. Abū Dharr was a companion of the Prophet, noted for his humility and asceticism. He has been co-opted in modern times as a precursor of socialism. On the tradition concerning the Ethiopian slave, see S. D. Goitein, *Studies in Islamic History,* pp. 203–4; B. Lewis, *Race and Color in Islam* (New York, 1971), p. 20.

23. In general, books written by ulema lay stress on the importance of consulting the ulema, while those written by officials attach greater value to the advice given by officials. A characteristic dictum is cited by the Ottoman writer Hasan Kafi Aqhisari: "The best of princes is he who frequents ulema; the worst of ulema is he who frequents princes" (*Uṣūl al-ḥikam,* p. 25). According to the editor, Dr. al-Hmoud, the saying is derived from the eleventh-century Cordovan man of letters Ibn ʿAbd al-Bārī.

24. Ibn Baṭṭa, *Kitāb al-Sharḥ wa'l-Ibāna.* On the two major festivals, and the ceremonies of Mina and Arafat, which form part of the annual pilgrimage to Mecca and Medina, see G. E. von Grunebaum, *Muhammadan Festivals* (New York, 1951), and, for a Muslim exposition, Muhammad Abdul Rauf, *Islam: Creed and Worship* (Washington, D.C., 1975).

25. Al-Ghazālī, *Iqtiṣād* (Cairo, A.H. 1320) pp. 107–8. This passage has been frequently quoted, notably by Santillana, *Istituzioni,* vol. 1, p. 22; Gibb, "Constitutional Organization," pp. 19–20; and Lambton, *State and Government,* pp. 110–11.

26. Lambton, *State and Government,* pp. 124, 140, 142ff.

27. Ibn Jamāʿa, *Taḥrīr al-Aḥkām fī Tadbīr ahl al-Islām,* ed. H. Kofler, *Islamica* vi (1934), p. 357. For discussion of this passage, see Kremer, *Geschichte der Ideen des Islams,* p. 416; Santillana, *Istituzioni,* vol. 1, p. 24; Gibb and Bowen, *Islamic Society and the West,* vol. 1, part 1, p. 32; Lambton, *State and Government,* pp. 138–43.

28. Santillana, *Istituzioni,* vol. 1, p. 24.

29. Lambton, *State and Government,* pp. 74ff.

30. The terms used for "tyranny," their synonyms and their antonyms, give some indication of how tyranny was perceived and defined in Muslim lands. The commonest term is *ẓulm,* which occurs very frequently in the Qurʿān. (On this and other terms used in the Qurʿān, see Izutsu, *Ethico-Religious Concepts.*) There it seems to have the broad general meaning of "misdeed," "wrongdoing," and hence "injustice." In post-Qurʿanic usage it is increasingly specialized in the latter sense, and is sometimes coupled with *jawr,* a word the primary meaning of which is "deviation," "straying from the path," whence also the derivative meaning of "wrongful or unjust treatment." A common messianic tradition speaks of a *mahdī,* a "divinely guided one," who in God's good time will come and "fill the earth with *ʿadl* and *qisṭ* as it is now filled with *ẓulm* and *jawr.*" (For a discussion of this and other messianic traditions, see Ibn Khaldūn, *Al-Muqaddima* (chapter 3), sec. 51, English trans. F. Rosenthal, vol. 2, pp. 156ff.) *ʿAdl* and *qisṭ,* usually translated "justice" and "equity," express the converse of tyranny. Similarly, the basic meaning of *ẓulm* is "the absence of *ʿadl,*" and its political content changes as does that of *ʿadl.*

Another word of common occurrence in the Qur'ān, with the meaning of "an insolent and overbearing figure," is *jabbār,* sometimes coupled with such other words as *mutakabbir,* "arrogant," "self-important"; *ʿanīd,* "willful";

shaqī, "fractious"; and *ʿāṣī,* "rebellious," "sinful." (On these terms, see Izutsu, *Ethico-Religious Concepts,* passim.) It is the converse of *taqī,* "godfearing," and *barr,* "pious," and is no doubt related to the Hebrew *gibbor,* which, however, has a positive and not a negative connotation. *Jabbār,* in the plural form *jabābira,* appears in the tradition enumerating the stages of deterioration in the Islamic institution of sovereignty (see p. 43 above, and p. 132, n. 1). The *jabābira* obviously represent the final stages of wickedness and oppression, before the advent of the messianic age. In general, the term *jabbār* is not much used in Islamic political literature, possibly because of its adoption as one of the divine names.

A term occasionally used in classical times and very much used in modern times is *istibdād,* which may be translated colloquially as "going it alone." As used in classical texts, it has a connotation of arbitrary and capricious, rather than illegitimate or tyrannical, rule. It is used of a ruler who decides and acts on his own, without due consultation with his religious and other advisors, and it is commonly contrasted with *naṣīḥa,* "advice," or *mushāwara,* "counsel," as *ẓulm* is contrasted with *ʿadl.* (For example see Ibn Sida, *Al-Mukhaṣṣaṣ,* vol. 21 (Cairo, A.H. 1316–21), p. 250. In Mamluk chronicles, *istibdād fi'l-amr* was frequently used in a neutral or even positive sense, to indicate that one or other amir had got rid of his rivals and taken sole charge. On the uses of *mushāwara* and *mashwara,* see B. Lewis, "Meşveret," *Tarih Enstitüsü Dergisi* xiii (1981–82), pp. 775–82, and idem, *EI*[2], s.v. "Mashwara." In the nineteenth and twentieth centuries, *istibdād* came to be the term commonly used by liberal democrats in both Turkish and Arabic, to characterize the autocratic rulers whom they wished either to restrain or remove. In modern usage, most of these Qurʿanic and other classical terms still occur, but they have become somewhat archaic, and others have taken their places. *Ghāsib,* which in classical usage normally denotes the forcible and illegal seizure or misappropriation of property, has acquired the political meaning of "usurper." Among many terms for repressive or oppressive government, *iḍṭihād* is probably the most common. A loanword of European origin, *diktātūr* and *diktātūrī,* is also widely used in Arabic of repressive regimes elsewhere.

31. Abū'l-ʿAbbās Aḥmad ibn Yaḥyā al-Wansharīsī, *Asnā al-matājir fī bayān aḥkām man ghalaba ʿalā waṭanihi al-Naṣārā wa-lam yuhājir,* ed. Ḥusayn Mu'nis, *Revista del Instituto Egipcio de Estudios Islamicos en Madrid* v (1957), pp. 129–91. On the question of Muslims in non-Muslim lands, see further the observations of J. Sadan, "'Community' and 'Extra-Community' as a Legal and Literary Problem," in Kraemer and Alon, *Religion and Government,* pp. 102–15.

32. From the Arabic root *lj',* "to seek refuge or protection"; cf. Meninski, p. 4884 (*mülteci* = "confugiens"). The term *malja,* "place of refuge," "sanctuary," usually linked with *ma'wa,* which has much the same meaning, formed part of the titulature of the Ottoman sultans, who in documents fre-

quently refer to their court as "the refuge of mighty sultans and the sanctuary of great Khaqans."

33. Abdel-Magid Turki, "Consultation juridique d'al-Imam al-Mazari sur le cas des Musulmans vivant en Sicile sous l'autorité des Normands," *Mélanges de l'Université St. Joseph* 1 (1980), pp. 691–704. For a lenient view on Muslims remaining in Christian Spain, see L. P. Harvey, "Crypto-Islam in Sixteenth Century Spain," in *Actas del Primer Congreso de Estudios Arabes y Islamicos* (Madrid, 1964), pp. 163–78 (citing al-Wahrānī).

34. Ibn al-Tiqtaqā, *Al-Fakhrī fiʿl-adab al-sulṭāniyya waʿl-duwal al-Islāmiyya* (Cairo, A.H. 1317), pp. 14–15. This passage is cited, in a slightly different translation, by J. Sadan, "'Community'", p. 114. Raḍī al-Dīn ibn Ṭāʿūs (A.D. 1193–1266) was a leading Shiʿite scholar of his time, and the author of many books. See Moojan Momen, *An Introduction to Shiʿi Islam* (New Haven and London, 1985), pp. 94, 314. In the same spirit, a later Egyptian historian cites a letter purportedly sent by Hulagu to the Mamluk sultan of Egypt, in which the Mongol describes himself and his armies as the instruments of God's wrath, sent to punish the Muslim monarch for his failures in Muslim observances and morals, and even quotes the Qurʾān to emphasize his points (Al-Maqrīzī, *Kitāb al-Sulūk li-maʿrifat al-mulūk,* ed. M. M. Ziyada et al. [Cairo, 1934–] vol. 1, p. 427, English translation in Lewis, *Islam,* vol. 1, pp. 84–85.

35. The treaty is usually quoted in Turkish and in French, but appears to have been originally drafted in Italian. The wording of these phrases in the Italian text is strongly reminiscent of the language of the Holy Roman Empire; "liberi, immediati, ed independenti assolutamente da qualunque straniera Potenza" and "senza però mettere in compromisso la stabilità libertà loro politica e civile." In the first phrase the Turkish text reads, "serbestiyet ve gayr-i taalluk mustakil vücuhla ecnebi bir devlete tabi olmamak üzre"; in the second, "akdolunan serbestiyet-i devlet ve memleketlerine halel getirmiyerek."

36. On *serbest,* see B. Lewis, "Serbestiyet," pp. 47–52.

37. Yirmisekiz Mehmed Efendi, *Paris Sefaretnamesi,* in *Kitabhane-i Ebuzziya* (Istanbul, 1306), pp. 33–36, modern Turkish version, ed. Abdüllah Ucman, in *Tercüman 1001 Temel Eser* (Istanbul, n.d.), pp. 28ff., contemporary French translation in Mehmed Efendi, *Le paradis des infidèles . . . traduit de l'Ottoman par Julien-Claude Galland,* new edition by Gilles Veinstein (Paris, 1981), pp. 77–82.

38. *Icmal-i ahval-i Avrupa,* Süleymaniye library, Esat Efendi no. 2062. For a description see V. L. Ménage, "Three Ottoman Treatises on Europe" in *Iran and Islam,* ed. C. E. Bosworth (Edinburgh, 1971), pp. 425ff.

39. Azmi Efendi, *Sefaretname,* in *Kitabhane-i Ebuzziya* (Istanbul, A.H. 1303), p. 15–16;

40. "Morali Esseyid Ali Efendi'nin Sefaretnamesi," in *Tarih-i Osmani Encumeni Mecmuasi,* no. 23 (A.H. 1329), pp. 1458, 1460, etc.

41. Cevdet, *Tarih,* vol. 6, pp. 280–81, 311, 395, 400. Cf. Lewis, *Mus-*

lim Discovery of Europe, pp. 52–53. For the reports of Hasan Paşa, the governor of the Morea, on these activities see Enver Ziya Karal, "Yunan Adalarının Fransızlar tarafından işgalı ve Osmanlı-Rus munasebatı 1797–1798," *Tarih Semineri Dergisi* i (1937), p. 133ff.

42. Şanizade, *Tarih,* vol. 4 (Istanbul, A.H. 1291), pp. 2–3.

43. Versions in al-Jabarti, *Muzhir al-Taqdīs,* vol. 1 (Cairo, n.d.), p. 37; idem, *ʿAjāʾib,* vol. 3 (Cairo, 1879), p. 4; idem, *Taʾrīkh Muddat al-Faransīs bi-Miṣr,* ed. and trans. S. Moreh (Leiden, 1975), p. 7 of text, 40 of translation; Niqula al-Turk, *Mudhakkirāt,* ed. G. Wiet (Cairo, 1950), p. 8.

The use of *ḥurriyya* in a political sense was still very far from being common usage. A French-Arabic word list, printed in 1802 for the use of the expedition, renders "liberté" by *ḥurriyya,* but with the restriction "opposé a l'esclavage"; in the other sense of "pouvoir d'agir," the list offers *sarāḥ,* from an Arabic root meaning "to roam or graze freely."

44. Thus, Meninski, p. 199, followed by Clodius, p. 558 explains *istiklal* as absolute authority, full power.

45. Carlo Botta, *Italya Tarihi* (Italian original *Storia d'Italia*) (Cairo, 1834), pp. 4, 8, 9, etc.

46. Cited by A. L. Tibawi, *British Interests in Palestine 1800–1901* (Oxford, 1961), pp. 147–48.

47. The Tunisian constitution was drafted in French, with the assistance of the French consul in Tunis, and shows the clear influence of French legal thought. The second Muslim country to experiment with constitutional government was Turkey, where a constitution was proclaimed by Sultan Abdülhamid in December 1876. There had been a number of decrees and other documents of a more or less constitutional nature in Turkey, dating back to the beginning of the nineteenth century, but this was the first full-scale constitution, drawn up and promulgated in due form. The Turkish example was next followed by Egypt, then still nominally subject to Ottoman suzerainty. The first of Egypt's several written constitutions was promulgated in February 1882. The first Islamic constitution to be established as the result of a successful opposition movement against the sovereign, was the Iranian constitution reluctantly signed by the shah in December 1906. On constitutional development in Islamic lands, see *EI*[2], s.v. "Dustūr" (by countries), reprinted in a revised version as a separate book (Leiden, 1966).

48. *"Meşrutiyet ve meşveret, şer-i şerifin ve-akıl ve-naklın emr ettiği bir tarik-i necat ve-selamettir."* Speech of 14 December 1909, Turkish press, 15 December 1909.

Index

♦

ʿAbbasids, 13, 33, 93, 96; *abnāʾ* of, 17; caliphate under, 45–51; *dawla* of, 36; kingship under, 55, 56
ʿAbbās II (khedive of Egypt), 137 n.21
ʿAbd al-Ḥamīd (al-Kātib), 35
ʿAbdallah (General Menov), 37
ʿAbd al-Malik (Umayyad caliph), 45
ʿAbd al-Raḥmān (amir of Afghanistan), 146 n.4
Abdülmecid (Ottoman sultan), 136 n.16
Abnāʾ, 17
Abū Bakr (caliph), 44, 75–76
Abū Dharr, 100
Abu'l-Faḍl Bayhaqī, 134 n.8.
Abū Yūsuf, 18, 61
Adab, 27–28, 128 nn.4 and 5
Adam, 44
ʿAdl, 143 n.60. *See also* Justice
Afghanistan, 146 n.4
Ağa, 17
Ağa of the Janissaries, 21
Age, imagery of, 15–16
ʿAhd, 80, 83
Ahdname, 84
Āʾīn-nāma, 119 n.7
Ahmedi, 148 n.8
ʿAjam, 118 n.5
ʿAlamānī, 107 n.2
al-ʿĀṣima, 147 n.7
Albanians, 39
Alberoni, Giulio (cardinal), 30
Alcalà, Pedro de, 60
Algeria, 74, 146 n.4
ʿAlī, 102
Amān, 77–78, 80, 84
Amasya, Peace of, 83, 150 n.28
"Ambassador," use of term, 76–77
American Revolution, 63, 140 n.45
Amīr al-muʾminīn, 50–51
Amīr al-umarāʾ, 51
Amirs, 43, 47, 50–51, 73
ʿĀmma, 67
Amr, 34
Apostates, war against, 77, 82, 84–90
Aquinas, Thomas, 25
Arabia: caliphate in, 43–47; kingship in, 53–56; pre-Islamic, 6, 27, 54, 85, 96–97. *See also* Arabic language
Arabic language, 118 n.6; *adab* in, 27–28; "body politic" in, 25, 32–41; "constitutional government" in, 114; development of, 6–8; "envoy" in, 76; "freedom" and "independence" in, 111, 112; frontier zones in, 147 n.7; "imperialism" in, 109; metaphors in, 12–23; "migration" in, 105–6; oath of allegiance in, 58; "outsider" in, 118 n.5; "peace" in, 78–80; poetry in, 10; "revolution" in, 96; ruler terminology in, 34–39, 43–60, 96–99, 124 n.31; and secularism, 2–3; "subject" in, 61–68; warfare terminology in, 71–75
Aramaic, 33, 38
Aristocracy, 64
Aristotle, 26
Armenians, 39, 80
ʿArsh, 22
Art, 10
ʿAskarī, Askeri, 62, 140–41 n.47
Assassins, 60, 74–75
Ata, 17

68; and theocracy, 29–30; and unbelievers, war against, 77–80, 82, 84, 85; warfare terminology in, 71–76
Islamic Bloc, 3, 4
Ismāʿīl Pasha (khedive of Egypt), 137n.21
Israelites, 54, 71. *See also* Jews
Istanbul, 30
Istibdād, 156n.30
Istiqlāl, 112
Italy, 76, 104

al-Jabartī, 142n.49
Jabbār, 155n.30
al-Jāḥiẓ, 55, 85–86, 144n.61
Jamāʿa, 13
Jamāl, Sheikh, 89
Janissaries, 21, 112
Jenghiz Khan, 57, 86, 88
Jerusalem, 145n.2
Jews, 39, 60, 78, 138n.26. *See also* Israelites
Jihād, 106; against apostates, 84–90; law of, 72–76, 145–47n.4; meaning of, 72; against unbelievers, 77–80; war against rebels versus, 82–83. *See also* War
Joseph, 55
Joseph II (Holy Roman Emperor), 110–11
Judaism, 6, 9, 17, 61, 71, 94
Jurisprudence. See *Fiqh*
Justice, 65, 70, 143n.60; concept of, 91–92, 99, 103, 113

Kaʿba, 71
Kāfī, Ḥasan, 140–41n.47
Kāfir. See Unbelievers
Kāfiristān, 146n.4
Kāmil, Ḥusayn, 137n.21
Kanun, 114–15
Karbalā', 121n.16
Kâtib Çelebi, 24
Khalīfa. See Caliphate
Khalifāt Allāh, 44–46, 133–34nn.3–7
Khan, 57
Khaqan, 57
Khāṣṣa, 67
Khawā'rij, 13
Khedive, 53, 137n.21
Khomeini, Āyatollāh Rūḥollāh, 28, 83, 115–16, 151n.5
Khuṭba, 127n.51
Khwārizmshāhs, 52
Kinda, 54
Kingship, 21, 39, 43, 97–98, 137–38n.26; development of, 53–56. See also *Malik*
Kings of Unbelievers, 55
Kıral, 98
Kiraliçe, 98
Knowledge, 28
Küçük-Kaynarca, Treaty of, 49, 98, 109
Kurds, 39
Kürgän, 57

Ladini, 107n.2
Lāji', 106
Law, 28. See also *Sharīʿa*
Leader. See *Zaʿīm*
Legitimacy: of non-Muslim rulers, 96–98, 103–8; and obedience duty, 91–94, 99–103
Leopold II (Holy Roman Emperor), 110–11
Levant, 76, 104
Logos, 38
Lûtfi, 136n.16

Mabeynci, 13
Machiavelli, Niccolò, 37
Madīna, 32–33, 59, 63
Mahdī, 19, 126n.43
Maghrib, 60
Mahmud II (Ottoman sultan), 136n.16
"Majesty," as title, 53
Malik, 39, 53–56, 97–98, 153n.16. *See also* Kingship
Mamlaka, 39
Mamluks, 60, 74–76; caliphate under, 47, 48; Islamic conversion of, 86–87; sultanate under, 48–49, 53

Old Testament, 18
Oratory, 10
Osman (Ottoman sultan), 22
Ottoman Empire, 11, 14, 74, 132n.29, 140n.43; as body politic, 24–25; caliphate in, 48–50, 135n.11; capitulations by, 84; and constitutional government, 113–15; consuls in, 76–77; European monarch terminology in, 98; "freedom" and "independence" in usage of, 109–12; *ghāzī* in, 74–75, 147–48n.8; Girding of the Sword in, 59; government concept in, 34–35; imperialism of, 108; Imperial Palace in, 13; *jihād* of, 146n.4; justice letters in, 143n.60; *khan* in, 57; migrations from, 106; *millet* in, 38–39, 41–42, 131–32n.27; muftis of, 30; as realm, 40; revolt against Mecca reforms of, 89; *sharī'a* law restoration in, 88; Sublime Porte in, 12, 20–21, 154n.19; sultanate in, 52–53, 136n.16, 137n.21, 144–45n.2; treaties of, 80, 82–83; vizierate in, 120–21n.11; youth movements in, 16–17, 113, 125n.33. *See also* Turkish language
Oxford English Dictionary, 61, 74

Pact, 80
Pādishāh, 57, 98
Paganism, 6, 85, 87, 92–93, 95–97, 105. *See also* Unbelievers
Pakistan, 106
Palestine Liberation Army, 122n.16
Pan-Islamism, 50
Parasol, 22, 126n.49
Pasha, 53
Pastoral image, 18
Patriot, patriotism. *See Waṭan*
Peace, 78–80
Persia. *See* Iran
Persian language, 76, 118n.6; "body politic" in, 25, 32, 41; "constitutional government" in, 114; development of, 6–8; metaphors in, 12, 14, 22; "revolution" in, 96; ruler terminology in, 53–57, 124n.31. *See also* Iran
Pharaoh, 79, 93, 96–97, 153n.14
Philosophy, political, 26–27, 32–33
Plato, 26
Poetry, 10–11, 27, 56–57
Polis, 32–33, 59, 63
Portugal, 104
Power: metaphors of, 11–14, 19–23, 127n.51; terminology of, 37–38. *See also* Government
"President," use of term, 59
Prince (Machiavelli), 37
Pulpit, 21

Qāḍi'l-quḍāt, 136n.17
Qādisiyya, battle of, 121n.16
Qā'id, 19
al-Qalqashandī, 97–98, 153n.16
Qāsim ʿAbd al-Karīm (president of Iraq), 60
Qdm, 11
"Queen," use of term, 66
Qunsul, 76
Qur'ān, 6, 7, 9, 123n.24, 140n.45; on caliphate, 44; and calligraphy, 10; and *fiqh,* 28; and fundamentalism, 118n.3; "holy" in, 71; *jabbār* in, 155–56n.30; *jihād* in, 72, 78, 129n.11; on kings, 55, 137–38n.26; on obedience, 91, 93, 94; on Pharaoh, 153n.14; political terminology in, 32–36, 38; *salām* in, 78, 79; "throne" in, 22; travel metaphors in, 18–19; on tyranny, 96, 97, 155–56n.30
Quraysh, 102

Raḍī al-Dīn ibn ʿAlī ibn Ṭā'ūs, 107
Ra'īs, 14, 59–60, 139n.36
Raʿiyya, 61–62
Rashada, 125–26n.43
Rāvandī, 47–48
"Rayah," 61
Razzia, 74
Reaya, 61–62, 140–41n.47
Rebels, war against, 77, 80–82, 84
Refugees, 106

Religion, 33; concept of, 2–4
Renaissance, 15
Resurrection, 15
Revelation, 114; and *jihād,* 73; and obedience duty, 91
Revolution, 36, 90; in Iran, 1–2, 113–16; Islamic, idea of, 1–2, 92–96; as metaphor, 13; Turkish, 16
Richard Coeur de Lion, of England, 97–98
Richelieu (cardinal), 30
Ridda, 85, 150n.32. *See also* Apostates, war against
Right and left, imagery of, 13–14
Robertson, William, 37
Rome, 75; ancient, 6–7, 9, 25, 45, 64
Rulers. *See* Sovereigns
Rumanians, 39
Russia, 8, 14; rule by, 105, 106, 108; and Turkey, war between, 49–50, 98, 109
Russian Revolution, 1
"Ryot," 61

Sādāt, Anwar al- (president of Egypt), 90, 153n.14
Sadık Rıfat, 37
Ṣadr, 120n.11
Safavids, 57
Safīl, 12
Safīr, 76
Ṣāḥib, 18, 97, 125n.39
Ṣāḥib amr, 34
Said Halim Paşa, 83
Saladin, 52, 144n.2
Salām, 78–80, 149–50nn.18–24
Salmān, 55
Samanids, 56
Samarqand, 33, 57
Samuel, 54
Sanizade, 111
Santons, 17, 71
Sar, 4
Sarajevo, 117n.1
Sarīr, 22, 126–27n.81
Satire, 10
Saudi Arabia, 53
Sayyid, 59
Scribes, 27–28
Secular, 3, 117n.2
Selim I (Ottoman sultan), 48–50, 136n.16
Seljuqs, 52, 59
Serbest, 109–11
Serbs, 39
Shāh, 56, 82
Shāhanshāh, 56–57, 98
Shakespeare, William, 34, 67
Sharīʿa, 4; adherence to, in Islamic states, 87, 88, 104–5; and constitutional government, 113–15; and *fiqh,* 28–29; *jihād* in, 72–73, 83; meaning of, 19; on obedience, 91, 100; on rebels, 81–82; sovereign's relation to, 31, 69
Sharīf, 67–68
Shawka, 37–38
Shaykh, 16, 59, 124n.31
Shiʿism, 49, 82–83, 97; and *ijtihād,* 129–30n.11; and *jihād,* 72; legitimacy in, 47, 102; and professionalization of religion, 30
Shurta, 7
Sicily, 104, 105
Sickness, 15
Sikka, 127n.51
Sin, 70, 91, 94, 103, 152n.9
Siyāsa, 11, 19, 122n.19
Slaves, 16–18, 60, 65, 74, 80, 89–90, 109, 142n.52, 146n.4; in Mecca, 89–90; and rules of war, 85; status of, 64–66; words denoting, 17–18. *See also* Mamluks
Slavs, 32
"Son," use of term, 17
Sovereigns: illegitimate, 96–98; powers and duties of, 31, 68–70, 91–92, 94–95, 112–13; terminology for, 31–39, 43–60, 96–99
Spain, 47, 104
Spatial metaphors, 11–14
Staff, 21
Subject, 61–63. *See also Raʿiyya; Tebaʿa*
Sublime Porte, 12, 20–21, 154n.19